MEMORIES AND HOPES

Leon-Joseph Cardinal Suenens

MEMORIES AND HOPES

Translated by Elena French

Veritas

Published 1992 by
Veritas Publications
7-8 Lower Abbey Street
Dublin 1

First published 1991 by
Librairie Arthème Fayard
Paris
France

ISBN 1 85390 129 6

British Library Cataloguing
in Publication Data.
A catalogue record for
this book is available
from the British Library.

The publishers are grateful to *The Tablet* for permission to reproduce an article entitled "Cardinal Suenens preaches the mission
at Oxford University", by Ronald Jenkinson, which appeared in
the issue of 26 February 1977; to Faber & Faber Ltd for extracts
from "The Four Quartets", from *Collected Poems* 1909-1962, by
T.S. Eliot. Excerpt from "Little Gidding", *Four Quartets*, copyright 1943 by Esme Valerie Eliot, reprinted by permission.

Cover design by creative a.d. Dublin
Printed in the Republic of Ireland by
Criterion Press Ltd, Dublin

Contents

Preface

I have often been asked to write my memoirs, and until now I have always refused. There are a number of reasons for this. Talking about oneself is not very agreeable. Moreover, while it is not always possible to reveal all the facts that would clarify this or that historical event, I do not feel called to paint my times in the manner of Rembrandt, playing clever games of chiaroscuro.

I have finally allowed myself to be convinced that there is a way out of this impasse. It is to follow the thread of one's memories without trying to be exhaustive, claiming the right to meander along, stopping now and then to draw the portrait of this or that person encountered along the way — somewhat in the manner of our Flemish painter Félix De Boeck, who could give soul to a face without worrying about non-essentials.

And so — by the grace of God!

These memories belong for the most part to the world of the Universal Church. They span first my years in Rome during the Second Vatican Council; and later my travels abroad (which occupied several weeks each year), in the wake of the Council and of the ecumenical encounters which resulted from it.

This book does not attempt to be all-inclusive. It does not cover, for example, my ordinary pastoral activities at the national and diocesan levels, to which I give most of my time. I have chosen the term "Memories", rather than "Memoirs", because this gives me the freedom to be selective in the things I write about and to choose my own landscapes. I will remind the reader that this is not meant to be a chronicle of daily life.

In writing, I shall let myself be guided by the image of the Rosary, since I have done all I could to promote the little FIAT rosary! I imagine these pages as a rosary of memories: there are larger beads and smaller ones, a thread that holds them together, and, at regular intervals, a "Glory be to the Father, and to the Son, and to the Holy Spirit." Much in the same way, you will find in this book a few large beads — meetings with famous people, in particular with the popes I have known well — and some smaller beads — things that happened in the margins of the more significant events; these will be new to the reader, and some are quite entertaining.

Much like the Rosary, life is a succession of mysteries — some joyful, some sorrowful. But the Lord has promised us a peace and a joy that no one can take from us. I can witness that, in my own life, he has kept his word so well that it will take me all of eternity — the time of the glorious mysteries — to give him thanks; and I shall not forget to add a Magnificat after the Te Deum , hoping that Mary will sing with me to help me stay in tune — in this life I was not blessed with the gift of music!

Shall we begin? ...in the name of the Father, of the Son, and of the Holy Spirit. Amen.

PART I

Before the Council

1

The Early Years (1904-1940)

My youth

Beginnings

I was born in Ixelles on July 16, 1904, and baptized in the church of the Holy Cross. At the age of eleven, I was confirmed in the church of the Holy Family in Schaerbeek. My mother was very pleased that I was born on the feast of Our Lady of Mount Carmel; from her I learned to value Mary's special protection.

For a while, I lived in a parish dedicated to Our Lady, in Petit-Willebroeck. My first school was the Collège de Notre-Dame in Boom; later, in Brussels, I went to the Marist Brothers' Institute, and finally to the Institut Sainte-Marie. It was by chance – another name for Providence – that I was repeatedly placed in the loving care of Mary, who delights in enfolding her children in the mantle of her protection.

My father was a brewer. He died when I was four years old. My mother never married again, having decided to dedicate her life to the upbringing of her only child. She lived a very simple life, since she only had a small income, which dwindled gradually over the years. We were always short of money, she and I, while I was at school, and I remember having to borrow schoolbooks, and never being able to buy the things I wanted.

As I had no history book, I once undertook a rather curious project: I compiled a list of all the popes. I did this on my own initiative, and for my personal satisfaction, by looking them up in the only book I owned, a dictionary – *Le Petit Larousse*. One by one, I found all their names and, much to my surprise, discovered among them a few antipopes!

Nor did I own a missal with which to follow the daily Mass. For many years, I attended Mass dipping into a collection of thirteen litanies contained in an old prayer-book!

Birth of a vocation

My vocation to the priesthood was awakened early, and was shaped by the solitude I shared with my mother.

On a BBC programme, in London, I was once asked about the birth of my vocation. Later, I was rather surprised to discover that *The Tablet* had published the interview. Here is the gist of what I said.

To begin with, my father's death made me intensely aware that life is very brief and heaven very real. As a small child, too, I was profoundly impressed by the idea of eternity. I have never forgotten a sermon I heard in which the preacher compared time with eternity. His images were so striking that the word "forever" has been impressed on my ears and on my heart as a refrain and as a living light. I understood once and for all that were I to live for eighty or even ninety years, this would still be nothing – compared to the endlessness of "forever".

So it was that I decided very early to opt for eternity and to live accordingly – whence my vocation to the priesthood! I was quite convinced that the best way to secure for myself a marvellous eternal life was to prepare many others for such a life by introducing them to the Gospel, the certain path to eternal happiness. It seemed to me that, to be welcomed in Heaven, it was essential not to arrive there alone.

Later, this view of eternity helped me to shed some light on the mystery of human suffering, which otherwise is meaningless and absurd. The image that comes to my mind is that of an infant in the mother's womb. I see him suddenly becoming aware of himself and of his condition. Jounced this way and that, he experiences a chaotic jumble of sensations and impressions. What are all those noises, the sudden stops, the movements – in other words, the mother's ordinary activities? None of it can have meaning until the day he understands that all of this turmoil was a novitiate preparing him for life; thus an opening onto the future sheds light and meaning on the past.

This image helps me see that our life here on earth, with its jolts and its aches, is no more than a preparation for our true birth into eternal life. As long as we are here, the process of our birth continues. Gabriel Marcel expressed this idea very nicely: "Life is like a sequence of words, but we cannot see the sentence or know its meaning until the final word is said."

The final vision will only be clear in Heaven. Meanwhile, faith teaches me that eternal life has already entered into my life on the morning of my baptism. I was baptized in the name of the Father, of the Son and of the Holy Spirit. The covenant was made; through baptism, I have entered into eternal life.

A day was to come when I would know that even from my mother's womb I have been loved with an eternal Love that has enveloped me at every step. And I know, too, that the first word of greeting in Heaven will be an invitation to enter for all time into the Joy of our Lord. Our life is played out, from beginning to end, at the very heart of the mystery of eternity.

This, in a few words, is what I told the journalist, in response to his questions.

What I did not tell the BBC is that I often visited the presbytery of the church where my uncle was priest; there, sitting astride a little wall that separated the church grounds from those of a nearby factory, I spent many hours daydreaming about all of these things. I imagined myself at the pulpit loudly proclaiming the Gospel for the happiness of all mankind. I must have improvised countless sermons, and delivered them to an audience of heavenly angels and a few little birds.

School
The elementary school I attended is today the Institut Champagnat. I will always be grateful to the Marist brothers who taught me there; they were excellent teachers and I have never met any

who could match their educational skills, in secondary schools or − even less − in higher education.

Our lessons were sometimes interrupted by visitors. The priest came to prepare us for major holy days. Less frequently, some important lay visitor went from class to class. The Prime Minister himself, Charles Woeste, former leader of the Catholic party, came to speak to us of our duties as future citizens. We only half understood his words, but we were proud to be treated as adults.

Perhaps it was his visit that awakened in me a lively and precocious interest in political debates; from the age of fifteen, I would occasionally go to the Parliament, armed with the required identity card, to hear them. The debates featuring the great political stars of the day fascinated me: Woeste, Devèze, Broqueville, Huysmans. I will never forget how shocked I was when, looking down from the gallery seats reserved to the public, I noticed senators and representatives calmly reading newspapers or writing letters, while, right beside them, the speaker was airing his oratorial talents!

In elementary school at the Marist Brothers', instruction had been in Flemish. When I went on to high school at the Institut Sainte-Marie in Schaerbeek, I had to face the difficult transition to French. But once I was over that hurdle, I had the advantage of being bilingual. Since the two languages were used interchangeably in my family, I was soon equally at ease in both.

My high school years were spent studying and reading. I read extensively − during the holidays, even a book a day! I embarked upon the fifteen volumes of the complete works of Louis Veuillot and read them all, never skipping a single line; I re-read *Les Soirées de Saint-Pétersbourg* ("Evenings in Saint-Petersbourg"), by Joseph de Maistre, three times; I knew *L'Homme* by Ernest Hello practically by heart, to the point that I could find any quotation almost instantly.

When my history teacher, Fr E. Hemeleers, allowed me free access to his books, I devoured Mgr Benson's books (*Master of the Earth, Paradoxes of Catholicism, Christ in the Church*). For a long time, I kept a list of all the books I had read. I did some writing as well, *ex professo*; somewhere, in one of my drawers, I still have a travel book and a war novel.

In addition to my love for books, I had one other hobby that was equally engrossing. In the quiet streets of Brussels, I played ball games after school, competing with the other neighbourhood children. It is difficult, today, to imagine Brussels as it was then; the atmosphere of that world has disappeared forever. We had no radio or television; cars were few and we were free to draw chalk lines across the empty streets where we played undisturbed. No one spoke of traffic-jams; indeed, the word had not yet been invented. The streets belonged to the people, and children shared in this privilege. Recently, I have heard a pedestrian described as "a gentleman who has found a parking space"; we were very far from such a world in those days! At night, the streets were lit by gas-light; a lamplighter armed with a long stick would go from lamp to lamp, lighting each one in the evening and extinguishing it again at dawn.

To return to my personal history, however: as I have already said, my vocation to the priesthood was never a problem. Towards the end of high school, a time came when I had to affirm and confirm my choice. An offer was made, involving my future; I refused the proposal, as you shall see. This is what happened.

A first cousin of my mother's had married, in the United States, a man by the name of William Robinson, who was director of the Boston-St Louis Railways. At the end of World War I, they came to live in Brussels. She had originally accepted to marry him with a sort of gentleman's agreement that she would remain in the United States until he retired, at which time they would both move to Belgium — which is what they did when peace was signed in 1918. Since they had no children, they offered to make me the sole heir of their considerable fortune on condition that, at the end of my schooling, I would obtain a degree in economics at the university and manage their finances.

Not for one moment did I consider accepting this offer; but

their friendship was very precious to me. In their home, I had the opportunity to breathe an air of ecumenism before its time, since my cousin's husband was a Quaker. They also encouraged me to learn English. My cousin, whom I called aunt, was Catholic by birth, but she did not practise. She was liberal in the American sense of the word. From time to time, she gave me a little pocket money, oddly enough insisting that it should be spent on frivolous things — in order, she said, to broaden my horizons. We talked for hours about the United States; she claimed that they should serve as a model for a United States of Europe! In those days I was a gaullist before the time of gaullism, and in the aftermath of World War I, I defended with youthful intransigence a Europe of nations! I have always remembered my cousin with gratitude and affection.

I finished my secondary education in classical studies at the Institut Sainte-Marie, and graduated at the top of my class. This particular detail played a decisive role in determining my future.

A third path: Rome
In our diocese, every candidate to the priesthood used to apply for admission to the seminary in Malines, where he would spend two years studying philosophy and four years studying theology. This was the usual path to priesthood. A few candidates were sent to the university in Louvain to obtain a religious and scientific education that would allow them to teach in secondary schools. Finally, the Cardinal reserved the right to send one candidate to Louvain to study at the Higher Institute of Philosophy which he had founded.

As the result of a misunderstanding, the Cardinal, unaware that the director of my school intended to request this particular privilege for the student who had graduated at the top of the class, granted it to a classmate of mine, who had graduated fourth. When he realised that there had been some confusion, and that objectively, I had been the victim of an injustice, he looked for some way to resolve this dilemma. Finally, he suggested that I should study in Rome. Thus I came to follow an unusual path that was to have a crucial effect on my future.

But I still had to obtain my mother's consent to this separation. It was a very painful decision for her: she could have asked that I remain in the country, at least reasonably close to her. To the priest who came to inform her of this offer to send me to Rome, she simply replied: "Decide without me, as though I did not exist." The same priest accompanied her to the station to see me off to Rome; when the train began to move off, she said to him, very courageously: "I'm so glad he did not see me cry."

Many years later, I came to understand the truth of these words, whose author I do not know: "When God upsets our plans, it is because he wants to grant extraordinary graces, according to his own plans."

All that followed was in some ways determined by this unexpected change. My long stay in Rome made a profound impression on me. I acquired a certain familiarity with the Roman world, which was a great advantage in later years, in particular at the time of the Council.

My Archbishop, Cardinal Mercier

One immediate result of this significant imbroglio was a meeting with my Archbishop, Cardinal Mercier, before my departure for Rome. He had asked to see me, perhaps in order to find out whether what he had heard about me was true... Almost immediately, he challenged me: "I am told that you have a gift for metaphysics!" I admitted truthfully that I did not even know what the word meant.

From the start, communication between us was easy and intimate. Cardinal Mercier knew well how to make the shy, short-trousered young man I then was feel relaxed and comfortable. Our meeting was interrupted by the church-bells in the nearby cathedral calling us to the noon Angelus. The Cardinal stood up to recite the prayer with me. This coincidence is an important part of my memory of our first encounter. Straightaway, his manner towards me became paternal. The Cardinal even suggested I should see a doctor and arrange to have my nose operated on where a flying ball had broken it during a game at school one day. He also told me that I was called to be a professor some day, and that a boring professor would not appeal to the students. He gave me a photograph of himself with his blessing. He wished me success in my studies and invited me to write to him from time to time.

I was happy to accept his invitation, and wrote asking for advice, as a son might. In particular, I requested his approval of my choice of a spiritual director in Rome, and asked him to suggest a motto for me. Here is the first letter he wrote to me; it reveals his fatherly heart, attentive and sensitive. It is easy to see why his memory has always remained so dear to me.

January 19, 1922

My very dear friend,

In the rush of these past two weeks, I have not had the leisure to reply to your two letters, so full of trust and filial piety. It is with joy that I turn to this task today.

I am very glad to know that you are happy and resolutely at work.

In Fr Sordet you have made an excellent choice of spiritual director; he is a man of God, knowledgeable, wise, experienced. I think you could not have done better.

If I remember well, before you left I gave you a copy of my little book, *A mes séminaristes* (To my seminarians). Let me know if you don't have it, and I will be happy to send you a copy.

I believe you will find in it some practical advice concerning the attitudes which you need to develop in order to prepare yourself properly for your future vocation.

Apply yourself to renunciation in all its forms, dear friend.

18

Renounce all that is not God himself, so that you may gradually realise the motto: God alone.

Very paternally, I bless you.

D.S. Cardinal Mercier, Archbishop of Malines

In those days, Cardinal Mercier enjoyed tremendous prestige, of a sort that is difficult for us to imagine today. His attitude during the war had made him a national hero; every head of state who visited Belgium called on him in Malines. In the religious world, the establishment of the Higher Institute of Philosophy in Louvain gave him immense prestige within the Church; his "modernity" made of him a pioneer in the dialogue between the Church and the world, a dialogue that was then in its earliest stages.

In my eyes he was, above all, the one who had re-opened ecumenical dialogue with the Anglican Church, after four centuries of silence. The name of Malines had acquired a new resonance because of his courage and initiative; and we were proud of him. The mere fact of being his successor in Malines has opened for me many a door and many a heart in Great Britain and in the United States. But I'm jumping ahead!

In the letter I just quoted, the Cardinal mentioned his book, *A mes séminaristes*. He thought he had given me a copy of it. I wrote back that he had given me his photograph, but not the book. Two months later, the Cardinal came to Rome to participate in the Conclave following the death of Benedict XV. I was at the station to meet him, with the president of the Belgian College. As he got off the train, he said to me: "Ah! I brought the little book. Brother Hubert will give it to you."

Brother Hubert brought it to the College, during the Conclave, with the Cardinal's apologies. As I expressed my surprise and asked the reason for the apologies, Brother Hubert explained: "The Cardinal autographed the book for you, but he apologises because he has forgotten your first name." He always referred to me simply as "young Suenens"! I could go on for a long time in this vein, filling the pages with *fioretti* ; but we must forge ahead.

Every summer I returned to Belgium for the holidays. This gave me the opportunity to visit him twice each year: once at the end of July on my way back from Rome, and again in October before leaving. My fellow-student from the diocese at the time was Father Carton de Wiart, later Bishop of Tournai.

The Cardinal received us separately. One day, as he was saying goodbye to me, he exclaimed jokingly: "Take full advantage of your time in Rome. Breathe in the air as deeply as you can; bring back all that can enrich you. The one thing you must not bring back is papal infallibility!"

The audiences followed the same pattern every year from 1921 to 1925. They played an important role in my life as a young seminarian, especially since the private secretary of Cardinal Mercier, Canon Dessain, took a liking to me straightaway.

He was of Irish origin by his mother, and had been in turn captain of the national football team, president of the Belgian football association, founder of the Club in Malines, and mayor of Malines. A late vocation to the priesthood, he was full of Irish humour and sportsmanship. He never failed to invite me to stay with him the night before my meeting with the Cardinal.

It was he who, for two years, instructed Queen Astrid in the Catholic faith. He had a vast experience of the world, and I benefited greatly from it. The Anglican participants in the "Malines Conversations" had stayed with him, and he told me many fascinating tales about that period, in addition to his own personal reminiscences. He shared all of this with me, simply because he had decided once and for all that I would one day succeed Cardinal Mercier! For my first Mass, he made me a present of a chalice with an Irish shamrock engraved on the knob. I still use it every day.

When Cardinal Mercier was dying, Lord Halifax came to see him at the hospital in rue des Cendres in Brussels. Together, they held the final "Malines Conversation". The Cardinal gave him his pastoral ring, as a sign of hope, to be given to Lord Halifax's eldest son.

Cardinal Mercier died on January 23, 1926. A few moments after his death, Father Lebbe, a well-known missionary who had spent many years in China, stepped out of the Cardinal's room. He was distraught, and these were his words: "There was a man who knew well how to become involved very effectively in matters that did not concern him at all." What he meant by this paradoxical statement was "There was a man who was willing to become involved in anything that concerned the glory of God in his Church." No doubt he was thinking of the very important role the Cardinal had played in hastening the establishment of a local episcopate in China.

Cardinal Mercier knew how to take risks. In the archives of the Archbishop's house, we later found a draft of a letter addressed to Pope Pius XI. This is what he wrote, very simply, to the Pope:

> In truth, Most Holy Father, Rome has nothing to lose: should our efforts fail, the humiliation of failure will rest with the Archbishop of Malines alone. If, through the workings of the Holy Spirit, a glimmer of hope were to appear, I would be ready at any moment to relinquish my initiative and transfer the talks to Rome or elsewhere.

Obviously, Cardinal Mercier was well aware of the difficulties involved; that is why he spoke of "a glimmer of hope". He wished to act with the prudence peculiar to great minds, and he knew when to take a chance. It is not at all surprising that he should have found the following quote from Mgr Pie, Bishop of Poitiers, very much to his liking, and repeated it frequently in private conversations: "When caution is everywhere, courage is nowhere to be found. Our ancestors were not so quiescent; we shall die of prudence yet, you'll see."

Memories and Hopes

The Belgian College in Rome

The atmosphere

The Belgian College has always been a training ground for bishops. There was no absolute rule, of course; however, the fact that these seminarians received their formation in Rome was for the Holy See a sort of guarantee of orthodoxy and catholicity. There I met, among my fellow students, Étienne Carton de Wiart, Auxiliary Bishop of Malines and later Bishop of Tournai; Louis Delmotte, former Bishop of Tournai; André Charue, Bishop of Namur; Carlos Himmer, Bishop of Tournai, Guy van Zuylen, Bishop of Liège; Maurice de Keyzer, Auxiliary Bishop of Bruges; Max de Fürstenberg, apostolic nuncio and later curial cardinal in Rome; and Emile De Smedt, who arrived the year I left and who later became Bishop of Bruges.

The president of the Belgian College in Rome was Mgr Charles de T'Serclaes; he was the descendant of an illustrious family which had played an important role in the history of our nation. In Rome, he was a legendary figure; he had written the *Life of Leo XIII* in three thick volumes. The Pope himself had read and annotated the proofs; thus the book had acquired a special importance in the eyes of those wishing to interpret the thought of Leo XIII, in particular with respect to the *ralliement* of French Catholics with monarchist tendencies, who accepted and supported the French Republic.

A conflict had once brought Mgr de T'Serclaes and Mgr Mercier into opposition. The latter had just created, in Louvain, the Higher Institute of Philosophy; Mgr de T' Serclaes saw in this a form of competition that disadvantaged those students who received their formation in Rome. He was in part responsible for the obligation to teach in Latin which was at first imposed on professors at Louvain. In the end, Mgr Mercier won the battle in favour of instruction in the vernacular, after the appointment of a new prefect to the Congregation for Education in Rome; but it was a very close thing!

I remember my president as a *grand seigneur* of another era, imbued with a very Ignatian spirituality and with a philosophy influenced by the scholastics of his time. He allowed us, however, a very precious margin of freedom in which we breathed easily while inhabiting a mental world that had little in common with his. He enjoyed humour and irony and used them well. I remember one exchange we had in which he gave a typically witty response. My fellow seminarians had appointed me to represent them in matters concerning the smooth running of the house. In this capacity, I once had to say to him "Monseigneur, the students are complaining about the coffee we are served; it is not good coffee." He surveyed me solemnly, adjusted his monocle and parried: "My dear friend, you are under no obligation whatsoever to call this beverage coffee!"

When he died, he was replaced at the College by Mgr Joliet, formerly bursar at the major seminary in Gand and later Auxiliary Bishop of Gand. I continued in my role of representative of the students; now the battle was no longer for good coffee, but rather to preserve the flexibility of College rules. I lost a few battles, but our personal relationship was not affected. The Belgian College, on the other hand, lost some of its charm and spontaneity.

Some years later, it was to welcome a certain Father Karol Wojtyla, who lived there for two years.

Studies

Lectures at the University were far too bookish and scholastic, and made little impression on me. I was much more stimulated and influenced by the free-wheeling discussions in which our elders at the Belgian College engaged for hours at a time.

We, the younger ones, studied philosophy; but our elders talked theology around us, at the dinner table and during recreation hours, and their impassioned discussions often lasted for days. Although we did not as yet understand many of the subtleties, we were acquiring a certain familiarity with a wide range of issues and concepts. Nothing was left unexamined: *"scientia maedia"*, the conflicts that pitted suarezians against thomists, the relationship between Church and State, and so forth.

We listened, for example, as Gérard Philips (then a student at the Gregorian University, later editor of *Lumen Gentium* for Vatican II) wrangled with Etienne Carton de Wiart (then a student at the Angelicum, later Bishop of Tournai). Ours was, in a way, formation by osmosis, by infusion.

There were many future bishops in the house, as I said. There were also unusual and fascinating characters, such as young Etienne Lamotte, who was already a specialist in oriental languages, and who eventually became famous for his interpretations of Buddhist thought. Even then he was as humble as he was knowledgeable.

In other words, the environment itself was a learning experience, a school of formation. But in addition, there were many strangers passing through Rome, opening our minds to new horizons: Fr Marcel Jousse, who told us about style in spoken language; Dom Lambert Beauduin, OSB, founder of Chevetogne; Fr Vincent Lebbe who spoke about China; and many others. All roads lead to Rome; travellers from every corner of the earth have met there, ever since Peter and Paul arrived along the Appian Way.

My seven years in Rome were rich in gifts. The atmosphere among the twenty or so students at the Belgian College was fraternal, and I greatly appreciated the freedom we enjoyed there.

Rome was above all, for me, the Rome of catacombs, saints, beatifications, papal audiences, international contacts. The seminary, as such, made relatively little impact on us, although I did discover there a few books that were very important to me and nourished me. In particular, through the writings of Fr Mersch, Fr Lebreton, Dom Marmion, we gained a new perspective on the Church, the mystical body of Christ. I discovered Eastern theology thanks to the writings of Fr Th. de Régnon, SJ, author of

Études de théologie positive sur la sainte Trinité. A number of books provided an ecumenical perspective; I read with tremendous interest *L'Histoire de Newman* by Thureau-Dangin. All of this provided nourishment on various levels – historical, theological, spiritual.

Since I was librarian at the College, I had to cross the library to reach my room. I often stopped on my way through, to sort books or put them away, finding some pretext to explore the top shelves, way up by the ceiling. One day I found a dusty old book called *La démonstration catholique de la vérité chrétienne* by Cardinal V.A. Dechamps, Archbishop of Malines at the time of Vatican I. He introduced me to a reversal of perspective in apologetics which has been analyzed and expanded by Blondel, who discovered Dechamps. The book belongs to its time, but it was precious to me then, for it helped to liberate me from a form of apologetics that I felt to be based on the wrong premises.

Life in Rome

The grandest and most spectacular days in Rome were those on which beatifications and canonisations took place. These made a profound impression on us, both because of their magnificence and because of what we learned about the persons being beatified, through the biographies that were distributed to us.

Many years later, I spoke up at the Council asking that the procedure for canonisation be speeded up, that the message of the saints be made more accessible to contemporary people, that more lay people be canonised, and that the process be made less costly! This made me rather unpopular with the department of the Curia that is in charge of these matters!

But at the time, I thoroughly enjoyed the sparkle of brightly-lit chandeliers in St Peter's, and the splendour of the triumphal entrance of the saints – despite the fact that their images, hanging at the back of the Basilica, were by and large in appallingly bad taste. Every human endeavour must have its own human limitations on this lowly earth!

One memory from this period still makes me smile today. As seminarians, we were given tickets to Vatican ceremonies. However, we were always seated in mediocre sections: it was assumed that seminarians, living in Rome, had more opportunities than passing pilgrims, who were therefore allocated the better places. It was all very reasonable, but nonetheless somewhat frustrating.

In the circumstances, we had to fall back on resourcefulness and ingenuity. I shall not reveal any of the stratagems we used, but I will tell you of the last bet we made with a group of French seminarians: the challenge was to see which of us could obtain the better seats in the Basilica, without proper tickets. At the end of the ceremony we were to meet beside the obelisk in St Peter's Square to compare notes.

I was certain at first that I had won the bet, since I had managed to view the ceremony alongside the Sistine Chapel choir members, without being discovered. Alas, I was shamefully outstripped by a French seminarian who had somehow managed — even though he was wearing an old sun-bleached cloak — to infiltrate the box reserved for the Queen of Portugal!

Finally, another of my Roman experiences comes to mind: quite unexpectedly, I became a journalist for a while. A Belgian newspaper with liberal-conservative leanings — *La Métropole* of Anvers — was looking for a correspondent in Rome to write a column entitled "Billet romain"; Mgr Fontenelle had written it in the past for both *La Métropole* and *La Croix* in Paris. Due to a concatenation of circumstances, I was asked to take his place. To my surprise and delight, Cardinal Van Roey — who had succeeded Cardinal Mercier in 1926 — gave me his permission, on condition that this would not take up too much of my time. I used the pseudonym Testis and wrote articles that covered a fascinating period of Roman life, that of the Latran treaty. I enjoyed this kind of work tremendously, and since then I have always had a soft spot for journalists.

A curious reporter — or is that a tautology? — once asked me: "Did you experience then the weaknesses and the petty sides of

Rome?" To which I responded: "Naturally, I saw that wherever there are human beings, there is weakness and pettiness. But this does not affect my faith in God or my profound love for the Church. I told myself that human beings are relative and God alone is absolute. We all carry our treasures in fragile containers. By God's grace, I was immune to the temptation of confusing what is essential with what is secondary, what is lasting with what is transient, the divine positive with the human negative. This grace also enabled me to maintain a sense of humour."

I could easily provide examples to illustrate the petty side of passing reality. Rome in those days was going through a time of such formalism and legalism that one could not help but wonder occasionally.

As seminarians, we were delighted to discover and point out that Fr Vermeersch, SJ, our very famous professor of moral theology, had had to pass an exam in order to obtain jurisdiction as confessor in Rome; he was examined by a jury appointed by the vicariate of Rome and composed of a few elderly prelates who themselves had studied moral theology from Fr Vermeersch's books!

This reminds me of my own absurd failure before the same jury when I took my first exam to be admitted to the tonsure, which in those days was the first step to priesthood. I failed lamentably when the examiner asked me what should be done if the candidate to the tonsure was bald. At a loss, I searched for solutions each less acceptable than the last, until finally the examiner informed me in a peremptory tone: "In that case, young man, one writes to the vicar requesting a writ of dispensation."

Looking back, the customs and ways of another time often seem strange and puzzling – all the pomp and the protocol, the elaborate ceremonial dress. Perhaps after all we are more the children of our time than the children of our parents.

Discovering the role of the Holy Spirit at the heart of the Church
Before I move on, I have a debt of gratitude to fulfil towards the

person who led me to discover, for the first time, the place and the role of the Holy Spirit. I was asked about this once in an interview for a Spanish magazine on spirituality; I answered that my discovery went back to meetings in Rome with Dom Lambert Beauduin, in the years 1922-1924. After Sunday vespers, at Saint Anselm on the Aventine, this man (who one day was to become the founder of monastic ecumenism at Chevetogne) would often speak to me, with contagious enthusiasm, about the Greek Fathers, about trinitarian theology, and about the Holy Spirit. I was a young seminarian and I drank in his words eagerly.

At the time, our spiritual climate was still deistic in its approach; the Trinity had very little to do with life, and, in God, the Holy Spirit disappeared into a sort of anonymity as a result of the theological explanations that were current at the time. According to the theory of appropriation, the role of each person within the Trinity — as regards external action — was defined by "the conventional attributes". Thus the role of the Holy Spirit became interchangeable, and lost any truly personal meaning.

Dom Lambert reacted against this impoverishment and urged me to read Petau, Waffelaert, and Régnon's four volumes of *Études de théologie positive sur la Sainte Trinité*. They opened a door to a true pluralism of the divine persons, discovered both in the mystery of their unity and in the richness of their living, inter-personal relationships.

This theologically dazzling revelation reinforced and enhanced for me the Christian world's new discovery of the spiritual writings of Sister Elizabeth of the Trinity. Cardinal Mercier had recommended these writings to his priests. In a concrete and practical way, Elizabeth revealed to us the undiscovered wealth of St Paul.

This newly acquired awareness of the Holy Spirit as such coincided with a first-hand experience of its charismatic action. Three names spring to mind in this context: Cardinal Mercier, Dom Lambert Beauduin,OSB, and Fr Lebbe, Belgian Lazarist of the Foreign Missionaries of Paris. The first initiated, with great difficulty, an ecumenical dialogue with the Anglican Church; the second was exiled by his own hierarchy because he had opened up too early the ecumenical perspectives to which he had witnessed in his paper *Église unie, non absorbée* (which Cardinal Mercier had read during the Malines Conversations); the third suffered greatly because he had supported the idea of a local clergy, and especially of local bishops, in China. I remember meeting Fr Lebbe on his way out of the Vatican, on the day the Pope decided to create the first Chinese bishops. He was glowing, and he called out to me: "I no longer believe in the Holy Spirit: I've seen him." I shall never forget the joy of a man who, after fighting for twenty-five years, sees his dream come true — a dream for which he had paid a high price indeed.

I was deeply affected by the experience of these three innovators, who struggled under tremendous pressure from various levels of the institutional Church. This may well be the psychological explanation for the fact that, when I was made bishop in 1945, I chose for my motto the words *"in Spiritu Sancto"*.

Teaching positions

Brussels

When I finished my studies, Cardinal Van Roey appointed me to teach at my old school, the Institut Sainte-Marie in Schaerbeek. The director had wanted me to replace Fr Eglem, who taught rhetoric. The latter did not leave until the following year, and so in the meantime I was given the only available position: class teacher for the first year of secondary school.

It was no easy thing for me to adapt to eleven- and twelve-year-olds, teach them catechism, and introduce them to the intricacies of French and Dutch grammar, spelling, calligraphy and drawing. But it was a good experience for me spiritually, because it forced me to shed my philosophical and theological baggage, or at least to become less encumbered by it. I owe a great deal of gratitude to my colleague there, Henry Bouveroux, for his advice on pedagogical matters and for his encouraging smiles. I had the happy inspiration to schedule all the drawing classes for the third term, in order to gain the time to learn something about it myself.

Malines

This trial did not last very long, however. Much to my surprise, in the middle of the school year Cardinal Van Roey appointed me professor of philosophy for the third term at the minor seminary in Malines, and I escaped having to teach drawing classes at all!

I will gladly admit that I was much more comfortable with moral philosophy, epistemology and pedagogy than with the Fables of La Fontaine. During the ten years (1930-1940) I spent in this new position, I was in contact with about a thousand future priests; vocations were still numerous in those days – 100 to 120 a year.

Much as I enjoyed the teaching and the time spent with students, I was very uncomfortable with the seminary's rules and regulations, the strict compartmentalisation between philosophy and theology, the authoritarian relationships with the seminarians, etc. A psychological wall separated teachers from students. I remember causing considerable concern by going out to play *balle-pelote* with the philosophy students. The structured lifestyle of the house did not encourage informal encounters.

Things improved somewhat once the seminarians were separated from the "humanists" when Saint Joseph's seminary was built outside the town. But there was still much that needed changing. I dreamed of natural and supernatural teaching methods that would be more in touch with reality, better adapted to the mission for which these priests were being prepared. It would take me volumes to explain it all, but I shall try to do so as I go along.

The Thierry Cogels incident. Even in this new seminary, one incident almost had dire consequences. I felt very strongly that the climate at the seminary was not conducive to a true human and priestly formation. I was not yet concerned, at that point, with "apostolic initiation", which was also totally lacking. I was disturbed by the artificial set-up of the seminary; by the enclosed, "boarding school" atmosphere in a building intended for 250 students; by the discipline that harassed and homogenised. All of this seemed counter-productive in view of our purpose, irrespective of the excellent qualities of those of my colleagues in charge of discipline.

One day, one of my students – Thierry Cogels – confided to me that he suffered greatly from this system. I advised him to write me a note describing the ways in which he felt stifled and oppressed. It was my intention to take this list to the administration to see if anything could be done to improve the situation.

When I read his letter, I found that all he said was true; however, it seemed too radical to be presented to the administration, too distant from their views on methods of education, and I left it in my drawer. Through sheer bad luck, a search of his room later revealed a draft of this note. He was accused of having an uncooperative attitude, and was threatened with expulsion. Naturally, he defended himself by saying that he had put these things in writing at my request.

As a result, I was reprimanded by the president of the seminary, and the incident appeared to be closed. I never did find out whether or not my appointment to Louvain, which came shortly after this incident, was a case of *promoveatur ut admoveatur*. The story has a happy ending, however; and much to my amazement, when I became Archbishop of Malines, my private secretary turned out to be Thierry Cogels!

A revolutionary seminarian. One of my former students, Prosper Truyts, who today is dean of the seminary, reminded me recently of an incident which I had quite forgotten. He tells me that when he was a young seminarian in his first year of studies, quite uncomfortable with the structured life of the seminary, he

31

happened to wander into the corridor reserved for faculty members, where students were only allowed to go for spiritual direction. I happened to be walking back and forth in the huge corridor, reading my breviary. He took a few hesitant steps in my direction and, out of the blue, spoke these words that he had been longing to express: "Professor, I am opposed to the Church!"

His was a full-blown vocational crisis, and he hurled his explosive remark as a challenge to the young philosophy instructor that I was then. He told me later that my response was the decisive factor which determined his vocation; with his intentionally provocative and defiant tone of voice, he was deliberately risking all for all. I closed my breviary, looked at him calmly and said: "Of course you are, my friend; who isn't?"

Immediately, he felt understood. What he was experiencing was not, in fact, opposition to the Church; he was suffering from certain limitations and a narrowness which, in part, would disappear before too long. We had understood each other perfectly. Many years later, when I said goodbye to the diocese as archbishop, he managed to be the very last person in the Cathedral to wish me farewell; he thanked me with deep emotion for the words which, some forty years earlier, had decided his future.

The last years of teaching at the seminary, 1936 to 1940, were darkened by the threat of an approaching world war. When the army was placed under alert, I was called up as reserve military chaplain.

When war actually broke out, in May 1940, I accompanied the Belgian army to Southern France, where, according to plans, the army was to regroup. The armistice put an end to hostilities, and I was back in Belgium by August 1940.

Here I received a new appointment: the Cardinal called me to inform me that the bishops of Belgium had appointed me vice-rector of the University of Louvain.

2

Louvain (1940-1945)

My role at the University during the War

During the War, from 1940 to 1944, I was in Louvain. At the University, I was in charge of the social and disciplinary aspects of the students' lives, and of protecting them from any harassment by the occupying forces. I knew little about the inner workings of the University; however, the position held a great attraction for me, in that it allowed me to provide a home for my mother in the vice-rector's house, thus putting an end to the loneliness she had painfully endured during the preceding years.

Life at Louvain University was quite lively during the War. Professor E. Lousse, who taught history, has described it in some detail. In his book, there is a chapter on the rector, Mgr Van Wayenbergh; another — which has a title too generous to be repeated here — is about the vice-rector. However, he has done such an excellent job of describing that period, that I need not delve into my memory for details of the War and of our difficulties with the invader.

University regulations stated (fortunately, as it turned out) that should the rector be unable to fulfil his functions, the vice-rector would automatically replace him and would be fully responsible for the administration of the University for the duration of his absence. I was called upon to fulfil this task when our rector was imprisoned for courageously refusing to hand over to the German authorities a list of students' addresses, which, as it happened, was hidden in my home. I was interim rector until the end of the War — a period of about a year and a half.

In addition to these functions, I held a private teaching position. In response to a request from the Royal Palace in Brussels,

Cardinal Van Roey asked me to provide religious instruction to the Princess Joséphine-Charlotte (later Grand-Duchess of Luxembourg), who at the time was about sixteen or seventeen years old. Obeying the Cardinal's wish, I went to Laeken every week, to the palace, which was held under military guard by the occupying forces. During that period, I wrote a brief commentary on the Creed, intended for the princess. However, our religion classes only lasted a few months: the occupying authorities suddenly exiled the royal family, refusing them access to the country until the end of all hostilities.

Clashes with the occupying authorities

Our relations with the invading forces were always tense. They became even more so after the University of Louvain opened its doors to students from the Free University in Brussels, which had been closed by the Germans. Because of the particular circumstances, a friendship developed between the rectors of the Universities of Brussels, Gand and Liège: we had to present a united front to the invader.

I have found in my files a report I wrote to the Belgian bishops. In it I describe my stormy encounter with Doctor Petri, supreme German authority in charge of universities. The meeting took place on October 15, 1943, and lasted one hour.

1. Petri opened the meeting by asking about the procedure for the appointment of a new rector. I replied that there is no new rector and that there will be none. I declared that I am and shall remain vice-rector in charge of ordinary business. He let the matter drop.

2. He then raised the question of student Deshormes. This young man passed with distinction his first exams in October 1941 before the central jury. He interrupted his studies in 1941-42. In 1943-44 I allowed him to register for the second year without previously requesting a certificate of dispensation from work as required by decree. I told Petri

that this case is not at all unusual, since we have never requested such a certificate from anyone.

Petri pointed out that this was, on my part, a very serious violation of the decree – there are sanctions, he informed me, against such an attitude. He proceeded to read the decree out loud, down to and including the paragraph concerning sanctions, and asked me to justify my actions.

I answered that my attitude is absolutely logical, since the *Werbestelle* themselves require a registration certificate from us for the year 1943-44 before they can issue their own certificate.

He responded that this is an exceptional case from which no interpretations can be made.

I answered that the *Werbestelle* have the same attitude throughout the nation and that identical cases have come up in both Liège and Gand.

Petri asked me how I came to know so much about what goes on in Gand and in Liège, and enquired whether we had consulted among ourselves. I replied that we have never held a special meeting on this subject, but that we meet every Friday at the University Foundation. Petri then said that the *Werbestelle* are merely executive bodies; their procedures cannot supersede formal texts and that, in case of doubt, I was under the obligation to ask for explanations before taking concrete action.

I answered that I have a right to assume that the German administration is a coherent affair, and that it is not my job to point out possible contradictions.

Petri then came to the heart of the matter, saying that he does not understand the attitude of Mr Nyns, who refuses any sort of control (whereas this is a sign of favour), who interprets his silence as a sign of approval, etc.

I answered that I am in no position to express an opinion concerning their conversations; however, it is natural that we should spontaneously cooperate with the ministry which, in the event, acted in agreement with the association of general secretaries and expressed the common view. We then discussed this issue of enforcement and control, and I pointed out to him that it is universally accepted that control and enforcement of a law is the responsibility of the authority that issues the law; it is, to say the least, strange that we are required to guarantee the authenticity of these German documents, and I pointed out to him the many contradictions that this could entail. I told him that we do have a form of basic control, since we ask students for last year's registration card or the last degree they have obtained.

He asked what our procedure will be for registration for exams in December. I told him that lists of exams will be displayed and students will sign up at their own risk, but we shall not ask for the certificate.

This discussion ended with a statement by Petri, who said: 1) that I am guilty of violating the decree; 2) that he notes as a central element of our discussion my comments concerning the *Werbestelle*; 3) that the fundamental issues are being discussed by Reeder and Nyns and that a decision will have to come from Reeder.

For my part, I responded that Louvain will follow the lead of Liège and Gand, and shall continue to register students. He asked for figures and whether there is a closing date. I said there was none. This seems to imply that he is not thinking of closing down the universities and, *ex silentio*, I conclude that the order given to Nyns to cancel registrations – about which I am supposed to know nothing – will not be enforced for the time being.

3. Petri then said that he has not yet received a satisfactory response concerning appointments and changes in courses; these must be submitted to them for approval beforehand. I answered that I know nothing about the past, and that in any case this does not concern me, but rather the board of governors. He wanted to know when the board would meet. I said, in July 1944. He told me that the chief of administration will write a letter concerning this point.

4. Finally, apologising for bringing up the subject, and with many oratorial precautions, he told me that there have

been complaints, both to him and in the press, concerning the high rate of failure among Flemish students, supposedly discriminated against in favour of Walloons. I answered with a shrug that this is a common but untrue rumour. He let the matter drop, apologised again, and the meeting was over.

A meeting with the military commander

In Louvain itself, our relations with the military commander, Baron von Thadden, were polite, due to his religious convictions. He was Lutheran, and president of the German Ecumenical Movement. Early on, he spoke privately of his anti-Hitler feelings to the rector, and this made communication between us much easier. He was a descendant of Bismarck and pointed out unhesitatingly the contrast between his ancestor and "the tyrant of Berchtesgaden". His sister was shot by the Nazis at the end of the War.

I have retained a vivid memory of the conversation I had with him, in my role as interim rector, on the day after the arrest of Mgr Van Wayenbergh.

He had summoned me to the Kommandantur, and it was feared that once again threats would be made in order to obtain the list of our students; and that should I refuse to comply, these would be followed by my arrest. However, von Thadden immediately said to me, "We are both Christians, you and I, and what matters above all is our communion in the Holy Spirit." And so, for an hour we talked together about the Holy Spirit, before going on to deal with our problems.

I thought of this conversation on the day when, as a newly consecrated bishop, I took for my motto the words "In the Holy Spirit". Years later, in the United States, I told this story to some twenty-five thousand people who had gathered for a Lutheran conference. The spontaneous response of the crowd was very moving.

In 1988, an excellent film was made in Germany about von

Thadden. In it I retold the tale of our meeting, as a witness to his authentic ecumenical spirit, lived concretely beyond the tragedy of war.

My theological discussion group

Outside the turmoil of public events, a small group met regularly in my home during the war, to exchange ideas on theological matters. The group, which was originally my idea, included Canons Cerfaux, Phillips, Dondeyne, as well as Fathers Malevez, SJ, and Levie, SJ.

I had invited these Jesuit theologians of great renown to take part in our discussions, first because I was certain that their contribution would be very enriching; but also to do a little "internal ecumenism" (*intra-muros*) between the University and the Faculty of Theology belonging to the reverend fathers. In the past, there had been some tension between them and the bishops concerning the granting of degrees, in competition with the University's department of theology. Later, Fr Dhanis SJ, future rector of the Gregorian University, and Mgr Thils, joined our group.

In a very friendly and open climate, we shared our intellectual and pastoral concerns, and quite frequently discussed the content of our courses. Directly or indirectly, all of this led to the establishment at the University of the Higher Institute for Religious Studies, intended for third-level lay students. Canon Cerfaux became its first director, and Canon Moeller (later secretary at the Holy Office) gave his first lectures, which met with astonishing success.

As a result of these meetings, it was easier for the Belgians to work together during the Council and to draft some of the Council documents jointly. I entrusted, for example, the preparation of *Lumen gentium* to a member of the group, Professor Philips.

Our theological discussions provided a few hours of freedom from the anxieties caused by the War and by the bombings – a brief respite, almost an escape. With my friend Franz Grégoire in particular, these discussions continued whenever we happened to run into each other in the streets – we simply picked up where we had left off.

I remember one very special session. Grégoire often tested his theology lectures on us, carefully watching all our reactions. One evening he expounded his views on Edouard Le Roy. Naturally – we might have guessed! – he told us that Le Roy was not at all the modernist he was caricatured as in those days. There was, he claimed, much truth in Le Roy's thesis, according to which "a concept does not contain all of reality; in its margins there remains a certain cloudiness, a certain fluidity, a left-over trace that escapes the clutches of conceptualisation".

Grégoire had a marvellous gift for making fine distinctions, bringing out subtle shades of meaning. He explained to us with much verve that the word "vague" can have seven different meanings, and that to confuse them would lead us to total disaster! Therefore, he concluded, there was some measure of truth in Le Roy's reasoning, and our approach should be different to fit each specific case – we should not attempt to squeeze authors into our own prefabricated conceptual geometries.

There was much lively discussion, late into the night. We were in total darkness – in more ways than one! For some reason that I can no longer recall, Cerfaux and Dondeyne would not accept Grégoire's views on this point. We parted, resolving to reflect on this further; our thoughts were clearly "not quite ripe" as yet.

The following day, walking down the street, I happened to meet Grégoire. Once again we engaged in a lengthy debate, right there on the footpath. Quite frequently, he would walk back with me from the Halles to my very doorstep, on the rue Saint-Michel, and we would go on and on talking, until my mother, who by then was quite used to this sort of thing, would come and tell us laughingly that "the soup was getting cold" and that "these gentlemen were requested to continue their debates at a more convenient time!" Grégoire would then depart graciously and the discussion would be put off to some later date.

On that day, he was glowing as he spoke:

> *Grégoire*: You know that discussion we had concerning Edouard Le Roy? Well, I've been thinking about it all night...
> *Me*: Ah? And did you find a solution?
> *Grégoire*: Yes! We were all terribly confused, because, yet again, we were not making clear distinctions. You see, we must make distinctions if we want to see things clearly.
> *Me*: So?
> *Grégoire*: Well, I had made a mistake! There aren't in fact seven different meanings of "vague". There are eight!

And there you have him in a nutshell!

Our friendship gave me much joy during those years in Louvain, as did my long talks with Professors De Meyer, Lousse and Simonart, and the occasional meal I had at the home of Professor Schockaert. Now and then, the latter had the great charity to invite his colleagues for a friendly meal that did not involve bringing one's own food coupons. The ultimate in luxury!

As I think of the contrasts between life at the University and the tragedy of war, another story comes to mind. One day, as I was walking along, I met Professor Etienne Lamotte who had been a fellow-student in Rome, and who had since acquired world fame as an orientalist. He looked so distressed that I asked "Tell me, Etienne, what's happened?" He replied: "I've just heard that Professor X died; he was the last of the only four experts who would have been able to read and understand the book I have just finished writing." Then he added timidly, "May I offer you a copy of my book? You don't have to read it, you know."

That day I fully understood the loneliness and the asceticism of great scholarship.

The end of the War
The War brought not only harrassment, searches, arrests and

shortages. It also brought bombings. One night, American bombers, intending to destroy railway crossings, made a disastrous mistake and ravaged many parts of Louvain. Cardinal Van Roey protested publicly.

Thirty-five people were killed within a radius of a few metres of my home at the Collège du Saint-Esprit. My mother and I barely escaped death by finding shelter beneath a staircase.

The day after the bombings, I remember going to see Professor Mertens, dean of the science department. When I knocked at his door, he was busy clearing away chunks of fallen walls. I enquired: "Are you receiving visitors? May I come in?" He responded, with courage and wit: "Come in, come in: my house is open to you... more open than ever!"

Despite all of this,the University resumed its activities with renewed enthusiasm. The rector, still banned from Louvain (where officially I continued to discharge his functions), returned nonetheless, without authorisation from the Germans, who chose to ignore his presence.

Eisenhower, doctor *honoris causa*

At the end of the War, the University of Louvain granted its first honorary degree to General Eisenhower, leader of the victorious forces, as a gesture of gratitude.

The situation was still quite tense with respect to the Russians, and the General was unable to leave his headquarters; he therefore asked us to come to Frankfurt to present him with the degree in the presence of his senior officers. He sent his private plane for us. This was my first airplane trip, and I was somewhat apprehensive — in those days, military planes were not as safe or as comfortable as they are today! I went with the rector, who was back in charge; Van der Essen, the secretary general of the University; and Mertens, the dean of the science department. The ceremony was quite impressive — there were about twenty generals present, and a military band to create the appropriate atmosphere. There were speeches, and lunch; then General Eisenhower took us back to the airport. This marked the start, for us, of a return to the normal university routine.

3

Malines (1945-1951)

Vicar general and auxiliary bishop
At the end of the War, Cardinal Van Roey appointed me vicar general and auxiliary bishop, to replace Mgr Carton de Wiart, who had been appointed Bishop of Tournai.

This was the beginning of a rather peculiar period, during which, as vicar general, I was in charge of checking the accounts of "Church factories", and of the censorship of books. Of course, as auxiliary bishop, I was called to the ministry of confirmations in the diocese, together with one other auxiliary bishop – at first this was Mgr Van Cauwenbergh, then Mgr De Smedt (who later became Bishop of Bruges), and finally Mgr Schoenmaeckers.

My most vivid memories of those fifteen years as auxiliary bishop are of confirmations throughout the immense territory of the diocese (at that time this included the area that later became the diocese of Anvers). All told, there must have been about 250,000 children confirmed! Each year, during the three or four months of good weather, about five or six hundred children from neighbouring villages would gather in some central location to be confirmed. It was a rich ministry, both from a religious and from a sacramental viewpoint. But it was also a painful one, since I knew full well that for the vast majority of these children, the day of their confirmation marked the end of their religious practice. As of the following Sunday, most of them would no longer take part in the eucharistic celebration.

This fact has troubled me deeply ever since, and all these years I have been searching for a pastoral solution. It is not enough to advance by a few years the age at which children are confirmed. I feel that there is a need for some sort of neo-catechumenate for those who have been baptised and confirmed, and have become

43

adults. This is where I can see an important role for "renewal in the Spirit", if it can be integrated into the very heart of the Church. But more about this later.

From my years as "administrator", I remember very specially one of my colleagues, Mgr Tessens, vicar general, whom I accompanied during the last moments of his life. I was at his bedside; he had received communion, but his agony continued. Since I had already recited all of the usual prayers for the dying, as well as the litany of the saints, it occurred to me to go back to the Eucharistic Prayer itself and then to repeat every word of the Mass, beginning with *"Introibo ad altare Dei..."* and continuing with the Gloria, the Creed and the entire Canon. He gave the responses with complete lucidity and a moving faith. This became a final offering of his life at the threshold of the Kingdom and of eternal Life. It had something of a pascal experience in which the liturgy acquired its full significance as mystery of death and resurrection. The following day, as I was telling Cardinal Van Roey about this, he said: "I would be happy if someone were to do the same for me one day."

My daily occupations left me some free time. I shared my life with my mother, who died peacefully on September 24, 1952, at the age of eighty-four. Her last words were those that John XXIII is also said to have murmured on his death-bed : "My Mother, my trust!" On her tombstone, I had the following words inscribed: *Donec veniat*, "In expectation of the glorious return of the Lord".

At the very instant at which her body was lowered into the ground in the cemetery adjoining the seminary of Saint Joseph in Malines, the bells of the church rang out for the Angelus. I was deeply moved by this coincidence. Later I asked at the seminary why the bells had rung so much later than usual. They told me it was because a lecture had unexpectedly lasted well past midday. Here was another of those chance events that are an expression of the loving care of Providence, whose fullness awaits us in Heaven.

Meanwhile, the gratitude I felt towards my mother helped me to understand the feelings Jesus had for Mary. On the day I was consecrated bishop, a few professors at the University of Louvain sent flowers to my mother. This thoughtful gesture went straight to my heart, and I have used this many times as an example when speaking to my Protestant friends: "Do not be afraid of honouring Mary; anything you do to honour her will go straight to the heart of her Son."

An unusual visitor
During my time in Malines as vicar general and auxiliary bishop — 1945-1961 — one event marked my life profoundly and affected its future course. This was the discovery of an apostolic organisation that I had been unaware of until then — the Legion of Mary.

Founded in Dublin by Frank Duff in 1921, it was introduced to Belgium in 1945; it made its appearance in the diocese of Malines in 1946, brought to us by a converted communist who had asked Cardinal Van Roey for permission to found a branch of the Legion in his diocese. He had made his request to the Cardinal by a letter dated May 7, 1946, from which I quote:

> I am a former militant communist, thirty-two years old; I have been a resistance fighter and a political prisoner in German prisons. I was converted last year by the Holy Virgin during a pilgrimage to her domain of Beauraing, a pilgrimage I undertook to thank her very specially for having saved my life in 1944.

He went on to describe how he had discovered the Legion of Mary. Finally, he requested permission to introduce the Legion for a few months, on an experimental basis, in one of the parishes of Brussels (the parish that was chosen was that of Notre-Dame de la Cambre, where Canon Gillet was parish priest).

The Cardinal granted his permission, which I passed on, along with an invitation to come and see me and tell me more about his plans. A few days later, he came to Malines and told me his story. He gave me the address of the secretariat of the Legion, rue Boileau, in Paris, in case I should require references or additional information.

I learned later that he wrote an amusing description of our meeting, which he sent to Canon Cordier in Nevers, and that the idea of presenting such a request to the Cardinal had come from a Belgian missionary bishop, Mgr Van Hee, SJ. The latter had become an enthusiastic supporter of the Legion of Mary, which he saw as an important instrument of the missionary apostolate. He was particularly successful in motivating Belgian missionaries to spread the Legion in what was then the Belgian Congo; here the Legion developed so well that it continued even throughout the worst moments of the struggle for de-colonisation.

Having said goodbye to my ex-communist, I walked out of the house and headed for my office at the Archbishop's House. Along the way, I ran into the man who had been military commander of the 9th Artillery Regiment of Malines, to which I was chaplain for a while. I told him about my visitor and about the Legion of Mary, and he said to me: "Monseigneur, I am quite ready to found such a group in Malines immediately, if my parish priest is willing." The very next day, he informed me by telephone that Fr Van de Werf had agreed and that a group could now be established. This became the core group from which hundreds of others were to spring in time.

Convinced of the apostolic value of the Legion of Mary, I followed its evolution closely and resolved to take an unusual and perhaps compromising step by giving it my active support. This was not something an auxiliary bishop would normally do.

Later, in Paris, I met the delegate of the Legion of Mary, Veronica O'Brien, and this meeting marked a turning-point in my life.

Pastoral publications
Between 1945 and 1960, I wrote several books in response to

pastoral problems which I had to face. I will introduce them briefly, in chronological order.

Theology of the Legion of Mary

The Legion of Mary was not well known in Europe. Veronica O'Brien, the Irish delegate who introduced the Legion to several countries — including Belgium — asked me to present it in writing, bringing out the spirituality of the Legion and its full apostolic richness. Since this consists essentially of an openness to the Holy Spirit through reliance on Mary, we were very much on the same wavelength, and I accepted her suggestion. Writing this book was a labour of joy, and I put the best of myself into it.

Cardinal Van Roey wrote an enthusiastic preface, and the book became a basic reference for members of the Legion. It was translated into about fifty languages and dialects, as the Legion gradually spread into more than two thousand dioceses throughout the world. To this book I owe the friendship of many missionary bishops whom I later met at the Council: we already had much familiar ground in common. This book was my first real literary effort!

A Heroine of the Apostolate: Edel Quinn

Next, I wrote a biography of the heroic life of a young Irish woman who introduced the Legion mainly to what used to be British Equatorial Africa. Her courage, and her lack of concern for herself, bordered on the miraculous. She died in Nairobi in 1944, in the odour of sanctity.

Her life seemed to offer itself as a catechism of images, illustrating my previous, more doctrinal essay. This book took a long time to write, as I did it concurrently with my official duties.

First I went with Frank Duff, founder of the Legion, to visit and question members of Edel Quinn's family. Then I studied the numerous testimonial letters from bishops, missionaries, and people who had known her at various times throughout her life. These were sent directly to me, as requested by the Dublin office of the Legion.

From Ireland, I also brought back her suitcase, sent on from Africa after the War. It had not yet been opened in Dublin. It contained a few favourite books, notes, and journals, which I studied very carefully as I tried to retrace her itinerary.

Finally, wishing to give the biography a touch of authentic local colour, I enlisted the help of a fellow-countryman, a great hunter in the eyes of God, who kindly filmed for me the landscapes of Kenya, Tanzania and Uganda, concentrating on the particular areas I singled out for him – and making sure to include a few lions and elephants!

I imagine Edel Quinn, smiling down on us from Heaven, as she watched the collaboration that went into her biography. The book itself was written by a Belgian bishop, while an Italian bishop – Mgr A. Riberi, who at the time was internuncio in China, and later became cardinal – wrote the preface. This blend had a definite taste of catholicity!

This book brings to mind a little story, a *fioretto*. To make it understandable to the reader, I must mention a habit that has evolved within a small group of my friends: each year, we randomly select a saint who will be for us "saint of the year", to be remembered and venerated from time to time. The purpose is simply to give life and expression on this earth to our communion with the saints.

In 1952, I had chosen at random for our saint of the year, Saint Martin de Porres. He was a lay brother, the son of a mulatto and a Spanish gentleman in Peru. His year was to end on December 31. On that night, as I was glancing one last time through Edel Quinn's journals, a picture which I had not noticed on previous occasions slipped out of the notebook and fell to the floor. There, on the other side of the card, was a relic of Martin de Porres! I took this to be a discreet and friendly smile of solidarity – I must remember to check it out with him in paradise.

The case for Edel Quinn's canonisation is under review in Rome. For me, the miracle of her life is quite sufficient to warrant a conclusion.

The Right View of Moral Rearmament
My next book was quite different. It was motivated by the appearance in Europe of a movement known as Moral Rearmament. In the aftermath of the War, it attracted a great deal of attention as a potential meeting point where men of good will could unite to build peace among peoples. The programme was attractive; but despite its undeniable idealism, some questions were raised concerning the underlying ideology, because its religious and "ecumenical" language was somewhat ambiguous. Would it be possible to preserve the inspiration while discarding some of these doctrinal ambiguities? The common denominator was on the level of natural virtues, away from any confused ideology.

With this in mind, I went twice to Caux, and later initiated further exchanges with the leaders of the movement in Switzerland, in order to clarify some of these points. However, there was to be no clarification. The Belgian bishops later published a note to warn any Catholics who might have been attracted by the positive aspects of the movement. I then wrote and published a booklet – the fruit of our otherwise fruitless conversations – entitled *The Right View of Moral Rearmament.*

The movement's major propaganda book included an introduction by Robert Schuman, who was at the time the French Minister of Justice and later a founding father of a united Europe. His name seemed to guarantee the absolute orthodoxy of the Movement from a Catholic viewpoint. I sent him a copy of my booklet, with my compliments. His friendly response clearly indicates the harmony of our views and reveals the mind of a great Christian.

Here is his letter, dated January 29, 1956:

> Your Excellency,
> I have just received the publication which you kindly sent me, and which I had not yet read; I do, however, already own a copy of your book on *The Gospel to Every Creature* which I read with great profit.
> There are definitely a certain number of misconceptions underlying the Movement for Moral Re-

armament which I had not noticed when I wrote the brief introduction to their book in 1950. Like you, I went to Caux once, in 1953. Despite the friendly welcome — which you describe so well — I never felt comfortable; it was somewhat like being in an overheated greenhouse.

Nevertheless, provided only concrete secular problems are dealt with, I believe useful meetings could take place, particularly where non-believers are involved, or those who are estranged by prejudices and resentments. There is a climate of brotherhood there, with a Christian inspiration. God can use such an environment to save souls.

On the other hand, I feel that for a practising Catholic, it can provide little more than the satisfaction of doing some good to others.

As for the methods used in Caux, they are distinctly American and Protestant; they remind one of the Salvation Army and will have no lasting appeal for our Catholic masses.

This is why I am not greatly concerned about the disadvantages of the Movement which you pointed out in your essay. Cooperation with non-Catholics *always* involves risks. What we must attempt to do is find, in various areas, a common denominator — not a common middle way.

Thus I feel that I am in total agreement with Your Excellency on all essential matters.

Perhaps, as a man of action, I tend to place greater emphasis on the practical usefulness of certain initiatives, such as greater closeness between races and peoples.

With gratitude and respectful devotion.

Schuman
Keeper of the Seal
Minister for Justice

La question scolaire (the school problem)
Equality for Catholic education, and indeed the very viability of a
Catholic educational system, seemed seriously threatened by a
debate that exploded at that time in the field of education. I felt
it would be appropriate to look beyond the specific demands put
forth, in order to define the principles that were being questioned, and in particular the concept of "neutrality".

While the battle raged — crowds of demonstrators filled the
streets, shouting "Down with Collard!" (the socialist Minister of
Education) — Cardinal Van Roey sent me on a secret mission to
the Minister in an attempt to defuse the conflict and find a viable
solution. I met with him several times to discuss the principles
underlying this crisis. Out of this came my little book on education, to which, once more, Cardinal Van Roey provided an introduction.

Years later, hearing that former Minister Collard was dying, I
sent him a note of comfort and encouragement, in memory of
this past encounter. He wrote back a few touching lines — his
handwriting shaky and barely legible — to thank me.

Since 1988, the agreement on education is included in our
Constitution and provides a fundamental guarantee for the
future of two separate educational systems — one official, the
other independent.

The Gospel to Every Creature
Wishing to broaden the perspective of *Theology of the Aposto-*
late, while remaining in the same general area, I called my next
book *The Gospel to Every Creature*. From beginning to end, this
is an appeal to every Christian to understand that no one is truly
Christian until he assumes his mission of Christianisation, of wit-
nessing to Christ and to his Gospel, in a way that is both direct
and personal. Without denying the importance of other approaches, I felt it was urgent to replace the concept of evangelisation in
the context of the Acts of the Apostles, and to emphasise a sense

of urgency for each and every one.

This book was written as a reaction against the theories of a group led by Montuclard which called itself *Jeunesse d'Eglise.* They suggested that evangelisation should be shelved until such time as social problems and afflictions were resolved. I pleaded, to the contrary, that Christians must find again, without delay, the active meaning of the baptism they have received. Mgr Montini, then Archbishop of Milan, welcomed and praised the book. He wrote an introduction to the Italian edition, in which he described it as courageous and optimistic. He spoke out personally and in public against the views expressed by Montuclard.

Love and Control
The idea for this book goes back to the World Health Congress, held in Brussels in 1958 in conjunction with the World Fair. The Cardinal had asked me to give the opening address in his stead, to an audience of some three thousand members of the medical profession who had gathered for this occasion. I decided to take advantage of this opportunity to launch an appeal to the medical profession, asking that priority be given to research on one of the most crucial issues for Catholic morality: the issue of family planning and birth-control. I explained to the participants that the question of birth-control is vital on a pastoral level, and I insisted that the scientific aspects be examined urgently in order to enable us to provide adequate moral guidelines.

I was both surprised and delighted by the positive reactions I received from every corner of the world. This led to the organisation of a series of international symposia of scientists and moral theologians who met in Louvain once a year. In the early years, I presided over their sessions. Another result was the creation of an institute for studies on family and sexuality, the Institut Universitaire des Sciences Familiales et Sexologiques, which is attached to the University.

I sent a copy of this book to Mgr Montini, Archbishop of Milan, and I discussed the content with him personally at his home. The book was translated into Italian at his instigation.

Mary, the Mother of God; Christian Life Day by Day

There are two more books, of a rather different sort, which I should mention here. The first, *Mary, the Mother of God*, is a Marian synthesis requested by Daniel-Rops for his encyclopaedia *Je sais, je crois* (I know, I believe). This too has been translated into various languages, most recently into Polish.

The title of the second book is *Christian Life Day by Day*. The Belgian episcopal conference appointed me to monitor Catholic programmes on radio and television. This is how I developed a special interest in the use of this technique of evangelisation. This brought about a collection of informal talks in which I attempted, in simple and direct language, to reach out to Christians in their daily lives, inviting them to listen, to give thanks, to be silent, to be willing to run risks, to guess, to show compassion, to smile, to forget themselves, to encourage, to enjoy.

I was surprised and delighted by the reactions to this publication, in particular from Germany and Italy, where reprint followed upon reprint.

Aside from these literary endeavours, my life as auxiliary bishop and vicar-general was quite ordinary and traditional. Daily work, both administrative and pastoral, depended largely on the tasks that the Cardinal distributed to each one of us every evening, together with his mail.

My Archbishop, Cardinal Van Roey

Cardinal Van Roey was an imposing prelate, overwhelming in his size, his theological scholarship, his judgement, and his classicism, as well as in his legendary uncommunicativeness. Cardinal Mercier had chosen him to be his vicar general as a bulwark to strengthen his canonical rearguard: to him he entrusted the care of women religious. Where Cardinal Mercier will be remembered for his qualities of imagination, daring and prophetic vision, his successor favoured the virtues of prudence, immutability and the preservation of tradition. But he obeyed with perfect loyalty all instructions arriving from Rome, even when he did not approve of them (as in the case of new rules concerning fasting, evening masses and so forth).

On a political level, the country was grateful to him for his clear and brave stand with respect to the invader during the War.

He was a member of the Preparatory Commission for the Council, but because of his advanced age, he attended none of the Commission's meetings. He did, however, to my personal knowledge, respond to at least one consultation. He called me in one day to tell me, in all sincerity, that in response to a questionnaire from Rome, he had stated that he favoured maintaining Latin for instruction in seminaries, and that he had answered "No" to the question as to whether he thought auxiliary bishops should be invited to the Council. He told me all of this without batting an eyelid — merely passing on an item of information.

He and I lived in two different worlds, and due to circumstances, I sometimes found myself caught between the two. The Nuncio had revealed to me, for example, under the seal of absolute secrecy that, on the death of the Cardinal, the diocese would be divided into two, in order to re-establish the separate diocese of Anvers which had been abolished in the sixteenth century. This involved, in the interim period, a certain number of preventive measures and adjustments (drawing of borders, distribution, etc.) that went against the express will of the Cardinal. Not long before his death, he had even asked the Prime Minister to use his personal influence to make sure that the vast diocese of Malines (which included three million inhabitants and close to three thousand priests) would remain intact, out of respect for the historical prestige of the seat of Malines.

We were in a time of transition, at the end of the era of Vatican I. Words such as "coresponsibility" or "collegiality" meant little, and the realities which they represent were not concretely experienced. It is said that Pius XII once exclaimed "I do not need collaborators, I need executors." Significantly, he was, in fact, his own Secretary of State. Cardinal Van Roey lived in this climate, never delegating power if he could help it. His closest collaborators kept a respectful distance. What mattered was to get on with ordinary day-to-day business. The manner of doing this was never questioned, and the articles of canon law were applied, as were diocesan statutes, with pragmatism and rigour. There was no time or place for "new perspectives" (an unheard-of concept), or for the slightest touch of humour.

Let me remind you that in those days seminarians still crossed the town of Malines, each afternoon, with their black hats firmly on their heads and their mantelets draped around their shoulders. In Rome, guidebooks invited tourists to admire — as one of the curiosities of the city — the students of the German College in their brilliant red cassocks (among them at one time was Hans Küng). One could also admire, in the gardens of Villa Pamphili, Belgian seminarians playing soccer, their cassocks rolled up to their knees.

The Cardinal, as I have mentioned, was also known for being a man of few words. John XXIII once disagreed with me vehemently on this point: "They all say he's so taciturn; well, he certainly isn't with me. We have often talked together comfortably, with the greatest ease." Duly noted!

It has been said — and this is a Conclave secret! — that our Cardinal had played a decisive role in the election of Cardinal Roncalli. I find this easy to believe: they had much respect for one another, and both had a great deal of solid common sense and a love of historical tradition. For his part, Cardinal Van Roey has said of Roncalli: "People do not know this man; they have no idea of his resources." (This was said during a private conversation between Cardinal Van Roey and Mgr Jadot.)

The Cardinal died peacefully, before the beginning of the Council, on the feast of the Transfiguration, August 6, 1961, at the age of eighty-five.

Preparing for the Council

A few months before the Cardinal's death, an unexpected event suddenly broadened my daily horizons: John XXIII announced that a council would be held in Rome in 1962.

Immediately, preparatory working commissions were set up in Rome. The Commission for Bishops and the Government of Dioceses was to study the necessary revisions in this particular area. The Commission consisted of auxiliary bishops, presumably because they were more available than bishops in charge of dioceses. I was appointed to it, along with a number of colleagues, most of whom eventually became archbishops and cardinals: Veuillot (Paris), Villot (Lyon), Krol (Philadelphia), Florit (Florence), Morcillo (Saragossa). Because of this, I made frequent visits to Rome before the actual opening of the Council.

We worked extremely hard to draw up the outlines of a draft text, *De episcopis*, which raised the major pastoral issues. There were problems in the early stages of our work: the President of the Commission, Cardinal Mimmi, was already quite ill, and died before the opening of the Council. The secretary, Mgr Gowlina, a Polish bishop in exile in Rome, was not really familiar with our problems. The items placed on our agenda by the Curia were either trivial or vague: "Should there continue to be suburban bishops in Rome?"; "Should a diocese be large or small?" – to the latter question we responded, with true Solomonic wisdom, neither too large, nor too small!

Finally we succeeded in handing over the actual job of drafting the text to Mgr Morcillo of Saragossa, future Bishop of Madrid, who produced an excellent document.

Within the Commission, we had to contend with a formidable defender of the *status quo* – the dearly beloved and very holy Father Cappello, SJ. In years past, he had taught all of us canon law – the articles of which he literally knew by heart – and we felt crushed by the sheer extent of his scholarship and knowledge. His presence gave us all a tremendous inferiority complex, while his holiness was a source of great encouragement. He was famous in Rome: his confessional in the church of St Ignatius was never empty. When he died, his many penitents gathered to strew flowers on his tomb; and it is murmured that the cause of his beatification is well under way.

After Cardinal Mimmi died, Cardinal Marella took over the presidency. He and I had long been friends; he had been nuncio in Paris, where Mgr Benelli had been his assistant and collaborator. He did not see how another council after Vatican I could serve any useful purpose; however, he reported with loyalty and objectivity all the suggestions that were made.

Since I was already in Rome to work on this particular Commission, I took the opportunity to get in touch with the secretaries of other preparatory commissions. As a result, I wrote a series of memos.

Of my own Commission, I requested the following:

— a definition of the specific role of the episcopate;
— greater flexibility, allowing others besides bishops to administer the sacrament of confirmation;
— a revision of the breviary;
— a revision of the *Pontificale*;
— a complete review of the concept and design of seminaries, in particular with regard to apostolic initiation;
— establishment of a permanent diaconate;
— the adoption of simple clerical dress;
— changes in religious life;
— a broadening of the concept of *Action catholique*;
— better preparation of Christians for marriage;
— a review of eucharistic fasting;
— a reform of the Roman Curia;
— a complete revision of the rules of the Index.

I submitted approximately fifteen memoranda to other commissions, concerning the following points:

— the new role of women religious in joint apostolic pastoral ministry;

- the bishop and the role of the director of diocesan works (the purpose of this being to clarify the role of the bishop);
- the permanent diaconate;
- collaboration with the laity, with suggestions for the establishment of lay councils at various levels — parish, diocesan, national and international;
- the role of women religious collaborating with the bishop;
- the future role of bishops' conferences;
- gradual integration of apostolic initiation in seminaries;
- age limits for retirement;
- relationships between bishops and major religious superiors (this particular note was drafted by the Bishop of Bruges, Mgr De Smedt, who was its principal author).

All of this preparatory work for the Council served as an initiation and a valuable learning experience which was very useful to me later, during the years of the Council.

Appointment as Archbishop

Immediately after the death of Cardinal Van Roey, the nuncio, Mgr Forni (who has since been made Cardinal), informed me that Rome was about to appoint an apostolic administrator who would decide the issue of the division of our diocese. Two days later, he informed me that I had been assigned to this temporary position, until such time as a new archbishop was appointed.

For several months, I concentrated on this task. The diocese was divided — two million inhabitants for Malines, one million for Anvers, with approximately two thousand priests remaining in Malines, while one thousand were assigned to Anvers whence they originated, with freedom of choice according to particular circumstances.

On November 24, 1961, I was appointed Archbishop of Malines-Brussels; I took up residence and assumed my new position on January 24, 1962.

I then took the initiative to decentralise, dividing the diocese

of Malines-Brussels into three territorial sectors: the Flemish Brabant, the Walloon Brabant, and Brussels. I appointed a vicar general or a bishop to be responsible for each sector. I did not see
myself as the bishop of each of these three different regions of
the diocese, but rather as the archbishop, supervising the implementation of common pastoral directives. In this I was assisted by
a representative pastoral council which met once a week for a full
day. This decentralisation into three religious sectors anticipated
by a quarter of a century the political federalisation of Belgium.

During this process of re-organisation, I discovered increasingly, within myself, to what extent our mission as bishops requires
us to be ever more open to the promptings of the Holy Spirit.
Only thus can we hope to live out fully our most fundamental
and central responsibility, which is "to be attentive to what the
Spirit says to the Churches" and to receive this guidance with
humble availability.

My motto — "In the Holy Spirit and in Mary" — acquired new
meaning day by day. At the heart of the Creed is a profession of
our belief that Jesus was born of the Holy Spirit and of Mary.
This is not a matter of past history. We must extend this mystery
into the Church, through all time, and never dissociate the institutional Church from the charismatic Church — these are but two
aspects of a single reality.

Many things were not then as explicit in my mind as they are
today. However, this motto is the key to all that followed. At various points in my life, it was to have the most unexpected applications. It was to bring light to every moment of my life, like a
watermark that illuminates the pages of a book and can only be
seen by holding up the pages to the light.

Appointment as Cardinal, and membership of the Preparatory Commission for the Council

Contrary to custom, Pope John appointed me cardinal only a few
weeks after I had been made archbishop. He did this in order to
make it possible for me to be involved in the preparatory work for

the Council, as a member of the Central Preparatory Commission.

At the time of my appointment, this Commission was half-way through its work. Much to my surprise, I discovered that the texts and drafts to be submitted to the Council in no way reflected the hopes that had been awakened by the announcement of this Council – they lacked life and vision.

Several European cardinals, who were already on the Commission before I was appointed, shared this feeling. Separately, we had all had the same reactions. Cardinals Doepfner, Koenig and Alfrink had already expressed their objections, but to no avail. Six of us then sent a joint letter to Pope John, telling him that the schemata prepared by the Curia were inadequate, and that the Council would certainly reject them. But the Holy Spirit was not yet at work.

Cardinal Tisserand presided over the Central Commission, which included fifty cardinals, about twenty archbishops, and ten major religious superiors. I made two statements to the Commission. In one I asked for the suppression of the monopoly of the "mandate" of *Action catholique*, arguing that this hindered the activities of all other apostolic movements. Much to my joy and surprise, my words were well received by practically all of the cardinals present at the meeting.

Later, I had to object to the minutes of the meeting – the secretary had simply omitted all of my argumentation from the report he had prepared for the Pope. This experience taught me, once and for all, how very important it is that every participant in a meeting should read and ratify the report intended for the Pope.

My second statement was less successful. This was only to be expected, yet I had felt compelled in conscience to raise the issue. Before speaking, I prayed in my heart *"Veni Sancte Spiritus"*, and thought "This is the end of me!" What I suggested was that the Council should set a retirement age for bishops, including cardinals. My statement was followed by a deathly silence. Cardinal Tisserand put the proposal to the vote. All of the cardinals voted *"non placet"* — even my friends. All of the major superiors of religious orders unanimously voted *"placet"*, as did a few archbishops. It may be interesting to note, from a historical standpoint, that at the opening of the Council one-fourth of all European ordinary bishops were over the age of seventy-five!*

I have one very vivid memory of the day on which I made this statement — at the coffee break, which, as usual, we took part of the way through our meeting, I felt very much a leper. Under the circumstances, I did not want to compromise anyone by seeking sympathy for my boldness, and I remember drinking my cup of tea alone, to the bitter dregs, my eyes firmly on the lump of sugar which obstinately refused to melt.

My proposal was clearly premature, but Paul VI later made it his own. It was just a matter of time.

---

* See *Documentation catholique* (1966), col. 2106.

PART II

The Council

4

The Council Under John XXIII
(1962-1963)

A surprise

When Pope John XXIII decided to convene a council, he surprised everyone, not least the curial cardinals, who were gathered in Saint Paul's-Without-the-Walls and were the first to be informed of his decision. Pope John told me of their "astonishment", and mentioned that he had previously "tested" his inspiration on Mgr Tardini, in confidence. Mgr Tardini, who later became cardinal, was a sensible man, and the Pope appreciated him for this. According to the Pope, Mgr Tardini's reaction was favourable.

Pope John's personal secretary, Mgr Loris Capovilla, was less encouraging. Observing the worried expression on his face, Pope John said to him: "I can see what you are thinking. You are saying to yourself: the Pope is too old for this sort of adventure. But, Don Loris, you are far too cautious! When we believe that an inspiration comes to us from the Holy Spirit, we must follow it: what happens after that is not our responsibility."

This is the story as it was told to me by Pope John. Mgr Capovilla gave his own account of this conversation, which, according to him, had a more intimate spiritual tone: "You have not yet shed your self. You are far too concerned that we should give a good impression, and that we should bring to completion the work that the Lord is suggesting or demanding of us, and for which he is requesting our service in full abandonment to his will. Only when you have crushed your ego will you be truly a free man".*

News of the Council came as a surprise to bishops throughout the world, who received a letter from Pope John announcing the forthcoming Council and asking for their suggestions. I wrote about ten pages in response, thinking that this was a private letter to the Pope. Once more, Pope John surprised the Roman Curia – and all of us – by ordering the publication of all our *desiderata*. As he said privately, this was so that "the Curia should hear what the world is thinking".

When published, the responses filled seventeen volumes. The bishops' letters, along with those of the major superiors of religious orders and the rectors of universities, were systematically sorted and arranged by continent. I cannot claim to have read all of this, but I have dipped into it. I imagine that few bishops have ever consulted these volumes; they are only available in Rome, and the entire collection was sent only to the primate of each Church. In handing it over to my successor, I told him of the use I made of it whenever some foreign bishop came to visit me in Malines: I looked him up to see what sort of person he had been before Vatican II! Needless to say, I read with particular care what Montini had wished for in those days when he was Archbishop of Milan.

Glancing through these volumes, one is left with the general impression that the wishes expressed concerned essentially canonical and liturgical reforms; the renewing wind of Pentecost was not blowing very strongly! Lacking in experience, we fumbled somewhat at the beginning of the Council. Pope John encouraged us, saying "When it comes to councils, we are all novices." One single bishop had had some previous experience of councils: he had been present at Vatican I, as an altar boy! We celebrated his

---

* Translated from an article in *Il Regno*: "Come nacque il Concilio di Papa Giovanni", *Documentazione*, February 15, 1969

one-hundredth birthday, and the Council gave him a fraternal ovation; he died after the first session.

Yet, we cannot say that Pope John opened the Council with no plan in mind. Not enough attention has been paid to the speech which he gave one month before the opening of the Council, and in which he provided us with a programme, in a nutshell. He called on us to see the Council as an *examen* of conscience concerning our faithfulness to the Master's commandment: "Go, take the Gospel to all people, and I will be with you to the end of time." In this speech, he spoke of the Church as a central theme – the Church from within, and the Church from without.

This passage was a summary of his thinking. But his intention was to leave the Council to its own devices, in all freedom. He left it to the Holy Spirit to guide Council members in ways that were pleasing to Him; these became increasingly clear, and a definite orientation emerged within the first few weeks.

By the end of the first session it was apparent to all that the Second Vatican Council would be, in the eyes of history, a Council centred on the Church; and indeed that all of the schemata, until then separate and distinct, would be reorganised and clustered around this central theme.

The opening of the Council
The Council opened on October 11, 1962, which in those days was the feast of the Maternity of Our Lady. Pope John had chosen this date deliberately; for him, the Council was a pentecostal grace, and therefore Mary was intimately involved. He had written a prayer for the occasion, and asked us all to share it with him and make it our own:

> Holy Spirit,
> sent to us by the Father in the name of Jesus,
> you help the Church by your presence
> and you guide it infallibly.
> Renew your wonders in our time
> as for a new Pentecost.

> Grant to the Holy Church,
> united in prayer, insistent and perseverant,
> with Mary, the Mother of Jesus,
> that the Kingdom of the Divine Saviour may spread –
> a Kingdom of truth and of justice, of love and of
> peace.

The whole of Pope John is in this prayer, and in its last line we already have in full his encyclical *Pacem in terris.*

For all the bishops who were present – and there were about 2,400 – the liturgical opening of the Council was an unforgettable experience.

The first working session was also memorable, but for different reasons. The Council immediately affirmed its own theological and pastoral identity by demanding the right freely to determine the composition of commissions among which the work was to be divided. The Roman Curia had presented us with ready-made lists, and were taken by surprise when both Cardinal Liénart and Cardinal Frings requested, in their opening statements, that the Council itself appoint the members of the commissions.

This was indeed a brilliant and dramatic turn of events, an audacious infringement of existing regulations! Cardinal Liénart had asked for permission to speak; Cardinal Tisserand, who presided over the opening session, faithful to his military training, had rejected such a violation of the rules, which did not explicitly allow for a discussion of this point. However, Cardinal Liénart ignored this refusal; his proposal, supported by Cardinal Frings, received such an ovation that the will of the assembly prevailed.

To a large extent, the future of the Council was decided at that moment. John XXIII was very pleased.

Steering the Council
Council regulations stated that ten cardinals would preside over daily meetings in turn. This proved to be impractical. Paul VI did

away with this function, which had become purely honorary. The president was replaced by a team of four permanent moderators, of whom I was one.

At the same time, Pope John had set up a sort of ministerial cabinet known as the "Secretariat for Extraordinary Ecclesial Affairs". This was headed by Cardinal Cicognani, Secretary of State, and included seven members: Montini (Italy), Siri (Italy), Meyer (United States), Wiszynski (Poland), Confalonieri (Italy), Doepfner (Germany) and Suenens (Belgium).

This central steering committee later acquired a new name, and became, on December 17, 1962, the Coordinating Council. It included Cardinals Liénart, Spellman, Urbani, Confalonieri, Doepfner and Suenens; Cardinal Cicognani was its president.

Cardinal Doepfner and myself are the only two who served on the Council's central steering committee from beginning to end – a privileged position from which to observe the progress and evolution of the Council.

The first working session with Pope John

Here is an account of the first working session we had with Pope John. The meeting took place in the evening, in the Pope's office, and lasted one hour. It was an interesting meeting, very revealing of the climate of that period.

Pope John first defined what he saw to be the role of the ten presidents appointed to preside in turn over the meetings. He told us also that he had appointed four under-secretaries to assist Mgr Felici – Secretary-General of the Council – in order to emphasise the international character of the Council.*

Pope John had agreed to the Curia's choice of Mgr Felici for the key position, even though this did not reflect his personal preferences. On one occasion, he referred to him as *"questo ineffabile Felici"*, a statement that was softened only by the kindness of his manner.

---

*The four under-secretaries were Mgr Villot (France), Mgr Krol (United States), Mgr Kempf (Federal Republic of Germany) and Mgr Morcillo (Spain).

Pope John then gave us a brief history lesson on the differences between Vatican I and Vatican II with respect to official representation. He was very pleased with the contrast, and with the large number of representatives of many different countries who attended the inaugural ceremonies. This for him was a sign that the world at large welcomed his initiative to convene the Council.

Then we turned to business. The Pope emphasised once more what he had already said in public concerning the spirit of the Council, which he hoped would be positive and pastoral. He handed out a memo from Cardinal Bea, which argued strongly that the Council should give great importance to the ecumenical repercussions of the documents it produced.

Cardinal Bea's memo was excellent, although somewhat heavy. He had already sent copies to me and to Cardinal Doepfner of Munich. Since our three names are associated here, this is as good a time as any to reveal that the three of us enjoyed a somewhat privileged position of trust with Pope John. I heard this privately from Cardinal Doepfner, who had been told in confidence.

Following the Pope's presentation, our discussion quickly took on an ecumenical tone. Cardinal Montini asked for special attention to the Oriental Fathers. I pleaded in turn that the Council should not be allowed to flounder in matters of secondary importance, but should, rather, concentrate on one central theme; I also asked that the ecumenical sensitivity expressed in Cardinal Bea's memo should infuse all of our work. What I was actually looking for was some sort of general mandate that would counteract tendencies towards dispersion. The Holy Father was delighted with this suggestion, and Cardinal Confalonieri at once proposed that I should be the one to draft such a document. I accepted, since this was in line with my own paper proposing an overall plan for the Council.*

---

*This paper was distributed to Council members and was entitled *De fine concilii et de mediis ad finem consequendum* (Concerning the aims of the Council and the means to achieve them).

We freely discussed a number of minor changes to the overall organisation of the Council. I felt in complete harmony with the Holy Father. The only proposal he did not agree to concerned the bishops' dress code. Several bishops had asked me to tell the Pope that their ceremonial attire was not at all practical; since they were travelling by public transport, they would have liked to attend Council meetings in ordinary clothes. Pope John rejected this suggestion: "We must remember", he explained, "that a Council meeting is a major liturgical assembly that begins with the celebration of the Eucharist. Besides, a council isn't something that happens every day!" Pope John had a sense of decorum that coexisted comfortably with his great simplicity.

His honesty was disarming. In the presence of the entire group, I asked him: "Holy Father, why did you appoint the prefects of Roman Congregations to head the Council Commissions? This can only inhibit the freedom of Council members in their work and in their discussions." He answered, laughing: *"Ha ragione Lei, ma mi ha mancato il coraggio"* ("You're quite right, but I didn't have the courage."). The relaxed atmosphere was both delightful and rich in surprises.

At the end, Pope John announced: "And now, Cicognani will give you a document that will be useful in guiding your reflections." Each one of us received a photocopy of my plan, along with a handwritten note from Cicognani summarising, in Italian, both the intent of the plan and the content of my letter of May 16. All told, we were handed seventeen pages.

And so we left the Pope. At my suggestion, we adjourned to Cicognani's parlour – right there in the Vatican – to hold the first meeting of our committee. We decided to meet in the same place every Friday at 5 p.m., with or without Cicognani.

As we were leaving, Cardinal Montini said "I thought our group was a mere formality; I can see now that it's much more serious."

* * *

In passing

Glancing through my papers, I found my first impressions of some of the members of this group:

> Cicognani − A disappointment; definitely more conservative than the Pope, frequently contradicts him. Even where the Pope opens doors, he hastens to close them. However, because of his age, we will be able to override him or ignore him. But he does not share our viewpoint.

> Siri − Says no to everything, even the most basic things. He is completely focused on "impossibilities" that are not impossible at all. He will be the greatest obstacle to overcome.

> Doepfner − He is very good; but Italian is our working language, and he is not brilliant in it.

> Montini − There is harmony between Montini, Doepfner and myself; we make up a trio. He's more interested in the Church *ad extra* than in the Church *ad intra*.

> Felici was not there for this first meeting with the Pope. A very good thing, which will allow us, I hope, to deal with him as an outsider, at the implementation level.

The two major tendencies

From the outset, two different approaches could be felt at the Council. In time, they became increasingly well-defined, and the media soon labelled the one "progressive" and the other "conservative". These are ambiguous terms, as is the word *aggiornamento*, often interpreted to mean that the Church was to be adapted to the surrounding mentality. I prefer to speak of a two-pronged tendency, consisting of a centralising approach (that of the Curia) on the one hand, and a collegial approach on the other.

These attitudes were most clearly expressed during the debate on the collegiality of bishops − pastors of particular Churches in communion with the Pope, who is Bishop of Rome and visible centre of unity within the communion of Churches. Everyone accepted the primacy of the Pope and wanted to be in unity with him. There was, however, a subtle distinction depending on whether the stress was on unity "with him" or "under him"; while neither side contested either of these principles, there was a difference in emphasis. The main difficulty stemmed from the following point: on an institutional level, the Church is both a universal Church and a communion of Churches – plural unity and unified plurality.

The collegial tendency within the Belgian Church

No one has ever questioned the fidelity of the Belgian Church to Rome; indeed, there was a time – during the Western schism – when it was considered legendary. At a theological level, it went hand in hand with a clear sense of episcopal responsibility.* Many factors contributed to this consensus among Belgian bishops and theologians on that particular point.

The Malines Conversations left their mark on our generation. In the course of the meetings, Cardinal Mercier read the famous *Memorandum* on "The Anglican Church, united but not absorbed", written by Dom Lambert Beauduin, OSB, who later founded the ecumenical monastery of Amay. The collegial approach was further strengthened by an important *Memorandum on the Episcopate* by Mgr Van Roey, who was, at the time, Vicar-General under Cardinal Mercier, and a participant in the Malines Conversations; no one could have accused him of being progressive. Moreover, thanks to the Department of Theology at Louvain and the ecumenical work at the Monastery of Chevetogne, we were mentally well prepared to give vigorous support to a collegial approach .

Dom Lambert Beauduin played a significant role in the decision to convene a council, a role that should not be underestimated

---

*See *L'Episcopat et l'église universelle*, with an introduction by Mgr Charue, Bishop of Namur, Editions du Cerf, 1962.

He had often spoken to us of the need to complete the work of Vatican I, and to bring about a better balance between primacy and collegiality. He had had long talks with Mgr Roncalli when the latter was Apostolic Delegate to the Balkans. In 1957 Cardinal Roncalli gave a speech in Palermo at the Congress on Christian Unity; here is what the future Pope said to the participants:

> Today, the fundamental weakness of the efforts for Christian unity is their inability to spread to the masses, who are in fact well able to appreciate their importance. My good friend from Belgium, the Benedictine Dom Lambert Beauduin, said, as far back as 1926, when I was just beginning my practical work of cooperation in the Near-East: "We must create in the West, in support of unity with the separated Churches, a movement parallel to that for the Propagation of the Faith." I had then just finished reorganising the institution for the Propagation of the Faith, in accordance with the wishes of Pope Pius XI; and now I feel that we should go back to Dom Lambert Beauduin's idea.

When he was informed of Dom Lambert's death, Pope John said to me: "Now he will see from up in Heaven what he had dreamed of down here." Dom Lambert, for his part, once privately told a friend, "If Roncalli is made pope, we shall have a council."

The Belgian Church thus basked in a climate of collegiality, shared by bishops and expert theologians alike. In all fairness, I must add that we were not alone: a French theologian, Fr Congar, OP, worked closely with our team of experts at the Belgian College. We were also in touch with Mgr Colombo, the Pope's personal theologian, and a few others, in particular Dossetti.

Later on, when we were preparing *Gaudium et Spes*, I invited a group of theologians to work with me for a week in Malines, on the actual drafting of the schema. In addition to Mgr Philips, we had with us Mgr Delhaye, Mgr Dondeyne, Fathers Tucci, SJ (Italy), Rahner, SJ (Germany), and Congar, OP (France).

The curial tendency under Cardinal Ottaviani

The centralising force, akin to the spirit of Vatican I, was represented most prominently at the Council by the head of the Holy Office, Cardinal Ottaviani. He saw himself as the one and only authentic interpreter of Catholic orthodoxy. For Pope John, he was indeed a heavy cross to bear. The schemata prepared by the Curia were profoundly marked by his theology.

These draft texts, which the Council was later to reject, were a source of concern even to one highly placed official at the Holy Office, who, on the eve of the opening of the Council, came to warn me and to tell me of his anxiety. I immediately asked him to repeat the reasons for his concern to the Belgian bishops who were with me at our College, and he accepted. I shall assume that I have his permission, from above, to reveal his name – the man in question was Father Dhanis, SJ. Former dean of the Pontifical Gregorian University, he was a highly regarded theologian, well known for his balanced and moderate views.

Before the opening of the Council, I was on good terms with Cardinal Ottaviani; I would even say, on friendly terms. It caused me much pain – as it did him (he personally told me so) – that we found ourselves in conflict; not on a personal level, but in Council debates.

It had become necessary to free ourselves from a theology that limited and restricted the mystery of the Church. What we were about to experience was not a "theology of liberation", but rather "liberation from a particular theology".

I admired in Ottaviani the strength of his convictions, his courage, the love he had for the poor and even, occasionally, for the victims of the Holy Office! There was, however, another side to the picture, which must be acknowledged; it is here that Pope John was in conflict with him and that the majority of Council members had to dissociate themselves from his views.

We were about to experience the end of an era, heir to the legacies of a long past – from Constantine in the fourth century, to Vatican I in the nineteenth, by way of the Council of Trent in the sixteenth. There would be continuity, certainly, in the essence; but there would also be new perspectives, and these would bring forth a vision of the Church enriched by a return to the sources. Those theologians who had caused consternation at the Holy Office (Congar, Daniélou, de Lubac, Rahner, etc.) would be present as experts to help define this new vision — and this was an added paradox.

Pope John himself had a few problems with the Holy Office as a young professor at the seminary. Later, he had seen his own bishop, Mgr Radini-Tedeschi, whom he called "the star of his priesthood", and whose private secretary he was for ten years, confronted with far more serious difficulties. After he was elected Pope, he had painful arguments with Ottaviani. Once, as Ottaviani officiated beside him as deacon in Saint Peter's, Pope John leaned over and whispered in his ear: "Our minds do not work in the same way; but let us be at one in our hearts."

In the final analysis, this was the central tension of the Council. According to Ottaviani, the Holy Office stood, in effect, above the Council, and had a monopoly on authentic theology — which he identified with his own theology. The Council had no business, in his opinion, questioning the schemata which had been prepared according to his own instructions. The Fathers were to discuss only the form, not the substance. He believed that Pope John was leading the Church to total disaster.

Ottaviani never fully recovered from the trauma of seeing Council regulations applied to himself on an equal basis. When Cardinal Alfrink, whose turn it was to preside (this was during the first session, when ten presidents rotated on a daily basis), interrupted him in mid-speech during a Council meeting because his allotted time was up, the psychological shock was so great that he did not reappear at Council meetings for several days.

Later, under Paul VI, there was a similar tension in the commission of cardinals and bishops who had been appointed to advise the Pope on birth-control. Ottaviani, who presided over the commission without ever saying a word, refused to transmit our conclusions to Pope Paul – even though they had been adopted almost unanimously. Finally, Cardinal Doepfner, vice-president of the commission, had to deliver them personally to the Holy Father.

I had another revealing experience later on, when I proposed to a post-conciliar synod the establishment of an international theological commission. In doing so, my intent was precisely to breach this monopoly which stood in the way of free dialogue at the highest levels. Much to my surprise, Ottaviani accepted my suggestion – only to add "*We* shall appoint the theologians"; this, of course, would have foiled my purpose entirely. My concern in this matter was to make available to the Pope complete and balanced information; I had no desire to see any particular thesis prevail over another.

As I have said before, one important reform – and an easy one to implement – would simply involve making sure that the minutes of all meetings in every dicastery are always read by the secretary to the participants, before they are submitted to the Pope, and that each participant has the opportunity to check that his views are transmitted correctly. Two episodes in my own experience – which I still remember vividly – have made me acutely aware of just how important it is to establish such a procedure. During the World Conference on the Apostolate of the Laity in 1957, I delivered personally to Pius XII a summary of the discussions that had taken place. Under John XXIII, I had to object to the minutes of a meeting of the General Preparatory Commission, and to send the cardinals and bishops a long memorandum supplementing the report from which my statement had been omitted.

I am absolutely convinced that a simple rule such as I have outlined above, requiring that all reports intended for the Pope be read and checked by all concerned, would prevent a great many misunderstandings and would give the Holy Father a chance to hear a wide range of opinions.

Co-responsibility is not a matter of sharing out power. Rather it is a matter of open and loyal communion, particularly when there is a risk of causing displeasure or disrupting long-established habits.

A plan for the Council

Preliminaries — the negative note
In response to questions concerning preparatory work for the Council, I wrote an article for *La Nouvelle Revue Théologique* (January-February 1985), hoping to clarify this historical point.

A few words, first, concerning the background. In March 1962, during an audience with Pope John, I took exception to the number of draft texts that had been prepared and were intended for discussion at the upcoming Council. There were, I believe, seventy such texts — far too many, in my opinion. Their quality varied greatly, and in any case, their sheer bulk would have precluded *a priori* any possibility of useful and fruitful work within the Council. Pope John asked me to clear the ground and to prepare a plan based on the prepared schemata.

After careful study of the documents, I drafted a preliminary note for Pope John. Its intent was to pare down the texts, and to give the Council a truly pastoral perspective. My note was both negative and positive; the *idem nolle* was as essential as the *idem velle*, and together they provided the groundwork for a more detailed plan.

The preliminary note was intended as a way of breaking loose from legalistic conceptions of the Council. It fully encompassed Pope John's approach — and he personally expressed his approval.

Here is the text of this "negative" note:

A NOTE ON THE SUBJECT OF THE COUNCIL

The choice of subjects
The announcement of the Council has raised great hopes among the faithful, and in the world at large.

The Council must respond to this double expectation; it must therefore, of necessity, deal with a double range of issues.

One series of issues would concern the Church *ad extra,* that is to say the Church in relation to the world of today.

A second series of issues would deal with the Church *ad intra,* that is to say the Church within herself, again with a view to assisting her in fulfilling her mission in the world.

Criteria for choice
May I be allowed to suggest, in all filial loyalty, that the issues to be included on the agenda should meet the following criteria:

Positive criteria
It seems to me that the Council should discuss:
- matters of *major* significance;
- matters of *vital* importance;
- matters of importance *for the whole Church;*
- matters that are related to the desired *pastoral renewal.*

Negative criteria
The world and the Church are awaiting with anguished hope the Council's answers to vital and urgent questions. It would be an immense and sorrowful disappointment, to the Church and to the world at large, if the Council were to become hopelessly entangled in matters of detail.

If this were to happen, we would no longer see the forest for the trees, and the Council's vital force would be smothered by such an abundant growth of secondary branches.

The need to prune
It therefore seems to me necessary to prune mercilessly all that is secondary, minor, of local interest, or purely canonical or administrative in nature. In practice — if I may be

allowed to speak with filial honesty – this means, in my opinion, that eighty per cent of the schemata, in their present form, are not "Council material". It is enough to read the documents to see that they deal largely with secondary issues.

Referral to commissions
I feel that these documents – concerning which there was much disagreement within the Central Commission – should be referred *either* to the Commission for the Reform of Canon Law, *or* to special post-conciliar commissions discussed later in this note.

Sketching broad avenues
In order to avoid the kind of painful floundering that characterised the early stages of Vatican I, I believe it would be useful to sketch the broad outlines of a few wide paths through the forest, and to bring out a few major issues for consideration by the Fathers.

The need for a restricted committee
The final choice of issues to be included on the agenda will rest with His Holiness the Pope. However, it would seem useful and practical to entrust a preliminary selection of issues to a restricted committee, appointed by the Holy Father, for his own personal and private use – a sort of "brains-trust" – whose mandate would be to suggest a list of major issues in line with the above criteria.

Choice of issues in relation to available time
Of necessity, the list of issues will have to take into account the intended duration of the Council. We must avoid, at all cost, the possibility that the bishops should feel that they have not had the opportunity seriously to address the items on the agenda, and that the Council has become bogged down in details.

Post-conciliar commissions

Whatever the duration of the Council, and whatever its outcome, it would seem appropriate to consider the establishment of post-conciliar commissions, and to announce this as soon as possible.

Purpose

At the conclusion of the Council, these commissions would undertake the following tasks:

1. to study any remaining issues left unexamined or unresolved at the end of the Council, as well as any new issues that may arise;

2. to follow up and monitor the concrete implementation of Council decisions in various sectors.

Membership

Such post-conciliar commissions would lighten the work of the Council; their establishment would give the Council's work the sense of purpose that everyone expects from it.

These commissions should include bishops representing the various continents, and appointed by the Holy See; there should not be too many members on each commission. Specialists and experts could later be called upon in a consultative capacity.

These commissions could continue the work of the preparatory commissions, along new lines, taking into account basic guidelines provided by the Council itself.

The commissions could be attached to congregations

It would be extremely useful, and would be of benefit to souls, if these commissions were set up as permanent bodies, attached to each Congregation within the Roman Curia. Thus, within each Congregation a breath of life would flow between the centre and the periphery, allowing diocesan bishops to make known their pastoral concerns, and to rethink from a pastoral perspective the problems facing Congregations; these Congregations are, by the very nature of things, primarily sensitive to the administrative and canonical aspects of their work.

The commissions could also receive from the Holy Father the mandate to prepare a reform of the Roman Curia. If we wish to achieve a genuine, concrete and lasting pastoral renewal, a reform of the Roman Curia, in line with the hopes and wishes expressed by bishops throughout the world, is essential.

A Council that would proclaim a few momentous truths, without providing the means to ensure their implementation once the Council is over, would be like a brief spring with no summer and no harvest.

Decentralisation through bishops' conferences

The greatest difficulties for the Council will not lie on the dogmatic level – where absolute unity is easy – but rather on the pastoral level, since it will be endeavouring to formulate, in every instance, one single rule, flexible enough to be adapted to local situations.

Would it be possible to hope that, for the good of the Church, a certain number of concrete adaptations on the level of pastoral implementation will be left to the bishops' conferences, subject, of course, to final approval by the Holy See?

The danger of stagnation

The move towards pastoral renewal has not been felt with equal intensity in different countries. It is to be feared that the number of bishops who have had a wide experience in this area may not be sufficiently large for their views to prevail within the Council. Our experience within the Central Commission is an indication that there is a powerful tendency towards fundamentalism, strongly opposed to pastoral renewal of any scope or significance. May the Holy Spirit enlighten His Holiness the Pope so that the tendency towards stagnation, even if it were to prove stronger in numbers, may not prevail in the final analysis.

A pastoral council

If I may be permitted, in conclusion, to express a wish – it is that the Council may be, above all, a pastoral council, that is to say an apostolic council. How greatly it would benefit the Church if the Council were to define, in broad lines, the manner in which the entire Church could become a Church in mission, at all levels – laity, religious, clergy, bishops and Roman congregations! It would indeed be a magnificent pentecostal grace for the Church, one that the beloved Head of our Church has wished for with all his heart and his Christian hope!

Working out the details

Having thus cleared the way, I was able to go ahead with a draft plan. By the end of April 1962, the plan was ready. I had introduced, as much as possible, the themes that were dearest to me, with a constant eye to promoting pastoral adaptations, which I believed to be of the utmost importance.

The document was confidential, and remained strictly personal and private until I decided that it might be useful to share it with a few cardinals, including Cardinal Montini, who were friends of mine. In my archives, I find a letter from Cardinal Liénart, dated June 14, 1962:

> I am absolutely delighted with your project, and I don't want to wait until this evening and tell you by telephone. I wholeheartedly support the apostolic spirit in which you have conceived the plan; the organisation of the various parts, as you have outlined it; and the wide horizons you have opened.

The other cardinals did not respond in writing, but their verbal reactions conveyed much the same message.

By order of Pope John, on May 19, 1962, Cardinal Cicognani, Secretary of State, distributed photocopies of this plan to a certain number of cardinals, for their information. Pope John wanted to rally the support of several influential cardinals, in the hope that when the time came, the plan could be presented under their joint sponsorship. To this end, he asked me to meet with a few cardinals, whose names he gave me.

A first meeting took place early in July 1962, at the Belgian College. I reported on the meeting to the Pope in a letter dated July 4, 1962:

Most Holy Father,
Your Holiness asked me to report on the reactions of several cardinals who have studied the proposed general plan.

We had a very cordial and relaxed meeting at the Belgian College. At the beginning of the meeting, Cardinal Doepfner suggested that perhaps it would be better to let the *schemata* be presented to the Council for discussion, as originally intended, without any overall plan. However, he quickly agreed with the unanimous and insistent views of Cardinals Montini, Siri and Liénart, all of whom vigorously supported the proposed plan, and strongly stressed the need for an architectural structure that would be both coherent and wide in scope.

All agreed that the Council should first deal with doctrinal matters, during its first session, and then focus on pastoral issues during one or more subsequent sessions.

All felt that the doctrinal part should begin with a study of the Church: *De Ecclesiae Christi mysterio* — in other words, the Church in her essence, with her various components.

It was unanimously felt that the Secretariat of the Council should not send the prepared draft texts to the bishops randomly, in no particular order; this would give a bad impression, implying that the Council will be dealing first with matters of secondary importance and that no central theme is to be brought out.

The Orthodox world shares the hope that the Council will begin with a constitution on the Church, so that the Second Vatican Council may indeed be the Council *De Ecclesia*. I am including a copy of a recent article by Pro-

fessor Florovsky, one of the most prominent Orthodox theologians of our time. A Catholic would perhaps have
expressed himself differently, but I find the convergence on
the central theme quite striking, and it is for this reason
that I am bringing it to your attention.

We now need to develop a more detailed plan, indicating
where and how the final schemata can be introduced at
appropriate points in the existing overall framework. The
cardinals mentioned above have asked me to undertake
this task; I set to work immediately upon my return, using
the existing draft texts as much as possible. On a separate
sheet, you will find some comments concerning the overall
picture; I have attempted to situate the plan more precisely
in the broader context as well as to explain its general
meaning.

It will then remain for me to deliver all of this to Your
Wisdom, Most Holy Father, and to pray that the Holy Spirit may guide you as you decide on the final orientations.

I have just finished reading *Il Diario del Concilio Vati-
cano I,* by Fr Dehon, which Your Holiness advised me to
read. I have found it interesting, lively, full of lessons concerning both what we should do and what we should not
do. The whole book is a glorification of the Holy Spirit,
whose work is done through instruments that are always
inadequate, and sometimes so human in their poverty.

In profound filial piety, I have the honour and the joy to
remain your humble and obedient servant.

There was a second meeting, again at the Belgian College. Cardinal Montini was present, with a few others, including Cardinal
Siri and Cardinal Lercaro. There was no difficulty in obtaining
their support for the plan, since the idea was to establish a general framework for Council discussions.

Pope John, for his part, had already adopted the main points of
the plan and made them his own. We can see them between the
lines of the memorable radio message he gave on September 12,
1962, to announce and introduce the Council, a few weeks before

its opening. On September 12, 1962, the *Osservatore Romano* announced the Council with the following headline: *"Ecclesia Christi, lumen gentium"*. Pope John described the upcoming council as flowing from the Lord's command: "Go,therefore, make disciples of all the nations; baptize them in the name of the Father and of the Son and of the Holy Spirit, and teach them to observe all the commands I gave you" (Mt 28:19-20). These words provided the central themes of my plan. Moreover, the Holy Father's speech included, and made his own, the proposed distinction between the Church *ad intra* and the Church *ad extra*, on which the entire plan hinged.

It is common knowledge that in the first few weeks, the Council was unable to find a sense of direction or to set its own path. In order to understand later developments, it is also important to remember that the Pope was not well; we were beginning to be concerned for his health.

The irresolute climate of the Council prompted Cardinal Montini to write a letter to Pope John on October 18, 1962, asking for greater structure and coherence in the organisation of the Council. At the end of his letter, he alluded to the plan I had submitted. The Pope sent me a photocopy of this letter, to be used as I saw fit. Its content is public knowledge today, and is of particular interest to historians, since it sheds light on certain aspects of the next pontificate.

The Pope's health was increasingly a source of concern, and I had to resolve a difficult moral problem: should I take the initiative and present my plan, or should I wait, since Pope John had wanted to be the one to choose the appropriate moment for making it public? The Pope was by then too sick to be approached directly. I wrote him a letter, expressing affection and concern, but making no mention of the plan. Just in case, however, I sent his secretary a copy of the statement I intended to make two days later at the Council, proposing the plan in general outline. I did not think that the Pope, sick as he was, would hear of this. Much to my surprise, Mgr Dell'Acqua called me to the Vatican very early the following morning, and told me that Pope John fully approved my text. Indeed, he had read it in bed and had added a few remarks of his own, writing them in the margin in Italian. I asked Mgr Dell'Acqua to have the Pope's annotations translated into Latin by his staff, in order to be quite certain to betray nothing of the Holy Father's thought. Thus I had no moral qualms as I made my speech, *in aula*, on December 4, 1962, proposing the central theme which the Council immediately approved. The unanimous endorsement of the Council was further reinforced on the following day, when Cardinal Montini — who had remained somewhat reserved during the first session of the Council — spoke with enthusiasm in favour of my proposal, as also did Cardinal Lercaro.

It has been said that John XXIII had asked Cardinal Montini to support my statement. I don't know whether this is true or not. I do know that while dining with Montini the previous evening, I had told him about the statement I intended to make, in view of the Pope's unstable health, but he had given me no personal reaction; thus his support, which carried so much weight, was for me a delightful surprise.

What follows is the text of the plan itself. In my speech to the Council, I summarised it to fit into the eight minutes allotted to each speaker.

TEXT OF THE PLAN SUBMITTED TO POPE JOHN XXIII

INTRODUCTION

The purpose of the following plan is to give the Council an overall coherent pastoral direction, one that will be easy for all to understand. It is designed as a triptych and includes: a basic introduction; the major themes, grouped under four main headings; and a final message, a sort of apotheosis of the Council.

A response to expectations

The themes that are emphasised are those that we believe to be foremost in the minds of the faithful and of the world. In response to expectations, we have attempted to situate the Council at the heart of the life of the Church and of the world, rather than in some "ivory tower".

Convergence around four centres of interest

The questions which were dealt with in a disjointed sequence, and which often reflected conflicting approaches and perspectives, have been brought together under these four headings, which represent four major centres of interest.

Use of prepared documents

This structure would enable us to make use of the prepared schemata as much as possible. A huge amount of work has gone into the preparation of these documents, and we must take full advantage of this important work. This can best be done by making it less disjointed, less of a fragmented mosaic, and by breathing some life into it. By and large, these documents are made lifeless skeletons by the legalistic, canonical and at times repressive manner in which they are presented. Within the framework of the plan, we can give them life and vitality, bringing them together into a coherent whole.

Of use to scholars and to the faithful

Themes that emerge clearly and are easy to retain are equally useful to bishops, to theologians, and to ordinary Christians, who, thanks to an easily popularised plan, will be able to follow the stages of the Council and to live in rhythm with the Church. These themes will also be very appropriate for use by pastors in their homilies; they will strike everyone's imagination by their relevance and simplicity.

Instruments of pastoral progress

These themes will allow us to look at the chief errors of our times - both *ad intra*, within the Church itself, and *ad extra*, in the world outside — in a positive and constructive way, without anathemas. They will make it easier for us to note certain gaps in our pastoral teaching and to make whatever adjustments are necessary.

DRAFT OVERALL PLAN

First schema: **De Ecclesiae Christi Mysterio**

It would seem necessary, as a starting point, to establish the links between Vatican II and Vatican I. The best way of doing this would be to open the Council with a discussion of a schema: *"De Ecclesiae Christi mysterio"*.

Reasons for this

a. Continuity with Vatican I. The First Vatican Council had already prepared a schema "De Ecclesia" , only one level of which has as yet been defined: that of papal primacy and infallibility. There was not enough time to "situate" the bishops or the laity within the mystery of the Church.

b. A better doctrinal balance. This would be both an effort in continuity and a search for balance, since the mystery of the Church would thus appear in all its fullness and in complete harmony.

c. A step toward our separated brethren. The Orthodox accuse our Church of minimising or suppressing the role of the bishops; Protestants accuse her of not giving lay people their proper role. In this schema *"De Ecclesiae Christi mysterio"*, we could usefully and positively respond to objections raised by these Churches by pointing to the bond between the Papacy and the Body of the Church, by showing the place and the meaning of the episcopal college, and by affirming the role of the laity (all of this will be dealt with later in greater detail).

d. Operari sequitur esse. Before focusing on "The Church at work", it seems essential that the Council should preface its efforts with a major doctrinal statement by the Church, on the Church: *operari sequitur esse.* The Church must define itself: *quid dicis de teipso?*

e. The Church is "Jesus Christ communicated and spread". This would immediately underline the essential: the Church is Christ alive today in his Mystical Body; it is Christ, our contemporary.

The one and only question which sums up all others for the bishops of 1962 is whether or not we are faithfully continuing the work that the Master has entrusted to us, the work that he wants to accomplish through us.

The central concept
The Council's work could fall quite naturally into two main areas:
– the Church *ad intra;*
– the Church *ad extra.*
The schema we propose introduces the collective *examen* of conscience that the bishops want to undertake concerning their mission. The basic question they must ask – and which could well be the central question of the Council, the crossroads from which its main avenues will lead outward – could be the following:

How does the Church of the twentieth century respond to the Master's ultimate commandment?

Euntes ergo
Docete omnes gentes
Baptizantes eos
In nomine Patris et Filii et Spiritus Sancti
Docentes eos servare omnia quaecumque mandavi vobis.

Go, therefore
Make disciples of all the nations
Baptize them
in the name of the Father and of the Son and
of the Holy Spirit
And teach them to observe all the commands I gave you.
This leads very naturally to the following plan:

Section A : *Ecclesia "ad intra"*

This same text from Matthew could be used to structure and divide the work:

- *Euntes ergo:* **Ecclesia Evangelizans (vel Salvificans)**
- *Docete omnes gentes:* **Ecclesia Docens**
- *Baptizantes eos:* **Ecclesia Sanctificans**
- *In nomine Patris et Filii et Spiritus Sancti:* **Ecclesia Orans.**

Section B : *Ecclesia "ad extra"*

In this Section, we could group together several major problems – listed further on – that would fall comfortably under the heading: "and teach them to observe all the commands I gave you".

Making use of existing schemata
This schema, *"De Ecclesiae Christi mysterio"*, has basically already been prepared in several existing schemata such as *"De Ecclesiae militantis natura"* and *"De membris Ecclesiae..."* (*Relatore* Cardinal Ottaviani). It would be enough to reorganise these schemata according to the observations of the members of the Central Commission. Since this will be, in fact, an introduction to the whole Council, it might be appropriate to broaden the text at various points; however, once re-worked, these schemata could provide the substance for an introduction.

Section A: *Ecclesia ad Intra*

I. *Ecclesia evangelizans* (or *salvificans*)

Go, therefore. In response to the Saviour's commandment, we must place the entire Church "in a state of mission". This part deals with missionary pastoral work.

A doctrinal statement
The Central Commission adopted, almost unanimously, the wish expressed by one member that the Council should develop a major statement concerning the missionary obligations of members of the Church, both *ad extra, vis-à-vis* non-Christian peoples, and *ad intra, vis-à-vis* those who minimise or even seek to eliminate all efforts to "convert", and who claim that "life witness" is sufficient, that the apostolate is an intrusion and an attack against the conscience of others, that all opinions are equally valid if they are sincere, that good faith in itself makes up for lack of theological faith. This is contrary to the Gospel and undermines at their very roots all efforts to "carry the Good News to all creation".

Let us now look at the *Ecclesia evangelizans*, part by part.

A. On the episcopal level
It is only natural that an examination of conscience and of pastoral renewal of any apostolate should begin with those who are apostles by divine right and, as such, are at the head of the pastoral work of their dioceses.

Main issues
1. It would be desirable to make an important statement on the apostolic college and the role of bishops within the Church. Such a schema *"de episcopis"* would, *in obliquo*, be very useful with regard to our separated Eastern

brethren, who feel that our Church has greatly understated the role of bishops in the Church. The schema *"de episcopis"* already exists under the title *"De episcopis residentialibus"* (*Relatore* Cardinal Ottaviani). This text would have to be re-worked, taking into account observations made by members of the Central Commission, and in particular by Cardinals Richaud, Doepfner and Bea.

2. It would be useful to affirm clearly the essential role of the bishop as head of the total pastoral effort of his diocese.

3. It would be useful to examine the *cura animarum* – the care of souls – from the standpoint of the bishop's duties. This schema exists: *"De Cura animarum in genere"*, part one (*Relatore* Cardinal Marella).

4. In the light of the principles defined, the following practical corollaries could be brought out:

a) An increase in the power of bishops *"in se"*. It would be necessary to combine the schema *"de episcopis"* prepared by the Bishops' Commission with that prepared by the Eastern Commission, since they are complementary.

b) An increase in the power of bishops *"quoad religiosos exemptos individualiter"* (in relation to religious exempt on an individual basis).

c) An increase in the power of bishops *"quoad religiosos exemptos collective prout adunantur in Unionibus Superiorum Maiorum"* (in relation to religious exempt collectively as associated in Unions of Major Superiors).

B. Regarding secular and regular clergy

This is the place to discuss matters affecting the clergy – vocations, seminaries and scholasticates, care after ordination, as well as possible assistance from permanent deacons, etc.

a) The Council of Trent has left a profound mark on seminaries. Saint Charles Borromeo gave them a form that has become traditional. Unfortunately, with time, seminaries became increasingly centres of piety and scholarship, and lost some of the practical pastoral aspects that the Council of Trent had intended them to have.

We must create a new kind of seminary; or, more precisely, we must enrich existing seminaries, which were conceived as centres for piety and study, by giving them an additional role as centres for practical pastoral initiation, in accordance with a methodology that will have to be developed.

Such a reform would have tremendous consequences, since the apostolic renewal of the clergy will affect everything else.

As regards religious more specifically, this would be the place to examine problems arising in active orders from the adaptation of religious rules of life to a modern apostolate, as well as all questions concerning the most effective collaboration between secular and regular clergy in the framework of present-day apostolic needs. Some of the existing schemata could be used here: *"De sacrorum alumnis formandis", "De vocationibus ecclesiasticis fovendis"* (*Relatore* Cardinal Pizzardo), as well as *"Quaestiones de religiosis", "Disciplina de renovatione vitae et spiritus"* (*Relatore* Cardinal Valeri).

b) On the question of permanent deacons: would it not be appropriate to leave open, for some countries, the option to experiment with the idea of a permanent diaconate? This would be extremely useful, if we truly want the message – and the sacraments – to reach all people.

An *ad hoc* commission could be appointed to look into the conditions for such experiments. If the Council opposes the establishment of a permanent diaconate at the universal level, let it allow experiments on a limited basis. In any case, the question deserves to be discussed by Council members.

C. Regarding nuns and lay brothers

Today the Church includes close to one million nuns and a

large number of lay brothers. They represent a vast potential of resources which are not being used as fully as they might be in the area of the apostolate. A major review is called for; it would require a huge effort of *aggiornamento* of the customs and rules of life of female religious (and of male religious) to adapt to the necessities of the apostolate today. It would be essential to stress the role they could play — if they acquired the necessary formation — as animators of lay adults.

D. Regarding the laity

1. A doctrinal statement
We need a major declaration on the role of the laity in the Church — all we have at present are three lines in the articles of canon law! A schema *"de laicis"* has been drafted, but it needs to be rewritten with greater breadth and soul. Moreover, this document should be harmonised with the one prepared by the Commission for the lay apostolate.

Our separated brethren accuse the Church of being far too clerical and of stifling the laity. They believe in "the priesthood of the faithful", to whom they assign an important role. Quite frequently, Catholics who leave the faith to join a sect will claim to have found a religion where they are respected, and in which they can actively participate.

Taking all of this into account, an important statement should be drafted, in a loving and paternal tone, recognising the rights and obligations of lay people by virtue of the baptism which they have received and through which they have been incorporated into the Church.

2. A 'catholic' terminology for Catholic Action
It would be appropriate to discuss the question raised by Pope Pius XII in 1957 at the World Congress on the Apostolate of the Laity, concerning the "generic" meaning that should be reserved, or as Pius XII said, "restored" to the expression "Catholic Action". In view of the explicit appeal

made by Pope Pius XII on this specific point, this question cannot remain unanswered.

Existing schemata, such as *"De laicis"(Relatore* Cardinal Ottaviani) and the schemata on the lay apostolate prepared by the Commission presided over by Cardinal Cento, could be used.

II. *Ecclesia docens*

We must reach out to those who do not know the Saviour, and carry the message to them, the full content of the message, in order to bring all of the Gospel to all living things. This is the goal of pastoral catechesis in the broadest sense of the term.

We must make the Gospel known to all people, by every possible means.

All people

— We need to look at the religious instruction provided within educational institutions of various levels, including universities.

— We must study the question of a universal catechism. Should there be one single catechism or would a simpler directory be enough? And what would be our wishes concerning the content of such a directory, from an apostolic point of view, for example?

— We must look carefully at the transmission of the Word of God through preaching.

All of these questions are discussed in various schemata, such as: *"De catechismo et catechetica institutione"* (*Relatore* Cardinal Cicognani); *"De catechetica populi christiani institutione"* (*Relatore* Cardinal Ciriaci); and *"De Verbo Dei"* (*Relatore* Cardinal Bea).

By every possible means

Under this item, we could include various techniques and methods of communication — press, radio, cinema, TV —

using parts of the existing schema on the media.

III. *Ecclesia sanctificans*

Major questions concerning the pastoral aspects of the sacraments would be included under this heading.

See, for example, the following schemata: *"De Ecclesiae Sacramentis"* (*Relatore* Cardinal Cicognani): *"De Sacramento poenitentiae"* (*Relatore* Cardinal Marella); *"De Sacramento ordinis"* (*Relatore* Cardinal Marella).

IV. *Ecclesia orans*

The question of *pastoral liturgy* should come under this heading.

The schema *"De sacra liturgia"*, prepared by the Commission, deals with the various aspects of this subject; it could be used here, provided the essential points are brought out and streamlined, allowing for an analysis of a few major issues selected because of their importance for the whole Church, both Western and Eastern.

See schemata *"De usu linguarum vernacularum in liturgiis"* (*Relatore* Cardinal Cicognani); *"De officio divino"* (idem).

Section B: *Ecclesia "ad extra"*

This part could come under St Matthew's text after the words "Go, therefore...": "and teach them to observe all the commands I gave you".

What the world expects
The Church must bring Christ to the world. The world has its own problems, and seeks with anguish for solutions;

some of these problems are obstacles to the spread of truth and grace.

Some of the major problems can be grouped as follows:

What do men and women seek? They seek love in their homes; daily bread for themselves and their families; peace both within each nation and among nations. These are basic aspirations. Does the Church have anything to contribute at these various levels?

Answers

We suggest that the Council should concentrate on the following four problems:

a. *The Church in its relationship to the family , and in particular to the married couple*

The state of grace is particularly threatened with respect to the ethics of marriage. We are faced with a crucial problem: that of birth-control. We must rewrite large parts of *"Casti Connubii"* taking into account new problems, making use of some statements made by Pius XII, and distinguishing between the duties and obligations of spouses and their responsibilities toward children.

It would be useful to do for *"Casti Connubii"* what was done for *"Rerum Novarum"*, which was revised with *"Quadragesimo Anno"*, then updated again with *"Mater et Magistra"*.

Several schemata have been drafted on the subject; for example, *"De matrimonio et familia"* (*Relatore* Cardinal Ottaviani).

b. *The Church and economics*

The Church is expected to condemn atheistic Communism. It will be most important, however, to bring out *the part of truth* that exists in Communism, and strongly condemn social injustice and inequality in the distribution of wealth. In her relationship to under-developed countries, the Church must show herself to be everyone's Church, and especially the Church of the poor. Moralists have written countless volumes attempting to define the *"de sexto"*; yet, we have practically nothing concerning the obligation to give our excess wealth to others, or the social purpose of goods created for the benefit of all. Inherent to authentic Christianity is a social and communal dimension which we must bring out vigorously.

c. *The Church and social issues*
The political world in which we live is a new one, and new problems arise concerning Church-State relationships. One of these important problems concerns the religious freedom which the Church claims for herself. What then should be her attitude with respect to the religious freedom of others? See schema *"De libertate religiosa"* (*Relatore* Cardinal Bea).

d. *The Church and international issues*
In a world which has known the horrors of two world wars, there is today a profound aspiration towards international peace, and a new sensitivity concerning all that can threaten such peace. It is essential to show the world that the Church is, *par excellence*, an instrument of peace.

It is expected that the Church will take a clear stand on issues like war, the nuclear bomb, the use of nuclear energy for peaceful purposes, and so forth. These are delicate problems, but they will have to be tackled in some way.

A Message to the World

It would seem appropriate and desirable for the Council to address a final solemn message to the world. Such a message must be compelling in style and in scope, and could be addressed to the following:

— firstly, to our separated Orthodox brethren;
— then to our separated Protestant brethren;

— next, to all those in the world who believe in
God;
— finally, to atheists, pointing out the meaning
of God and of his presence.

The message could end by invoking Christ in his Glory,
King of humanity and Master of the Universe, "Pantocra-
tor", the Beginning and the End of the whole cosmos, in
accordance with a vision that is dear to contemporary men
and women.

The message could end with some sort of collective act
of faith in Christ alive in his Church, in accordance with
his promise: *"Et ecce vobiscum sum usque ad consumma-
tionem saeculi."*

Through such an eschatological vision, the Church
would express her awareness of being a pilgrim Church —
"peregrinans et in via" — and turn to the Lord with humble and courageous faith, *"donec veniat, usque ad diem
adventus Domini".*

* * *

A thoughtful gesture

I would like to conclude this historical background to the Council
by mentioning another instance of Pope John's thoughtfulness in
relation to the proposed plan. On a previous occasion, he had
sent me a book by an Italian spiritual writer named De Luca. This
was intended for my "spiritual reading", and was an expression of
his affectionate desire to share with me his enthusiasm for this
particular author.

To thank me for the work I had done, he now instructed Cardinal Cicognani, his Secretary of State, to send me the *Acts* of
Saint Charles Borromeo, in five magnificently bound volumes —
an edition he had supervised personally. The letter that accompanied these alluded pointedly to the date chosen for sending the
gift: it was the day on which Pope John made his statement con-

cerning the organisation of the Council, in which echoes of my plan could be found between the lines. Here is the letter, dated September 11, 1962:

Your Eminence,

The Holy Father has instructed me on this day to send you on his behalf the complete edition of *The Acts of the Apostolic Visit of Saint Charles Borromeo to Bergamo (1575)*, published under his personal care.
It is with pleasure that I perform this duty and congratulate you on this further mark of the benevolence of our Sovereign Pontiff, *at the very moment in which he addresses a radio message to the world at large, one month before the opening of the Ecumenical Council.*

Yours, etc.
Cardinal Cicognani

Instructions to wait, and an amendment
During the first week of the Council, Pope John had said to me: "The plan is here, in this drawer [which he opened, as if to confirm his words]. I will let you know when the time comes. For now, the Pope's duty is to listen with open ears [and he placed both his hands behind his ears] and be attentive to what the Holy Spirit is saying to the bishops." I willingly obeyed this command to be patient.

Despite his exhaustion, while on his sick-bed Pope John wrote a few lines in the margins of my draft, mentioning his predecessors Pius XI and Pius XII; it is customary to link pontifical documents to statements made by preceding pontiffs. Towards the end of the document, he corrected my allusion to the opposition encountered by Cardinal Mercier in the wake of the Malines Conversations, giving my words a more moderate tone. Finally, where I had proposed the establishment of a secretariat to study social questions, he suggested as an alternative an under-secretariat.

B. BETWEEN SESSIONS

Pacem in terris

Wishing to communicate his personal message to the world, and feeling that his end was near, Pope John drafted a somewhat "different" encyclical, intended not only for the faithful within the Church, but for all men and women of good will. This encyclical, known as *Pacem in terris*, had wide repercussions, and was extraordinarily well-received the world over.

Pacem in terris was Pope John's personal spiritual testament, and he wanted it to reach the widest possible audience throughout the world. He was very happy indeed to accede to the wish expressed within the United Nations headquarters in New York that a Vatican Prelate should introduce the encyclical to the Organization.

Early one morning, I received a phone call with a request from Pope John, asking me to be his messenger and his spokesman to the General Assembly, and to present to U Thant, then Secretary General of the Organization, an autographed copy of *Pacem in terris*.

The Holy Father had given me no instructions, except to expand more particularly on the last section. He only saw the text of my presentation after I had delivered it.

It is not an exaggeration to say that *Pacem in terris* was Pope John's personal message to the world. In it he invested the very best of himself, in the service of the whole of humanity.

The commentary on the encyclical at the UN

A date for the presentation of the encyclical in New York had already been set for the following week. It was not very convenient from my point of view, since Archbishop Ramsey of Canterbury, Primate of the Anglican Communion, had agreed to come to Malines on the day after the presentation for a first friendly ecumenical encounter. Nevertheless, I accepted, on the understanding that I would give my speech in New York in the morning and take an evening flight back to Brussels. Luckily, the Americans, who had not expected Pope John to send them a cardinal, proposed a later date to give themselves time to make arrangements for this solemn occasion.

I was met at the airport by the organiser of this event, Curtis Roosevelt, grandson of the former President of the United States, and by Cardinal Spellman. While they were waiting for me together, Curtis Roosevelt asked the Cardinal whether he and I were friends. Later he told me the humorous answer he received from the formidable Cardinal Spellman. Spellman first spoke a few words of friendly praise, indicated that he knew me well (and indeed we had a friend in common, Peter Grace), and finally concluded with a smile and these unexpected words: "We discussed all sorts of things at the Council...and we never once agreed!"

I must say, I have wondered once or twice whether Cardinal Spellman's speeches to the Council, always couched in the most impeccable Latin, had not been written for him by some theologian at the Holy Office!

Cardinal Spellman was not present at the UN meeting, for the very simple reason that, as a truly patriotic American, he had always refused to set foot in that building. His gruffness was very useful to me that day, however, for he high-handedly dismissed the crowd of reporters who met me at the airport with a barrage of questions, and put an end to my ordeal.

As I think of him, I remember another little scene, which took place in a Vatican elevator. We were in the elevator together, in our most ceremonial garb, going up to a meeting with a curial cardinal on the third floor. The elevator stopped at the second floor and a young priest came in. Surprised to find two cardinals, he asked very ceremoniously if he might be permitted to go up with us. Spellman immediately replied: "My dear friend, for such a favour you must apply *in scriptis* [in writing]!"

To resume my story after this brief parenthesis: the solemn session at the UN took place the day after my arrival. This was the first time I gave a public address in English. I spoke for about an hour, giving a summary of the encyclical and bringing out a few central points. The purpose of my speech was to emphasise the universal aspect of the message of the encyclical. Pope John had written it as an open letter to all men and women of good will. In it he revealed his paternal love for all human beings.

I introduced the encyclical by comparing its contents to a symphony of peace, with all its various components. In the eyes of Pope John, I said, peace must have truth as its foundation, justice as its dominant force, love as its motivation, freedom for its vital space. Peace demands respect for the individual.

I quoted from Saint-Exupéry: "Only when respect for the dignity of man lives in our hearts will we be able to imagine a social, political and scientific system that will embody respect for every human being." I pointed out that peace begins in people's hearts, but must spread out in concentric circles and reach to the very ends of the universe.

And I added: "No man of good will can accept that two out of three human beings should suffer hunger. Civilisation is not worthy of its name if it remains indifferent to this social and collective sin. We are still very far from mutual understanding, from an authentic spirit of friendship. We cross paths, as we hurry along our busy ways, without a word or a smile. In our century, man has discovered interplanetary space, and yet we have only begun to explore that space which separates us from one another. Man has built gigantic bridges to span rivers and torrents, but we have yet to learn how to reach across the abyss that separates one people from another. Our century has discovered nuclear energy, but it has yet to discover the creative energy that comes with peace and harmony. The encyclical is entirely aimed at making this world a better place to live in."

There followed a question-time. Ushers collected about forty questions in writing; I asked the chairman, Curtis Roosevelt, to sort them and organise them into some kind of order. I must admit that this dialogue with an audience which included every shade of opinion and every religion was for me a powerful experience, and I remember it with deep emotion.

The first question went as follows: "Does Pope John bless the UN?" to which I responded, "The Pope knows well the saying that 'A voyage of a thousand miles begins with one single step.' He blesses the UN as a first step in the right direction." This got a round of applause.

The second question was this: "Does Pope John bless communism?" My answer was: "You have just heard me say that the encyclical makes a distinction between the doctrine of a movement, the movement itself, and, beyond that, the people involved in it. The communist doctrine is incompatible with our faith. A movement can be more or less imbued with a particular doctrine. As for the people themselves, they are often worth much more than the doctrines they espouse." Then I added, "We Christians are always worth less than our doctrine," which brought a delighted response from my listeners.

Another question came from a woman who, speaking "on behalf of thirty million women", wanted to know whether the Church counts on women to bring about peace in the world. A quote from Lenin sprang to mind, concerning the role of women in all revolutions: "Revolution is unthinkable without the participation of women"; commenting on this, I said "If Lenin considered women essential to the success of any revolution, then how much more vital they are to the establishment of peace in the world." The woman seemed well satisfied with my answer.

At the end of an hour of public dialogue, the chairman put an end to the discussion, which by then had covered about fifteen different issues. The Apostolic Delegate, who was present at the session, said a few friendly words of thanks in private, and I was at last free to breathe a deep sigh of relief.

The morning's public session ended in an excellent atmosphere. It was followed by a number of private conversations with members of the US Senate and House of Representatives. Finally, we went up to the thirty-fifth floor of the building. Here, Secretary General U Thant, to whom I had delivered the copy of the encyclical autographed by Pope John, offered us lunch.

We left in great haste as soon as lunch was over. Preceded by a police motorcade, we sped across New York at a tremendous rate, to a little airport from which a helicopter flew me over the city to catch my flight for Chicago. Here, a private airplane was waiting to take me to the University of Notre Dame in Indiana, where I was scheduled to give a lecture that same evening. I was once and for all convinced of American efficiency.

I wrote a report to the Pope, who by then was seriously ill and in bed. I know that my report gave him great joy, for this was "his" encyclical and it meant very much to him. In many ways, it was his farewell message to the world.

"Working holidays" in preparation for the council

Late in December 1962, Pope John had established a committee of a few cardinals to supervise the preparatory work, and to give him advice concerning the documents that were being drafted. He had personally assigned specific tasks to each one of us. To me he had entrusted the schema on the Church *ad intra* – which was to become *Lumen Gentium* – as well as the final schema on the Church *ad extra* – which was to become *Gaudium et Spes*. It was an engrossing task, since these two were in fact the key documents of the Council. Pope John had deliberately assigned them to me so that I would incorporate, as much as possible, the suggestions I had made in my plan for the Council. This was easy to do as far as *Lumen Gentium* was concerned, since much of the document had been drafted originally by a group of Belgian theologians, and the actual re-writing of the final text was done by Mgr Philips.

Schema XVII, which eventually became *Gaudium et Spes*, gave us much more trouble. The early drafts all seemed inadequate, and three times I rejected the texts that were proposed.

To establish an authentic dialogue between the Church and the world, we would need a document of tremendous scope; because of this, it seemed necessary to begin with a text that would situate the Church as such within the world. I wanted to emphasise that Christians are in the world but not of the world, and that, as we engage in dialogue, we must never lose sight of the Christian's own identity. This is why I suggested that the theology of the Church's presence in the world should be developed in the first part of the document; a second part would then deal with specific problems, such as human rights, the family, culture, justice and peace, and so forth.

In Malines, I gathered together for a week a group of theologians: Mgr Philips; Congar, OP; Mgr Dondeyne; Tucci, SJ; Rahner, SJ; and Mgr Delhaye. The fruit of our discussions was a text drafted by Mgr Philips, which I sent to Cardinals Cento (of the Commission for the Laity) and Browne (of the Commission on Doctrine). In the end, a different working plan was adopted, and *Gaudium et Spes* saw the light in its final form, drafted by Mgr Haubtmann with the assistance of a special drafting committee.

A last letter to Pope John
During my last conversation with him, the Holy Father had asked me to keep him informed on the work of our Commission. This letter was written in response to his request.

Malines, February 19, 1963
Most Holy Father,
I was deeply moved by the trust and paternal concern expressed by Your Holiness on the occasion of our unexpected audience, just before my departure. At that time, Your Holiness asked me for a written progress report, which I am now enclosing in the hope that it can be of use.

It is now – during the interval – that the future of the Council is being decided with respect to the issues that will be discussed, and to the duration of the Council itself. As regards the material, I believe the Commission has done an excellent sorting job, but it is important to supervise the implementation.

As regards time, after the experience of the first session,

the regulations will have to be amended; they were conceived in far too formal and legalistic a manner, and one that has satisfied nobody.

I hope to have some concrete proposals to submit to Your Holiness in a few weeks' time, concerning the *aggiornamento* of the regulations; consultations are now under way with competent experts on the organisation and management of international parliamentary assemblies.

The essential point has, however, been established, since the central theme will be *"Ecclesia Christi, lumen gentium"*.

In the enclosed note, I have brought out certain aspects of *Ecclesia Christi, ad intra* and *ad extra*, to which I would like to call Your Holiness's attention.

Thank you, Holy Father, for having saved the Council at major turning-points; for having known so wisely when to be silent and when to speak; and for having proved – at times, *ex absurdo*, which according to Aristotle is the most powerful argument! – that the episcopal college needs a chief, and that the command *"et tu confirma fratres tuos"* ("and you, confirm your brothers"), after twenty centuries, still carries its compelling quality.

In conclusion, may I call Your Holiness' attention to a matter that has caused much controversy throughout the world? Following the Liège trial, which attracted so much attention because the "compassionate killer" of a child was not punished by the law, I felt it was appropriate to devote my pastoral letter for Lent to this serious issue. I have taken the liberty of presenting a copy of this letter to Your Holiness. In the draft paper that is being prepared on *The Church and the Human Person*, I think it would be important to include a paragraph concerning precisely the inviolability of the human person: it would not be difficult to summarise in a few lines the essential arguments of my pastoral letter. Thus it was both in a national and in a conciliar perspective that I felt the duty to write these few pages.

With feelings of the deepest respect, I remain yours, etc..."

C. POPE JOHN IN PRIVATE

First encounter

When John XXIII appointed me Archbishop of Malines, I had not yet met him. I wrote a letter at the time, to thank him and to express my allegiance, as is customary. Some time later, I sent him a copy of my first pastoral letter, entitled *What do you expect from the Council?*

At our first meeting, he told me that when he read the letter, he immediately felt a great liking for its author, and recognised between us a communion of vision and of hopes for the upcoming Council. He added that he enjoyed the style as well; it reminded him of some French writer or other – I think it was Maurois.

A few weeks later, at the end of a second audience, he informed me that he was going to make me cardinal at the next consistory, to give me a chance to be more effective at the Council, where cardinals would be given the privilege of speaking first – bishops, who would only speak after the cardinals, would have a harder time holding people's attention on issues that by then would have been thoroughly explored. At that stage, only the eloquence of a Mgr De Smedt – who used Latin with virtuosity – or the words of a particularly cogent speaker could be expected to hold the interest of the audience.

In time, Pope John became a grandfather, rather than a father, to me, through his affection, his simplicity and his trust. He made one feel comfortable immediately, and disregarded all the complications of protocol. He was very detached from himself, from his role. He said to me one day, "I have not yet understood why I have become pope, and I believe God is having some trouble explaining it to himself!"

He described for me one day, with great vivacity and the greatest detachment, his deepest personal emotions at the moment of the last ballot between himself and Cardinal X – whose name he revealed to me, thus breaking a conclave secret! He accepted his election with deep inner peace. When his secretary, Don Loris

Capovilla, met him for the first time as the newly-elected Pope, and burst into tears, John XXIII calmly said to him, "There, there, do stop crying. Who's been elected Pope — you or me?" And he serenely went off to give his first blessing from the *loggia* to the crowds gathered in St Peter's Square. "I couldn't see a thing; I was completely blinded by the television lights pointing straight at me", he told me. "It was like looking at a crowd of souls in purgatory!"

A revealing letter

This profound detachment with respect to his own person found expression in his humourous remarks, and in the whimsical reactions that never ceased to surprise those around him. I believe the key to his personality is to be found in these unguarded moments.

On the very eve of the conclave, Roncalli, then Patriarch of Venice, wrote a letter to his friend Mgr Piazzi, Bishop of Bergamo. I find parts of this letter particularly revealing, and I reproduce it here, because I feel that it is an excellent introduction to a chapter on Pope John as he was in his private life. It is dated October 23, and reads as follows:

> A quick note as I enter the conclave. Treat it as a request for prayers from the Bishop and the diocese that as a good Bergamesque I hold most dear. Thinking of all the lovely images of Mary dotted around the diocese, calling to mind our patron saints, bishops, famous and holy priests, religious men and women of outstanding value, *my soul finds comfort in the confidence that a new Pentecost can blow through the Church, renewing its head, leading to a new ordering of the ecclesiastical body and bringing fresh vigour in progress towards the victory of truth, goodness and peace.* It little matters whether the next Pope is from Bergamo or not. Our common prayers will ensure that he

will be a prudent and gentle administrator, a saint and a sanctifier. You understand me, your excellency. Receive my greetings and my embrace."*

The italics are mine. That paragraph already contains a whole programme for a life and a pontificate; we must weigh each word with the greatest care.

Did he know he would be elected? I think he probably had a premonition. Be that as it may, here is an amusing anecdote as told by Mgr Jadot, former Apostolic Delegate to Washington, that also dates back to the day before the future Pope entered the conclave.

Early in February 1959, in Rome, I met with Mgr Sigismondi, Secretary of the Congregation for Propaganda.
We discussed the new Pope. Sigismondi told me that on the eve of the conclave in October 1958, Cardinal Roncalli had invited him to dinner and had asked who was being mentioned as *papabile*. As he became more and more insistent, Sigismondi finally told him straight out that his name was not among those considered likely to be elected.

A few days after the election, John XXIII called in Sigismondi to discuss Propaganda business. Sigismondi arrived looking a little sheepish, and Pope John gently teased him. No need to be alarmed, he said; a similar incident had actually happened to himself at the time of the election of Pius XI in 1922. Cardinal Ratti, the future Pius XI, had questioned him on the eve of the conclave about any rumours that might have been going around, and Roncalli had told him that Ratti's name did not appear on the list of *papabili*. Pope John then added "I'll tell you what Pius XI said to me then. He said, 'You have many good qualities, but you do not have the gift of prophecy!'"

---

*As quoted by Peter Hebblethwaite in *John XXIII— Pope of the Council*

Memories and Hopes

A few significant anecdotes
From the outset, his lifestyle, his witty remarks, his unexpected reactions, made John XXIII a great favourite with reporters. The image they created was half-way between history and legend, but it did include a number of authentic *fioretti*. I wrote down a few of his surprising reactions myself, some of which have never been published before.

A long wait for Fulton Sheen
The new Pope's first audience was with the famous American television bishop, Fulton Sheen. The latter had to sit in the waiting room for a long time while a group of professional photographers took the first official portrait of the new Pope. The whole thing lasted much longer than had been expected. At last, the door to the Pope's office opened, and by way of apology, the Pope greeted the bishop with the following words: "Ah! Monseigneur, I do not understand God. He has known from all eternity that I would some day be pope; why didn't he make me more photogenic?"

The first audience with the Belgian bishops
From our first audience with him, the Pope made us feel very much at ease. After each Belgian bishop had been duly introduced, Pope John asked for the speech that had been prepared for him. Before reading it, he introduced it as follows: "And now, my dear bishops, I shall read you a speech that was written especially for you by the services of the Secretariat of State. It will tell you what they think of you over there... Then you must tell me whether or not it is all true, and what you think of it!"

The ice was broken instantly!

An audience at Castel Gandolfo
On one of my visits to Castel Gandolfo during the summer that preceded the Council, I found Pope John alone and a little overwhelmed by the summer heat. He was busy reading galleys of

documents intended for the Council. He spoke to me about them, criticising their lengthiness and their abstract argumentations, so contrary to the pastoral aims of the Council. He kept repeating with a half-comical, half-serious smile:" *O questi professori!*" – "Oh, these professors!"

Mine was the only visit scheduled for that day in his desert at Castel Gandolfo, and he made it last longer by showing me some of the books in his library. Suddenly he picked up a few volumes bound in white – his pastoral letters, written during the time he was Patriarch of Venice. Leafing through one of them, he looked up at me and said: "Do you know what I feel when I look back at the things I wrote in those days? Well, I really shouldn't say this myself, but I feel sincere."

That same morning, he said to me also, "I know what my own part will be in this Council... it will be suffering." I had no idea what sort of suffering he had in mind; and I imagined he was thinking of the struggle he would have to engage in to prevent his entourage from slowing down or blocking the Council.

An open microphone

During a solemn audience granted to the participants at a scientific symposium, Pope John read a speech that had been prepared by the Secretariat of State. When he finished reading, forgetting that the microphone was still on, he turned to the prelate who accompanied him, and all the participants heard him comment: "Well, my friend, I could have written that speech myself, you know."

An improvised audience

My American friend, Peter Grace, phoned me one day from the States. He told me that a very important man, a Methodist rancher from Texas, was in Rome with his family; his fondest dream was to have a private audience with Pope John. My friend asked if I could help. I called the number he had given me in Rome and invited this unknown Protestant family to come with me on the following morning to the Vatican, at their own risk and peril. I was to see the Holy Father, but I could not guarantee a private audience.

When I had finished discussing Council business with the Pope, I told him that in the waiting room was a very wealthy Methodist family about whom I only knew one thing: their dream was to have a private audience with the Pope.

Pope John asked no questions; he simply said: "Bring them in." While I went to fetch them, he personally arranged the chairs in a circle for the visitors. Then he spoke to them for twenty minutes about the responsibilities of rich people toward the poor, and about the evangelical use of wealth. Such was his liveliness and verve, that I had trouble keeping up with him and translating what he said. I know that the family returned to the States full of enthusiasm; in the entrance hall of their home is a huge portrait of John XXIII. They have since come to thank me in Malines.

Keeping up with protocol

The Grand Duke and Grand Duchess of Luxembourg told me that at the end of their audience, Pope John stood up to accompany them to the door. He already had his hand on the doorknob when suddenly he drew it back, exclaiming: "Ah! I am so absent-minded: I forgot that I am the Pope, and I'm not allowed to open doors myself!" Then he rang to call the prelate who was waiting in the pontifical antechamber.

The day after a royal visit

On one occasion, as I arrived for an audience, the Pope greeted me very cheerfully, then told me about a visit he had had from the King and Queen of Belgium. About the King, he said: "I like him very much; he is so kind, so friendly. I could feel all the respect and affection he has for you." Then he spoke of the Queen with visible emotion. I could see that the Holy Father had a deep affection for both. Once I saw him raise to his lips a telegram that the King had sent him on his feast day.

John XXIII and canonisations

Three professors from the University of Louvain once presented an important collection of biblical studies to Pope John. The Pope thanked them, but asked no questions and made no comments about their work — clearly, his mind was on something else. Suddenly, he said to them, out of the blue, "I should like to canonise Barbarigo: he was beatified in the eighteenth century, but I think the time has come to canonise him. But there you are — they need two miracles. It's been so long ... Barbarigo no longer knows how to make miracles! So I was thinking..." Pope John turned toward the portrait of a pope that was hanging on the wall right beside him, and, pointing at him, continued: "My worthy predecessor, here, decreed that two miracles are necessary for a canonisation... Well, I, his unworthy successor, can perfectly well decree that Barbarigo is dispensed from this requirement!"

And so it was that Saint Gregory Barbarigo was canonised.

On another occasion, Pope John mentioned that he wanted to proclaim three Italians at once to be Doctors of the Church: Lorenzo Giustiniani (which caused great consternation among biblicists), Bernardino da Siena, and a third one whose name I now forget. "Imagine", he said to me, "I thought one of them had only written four books, and they've just brought me his Complete Works in eight volumes. Please admire my humility and my ignorance!"

Ecumenical *fioretti*

The exchanges between Pope John and the separated Christians whom he invited to the Council could easily provide a rich harvest of *fioretti*. The very fact that he invited them is a clear sign of his deep desire to re-establish visible unity.

One of the observers, the head of the Methodist Church, was on friendly terms with Pope John. He personally told me of his embarrassment when Pope John asked him unexpectedly: "Corson, my friend, how much longer do you think it will be before unity is restored among Christians?" The Methodist's reply was somewhat hesitant, so Pope John simply said, "Well, at any rate, between you and me – it's done!"

John XXIII – the pragmatist

An article by Father Thomas Stransky, of the Secretariat for Christian Unity, tells us the following story. When the Secretariat requested ecumenical orientations from the Pope in order to situate themselves legally within the framework of the Curia, the request was put forward by Cardinal Bea, and the Pope responded: "Don't ask me too much – conquer your own territory!"

Pope John wanted to be open to the unpredictable workings of the Holy Spirit, and to let the Spirit act freely. He was not a theoretician, and was not embarrassed to say so. An Orthodox Archbishop once said to him, at the start of a conversation, "Holy Father, I am not a theologian." To which Pope John quickly responded: "Neither am I, but please don't tell the Holy Office!"

He once said to me, with a smile, "The Holy Office is doing its best to find heresies in my writings and in my projects... but they haven't managed to find any yet!"

The tension between centre and periphery

Pope John was made out to be a progressive pope; in fact, by personality and by instinct, he was rather on the conservative side. He had, however, spent many years away from Rome; he had experienced more than once the closed-mindedness of the Curia, and was well aware of the inadequacies of the central administration of the Church. When he asked Mgr Tardini, himself very much a man of the Curia, to be his close collaborator, he said to him: "You are much more familiar with the 'centre' than I am; on the other hand, I know the 'periphery' much better than you do – so let us work together."

On an unscheduled visit to the offices of the new Secretariat for Christian Unity, he met a newcomer and foreigner – the future Cardinal Willebrands, who was later to play an important role in the Church. Willebrands told me that the Pope said to him, "My friend, you will suffer here, because so many people in Rome have never seen anything outside of Rome!" This remark is a key to Pope John's psychology, and points to the reasons why those on the "periphery" felt so comfortable with him.

Above all, Pope John was in a category of his own; it would have been impossible to put a label on him. He had an unusual amount of "genius of the heart", for which people of all tendencies and persuasions loved him as a father, beyond all differences and divisions.

His instinct was towards collegiality, and he wanted the bishops to assume their responsibilities fully. One day, after he had spoken to me for a long time about the changes and cuts that seemed desirable to him in the organisation and the text of the breviary, he concluded with these words: "I have told you my personal preferences; but, of course, it's all in the bishops' hands."

I felt very much in harmony with him concerning the relationship between the "centre" and the "periphery", and I asked him whether it would not be a good idea for the Council to request a review of the organisation of the Curia. I wrote down his answer: "Yes, do this, take the initiative, but make sure you are supported by a few other cardinals; and choose a few old ones as well, so it won't look like something coming from the young guard. Then send me something in writing, privately. That's very good, you must help me in these matters."

In a letter I wrote to a friend in March 1963, I find these words, which vividly bring back Pope John in all of his spontaneity and simplicity:

"An absolutely delightful audience, a very warm welcome, and immediately the Pope was telling me that he had been present at the Council meeting, the previous day, and had seen with great joy that things were going very well indeed. He seemed very pleased with his commissions.

Then he said to me, "You gave me some brilliant ideas for the

Council, at the very beginning; then we got off to a very disorderly start. Well, what I most appreciated is that you did not insist, at that moment; you did not push your ideas and try to make them prevail. The time had not come. I admired that very much. It is very much to your honour that you did not try to force things. The time has now come, since the plan has been adopted."

John XXIII and his critics

Pope John suffered a great deal from the fact that, within the Curia, he was held responsible for the success of the Communist Party in the Italian elections. According to his critics, the Pope did much for the cause of communism when he accepted to meet Khruschev's son-in-law; this was viewed as a friendly gesture towards the communists.

I was able to see for myself how painful this was to Pope John on one occasion, when he spontaneously brought up the issue. Interrupting our conversation during an audience, he suddenly opened a drawer in his desk and took out a typewritten document. "I'm going to read you the minutes of my meeting with Ajubei", he said. He read out the whole report, which had been prepared by the interpreter (and which has since been made public); then he asked me, "Don't you think that the Holy Spirit guided me?" and gave me a commentary on his remarks. When Ajubei had asked for some sort of diplomatic *rapprochement*, Pope John answered: "We must move step by step in that direction; but we must not forget that the world was created in six days!" Evidently, Pope John wanted his friends to be well-informed on the subject, so they would be better able to defend him.

This, however, was only one of many such episodes. More than once there was tension between him and certain members of the Roman Congregations. Mgr De Smedt – former Bishop of Bruges – was the last bishop to be received in audience by Pope John, who by then was gravely ill; he told me that the Pope said to him, with great sadness: "There are so many people here who have the

Pope's name constantly on their lips, and use it whenever it suits them; but they take no notice of him when they don't feel like it."

A photograph and a last visit
One morning, Pope John's secretary, Mgr Capovilla, told me that the Pope had asked him to give me a photograph which had been taken in his office. I went up to the third floor of the Vatican with him to get it. In the photo, Pope John stood smiling, leaning down towards me as I knelt before him to kiss his ring. Cardinal Urbani was also in the photo, standing by and watching. To understand the rest of the story, the reader must know that a cardinal does not kneel before the pope, he merely bows; I had therefore knelt either through absent-mindedness or in an exuberant impulse of faith.

Pope John had signed the photograph for me. I was just about to leave the secretary's office, when he said to me "You should look at the back of the photo; the Pope has written what he thinks of it." I turned it over, and indeed, there were a few words written on the back in the Pope's handwriting: *"Non placet mihi"* ("I don't like this"). Those were the days when, at the Council, we voted on the documents being discussed by saying *"placet"* or *"non placet"*. Underneath, he had added a few words in Italian, teasing me about kneeling, forgiving me good-humouredly, and concluding with an affectionate absolution and a blessing for my archdiocese.

Once more, I started to leave the secretary's office, and I asked Mgr Capovilla to thank the Pope kindly for me; but he suggested "You should thank him personally. He's there in his office; he has a cold but he's hard at work." I was happy to comply. This turned out to be my last meeting with Pope John; I never saw him again.

He explained that he was reading some documents on the relationship between Church and State. On an impulse, I told him that I did not think this issue should be discussed at Council meetings, because circumstances are so different from one country to the next. *"Allora, va bene"*, he said, and tore up the galleys right there in front of me, with a sigh of relief and a conspiratorial smile.

I stayed with him for almost two hours that morning. He showed me the paintings in his room, and commented on the lithograph of the Basilica of the Lateran. He had a great fondness for this Basilica, and wanted to be buried at the Lateran, the Cathedral of Rome. He even pulled out some drawers to show me family mementoes and souvenirs from his travels.

Finally, I asked him if he had started reading one of my books — he had promised to do so. He pretended to be offended by my question, as if I were doubting his promise. He took my arm, led me across several adjoining rooms to his bedroom, and said to me: "There, if you will not trust me — check for yourself..." My book was right there, on his night-table!

Words of encouragement about *The Nun in the World*

I had had the opportunity to tell Pope John, in a private conversation, that I considered it a matter of the greatest urgency to eliminate certain canonical obstacles from the lives of active women religious, in order to allow them to play their rightful role in strengthening the missionary dimension of the Church.

I had even remarked that, for this call to be heeded, a written preface to my book would have been a great help — I had added that I knew perfectly well that popes do not write prefaces! He responded to my utopian wish by an official letter from Mgr Dell'Acqua, of the Secretariat of State, giving full support to my book, the contents of which were well-known to the Pope.

He renewed his support through Cardinal Cicognani, Secretary of State; when I gave him a copy of the book, he said, "His Holiness hopes that your book will promote the necessary adaptation of women religious to their apostolate in the world of today."

Finally, Pope John expressed his support a third time, in an ingenious and subtle manner. In the speech he gave on the occasion of the beatification of Blessed Elizabeth Seton, he inserted a short sentence about my request. Here is a letter from the Cardinal Secretary of State on this point, dated March 22, 1963:

Your Eminence;

The Holy Father has received your recent letter concerning the *aggiornamento* of congregations of women religious, about which you have just written a book.

His Holiness read your letter with great care. *As you have no doubt noticed, he accepted your suggestion and inserted a brief sentence to this effect in his speech to the pilgrims who came to Rome for the beatification of Blessed Elizabeth Bayley Seton.*

Please accept, Your Eminence, the expression of my feelings of veneration, with which, in kissing your hands, I have the honour to be your most humble, most devoted and very obedient servant in Our Lord Jesus Christ.

A.G. Cardinal Cicognani

On the threshhold of eternity

A few days before his death, Pope John gave me one last sign of his paternal affection. As he was dictating his last will to his secretary, he instructed him to send me the large stole, bearing his coat of arms, which he wore at the opening ceremony of the Council — of "his" Council.

His agony and his death were his supreme message to the world.

It has been said that the days of Pope John's agony were a paschal liturgy; and for good reason. After teaching us how to live, he taught us how to die. The words he spoke on his bed of pain are worthy of being inscribed forever in our memories:

This bed is an altar.
An altar must have a victim:
here I am, ready.
I offer my life for the Church,

121

for the continuation of the Council,
for peace in the world,
for the unity of Christians.

The Council's farewell to John XXIII

The Council was duty-bound to hold a solemn assembly in homage to the one who had been its initiator. Much to my surprise, I received a letter from Cardinal Cicognani, Secretary of State, on behalf of Paul VI, asking me to give the eulogy in memory of John XXIII at the opening of the second session, which would coincide with the inauguration of the new papacy.

I immediately replied with a telegram, thanking the Pope and asking for details concerning the length of the speech and the language in which it was to be delivered. I received the following telegram in response: "His Holiness thanks Your Eminence for filial message. Speech in French may last forty-five minutes. Respectfully. Cardinal Cicognani."

Here is the letter explaining this request, and emphasising my bonds with the late Pope:

Secretariat of State
to His Holiness

The Vatican, September 7, 1963

Your Eminence;
His Holiness Pope Paul VI has decreed that a commemorative ceremony in honour of Pope John XXIII, of regretted memory, should take place on October 28, anniversary of his elevation to the sovereign pontificate.

A Mass will be celebrated in St Peter's Basilica in honour of the late Pope. At the end of this Mass, a speech will be given in the presence of the Holy Father; of the cardinals and bishops, from every part of the world, gathered in the aula of the Council; and of the members of the diplomatic corps, dignitaries, clergy and faithful, who have been invited to participate in this solemn and moving occasion.

His Holiness feels that no one could evoke, better than Your Eminence, the person of Pope John XXIII, before this illustrious gathering in the assembly hall of the Council for which he offered his suffering and his life. It was Pope John who, having entrusted to you the episcopal seat of Malines-Brussels, elevated you to the position of cardinal and immediately associated you closely with the work of the ecumenical Vatican Council, first in its preparatory stages, then in its actual unfolding. It was to you that he turned once more to introduce his encyclical *Pacem in Terris* before the prestigious assembly of the United Nations Organisation in New York. For all of these reasons, the Holy Father, whose profound esteem and great affection for your person you are well aware of, has instructed me to ask you, on his behalf, to deliver in his presence the commemorative speech in honour of his predecessor, who remains for all the Pope of peace and the Pope of the Council.

It is with great pleasure that I undertake to transmit to you this further expression of the Holy Father's trust. I am of course at your full disposal for any information you may require, and I send you my very best wishes for the success of the important task with which you have been entrusted.

Please accept the expression of my deepest veneration, with which, in kissing your hands, I remain your most humble, devoted and obedient servant in Our Lord Jesus Christ.

A.G. Cardinal Cicognani

The second session of the Council opened with a solemn assembly in memory of John XXIII. The Vatican distributed copies of my speech to all the bishops in the main Council languages. Here is what I said; no speech I have ever given has been for me a more intense emotional experience.

* * *

Reactions to the speech

I must admit that this was one of the greatest moments of my life, not only because of the very positive reactions of the Council Fathers — who five times applauded my words — but because of the implications of my message: between the lines, there was an appeal to Pope Paul VI, asking that the Council should be allowed to continue on the path set by his predecessor. At the end of my speech, the Pope embraced me.

Many bishops thanked me in person, or wrote to me later. Here is a letter from Cardinal Conway, primate of Ireland, dated November 1, 1963:

> Dear Cardinal,
>
> I feel I must write to tell you how deeply moved we all were by the memorable homily which you gave last Monday, in St Peter's Basilica.
>
> You succeeded in bringing back for us the real presence of the late Pope in a way that was extremely moving. I personally noticed that several of the Council Fathers had tears in their eyes, and the deep emotion of the assembly in response to your words was almost tangible. This speech will remain a historical event for our times.
>
> May I also add, Your Eminence, that the Irish Bishops were deeply touched by the charming reference to our native land, and I know that they would like me to thank you.
>
> With all best wishes,
>
> William Conway, Archbishop of Armagh

5

The Council Under Paul VI
(1963-1965)

A. ON A PERSONAL LEVEL

Pope Paul's first Angelus

Pope Paul's thoughtfulness was the source of another important memory from this period – of the morning he gave his first blessing to the assembled crowd, from the *loggia* in St Peter's. I was with him earlier that morning. I had asked permission to speak to him of my dreams for the Church, of his role, and of the difficulties he might encounter – without reticence or oratorial precautions, as though he were not Pope; I had added that in future I would abide by the proper rules of protocol, if he so wished.

Our conversation was very intense, friendly and open.A chamberlain interrupted the audience to announce that it was the hour of the Angelus, and that the crowd was waiting for the Pope's first blessing. Pope Paul rose immediately and beckoned me to accompany him to the window. It was a gesture of humility and of friendship, perhaps also inspired by gratitude for the honesty with which I had spoken; it may also have been a way of emphasising his wish that the Council should proceed along the course set by his predecessor, John XXIII.

It was not at all customary for a cardinal to appear beside the Pope at the hour of the benediction. Since this event was broadcast on television, it received a great deal of attention and comment, and the press made highly imaginative conjectures concerning the significance to be attributed to this gesture.

The appointment of moderators

During the Council's first session, a system of rotation was applied whereby our daily meetings were chaired, in turn, by one of ten cardinal-presidents. This procedure had proved impractical, and Pope Paul decided to make some changes. He told me he wanted the Council to be directed by two "legates", Cardinal Agagianian and myself – in effect representing the Council's two tendencies. He told me he might consider appointing a third "legate", in which case he would choose Cardinal Doepfner, of Munich. He did not mention at that time the possibility of a fourth, but later he also appointed Cardinal Lercaro, of Bologna. Strictly speaking, the term "legate" is not applicable when the Pope is in Rome, and the Curia suggested that a more appropriate word might be "moderator", which was adopted. Cardinal Cicognani, Secretary of State, was to send us our terms of reference, detailing our duties and prerogatives. No such document was ever drafted officially; in time, this led to situations that were legally confused and psychologically delicate.

A letter to me from Cardinal Lercaro, dated September 25, 1963, indicates precisely the state of affairs at that early stage:

> I have called for Fr Dossetti; I hope he will arrive on Thursday. He will contact you immediately upon his arrival. He told me he would bring a draft of the "Rules for the four moderators"; these reflect the Pope's thinking as he expressed it to me on August 31, and confirmed it again in a conversation I had with him earlier this evening. I sent the draft to him on September 6.
>
> The Holy Father asked me last night to prepare an outline of our terms of reference, defining our responsibilities as moderators in accordance with his views; I think it would be useful for you and Cardinal Doepfner to read the text and study it.
>
> I hope to be in Rome tomorrow, in time for the meeting...

Knowing full well that such confusion, if unresolved, could lead to a reconsideration of the very function of the moderators, I had already stressed in a letter to the Holy Father the "brains-trust" aspect of our group, which I believed to be firmly established. I had understood, as had Cardinal Lercaro, that the moderators would constitute a sort of committee to supervise the Council's progress and ensure its inner cohesion. In any case, their role involved something other than merely taking turns presiding over Council meetings. The Curia, for its part, was hoping to reduce it precisely to this.

Here is the letter I wrote to the Pope on September 15, 1963; I give it here in full, although not all of its content concerns this issue:

Malines, September 15, 1963

Most Holy Father,

Allow me to express my profound gratitude for the recent appointment by which Your Holiness has called on me to cooperate in the success of the Council. I feel most comfortable as part of this new and happily-constituted foursome; it will be easy to look at both the *"idem velle"* and the *"idem nolle"* , and we shall truly be able to do solid and positive work, following an inner logic and a shared sense of the hierarchy of the most imperative pastoral values. I thank Your Holiness for the trust, the respect and the affection that are implied in this appointment, and I fully appreciate its importance and the responsibility involved.

I will dedicate myself wholeheartedly to the task you have entrusted to me. I hope to have the opportunity to assure Your Holiness of this in person very soon — I shall be in Rome on the afternoon of the 25th for a meeting of the Coordinating Commission. I cannot leave Brussels before the morning of the 25th, because of a solemn ceremony in honour of John XXIII, scheduled here for the evening of the 24th, in which I must take part along with Cardinal Alfrink and Jean Guitton.

Thank you also for your thoughtfulness in asking me to deliver on October 28 the official speech honouring John XXIII. I will simply need to let my heart speak – my heart and my deep veneration for the Pope of the Council, of unity and of peace. I await instructions concerning the length and the language of the speech. I think Latin would be awkward in the circumstances, particularly since the audience will include a vast majority of lay people.

I look forward to discussing with you the problems of the Council and benefiting from your direct guidance. The task of preparing the general section of draft text 17 was entrusted to me by the Coordinating Commission; a team of theologians has worked with me at my residence for several days, including Frs Rahner, Congar, Tucci and several professors from Louvain. I have a feeling that the result will be quite good and will provide an excellent basis for discussion.

We have also reviewed the draft text, *De Ecclesia*, which had been entrusted to our experts by the Theological Commission; that too is well under way. It will be the *pièce de résistance* of the Council – *operatio sequitur esse*. I remember that you reminded us of this principle when we were working on the plan: the pastoral and ecumenical consequences will be far-reaching. It is indeed a special grace to be in a position to serve the Church at this turning point in its history, and to be able to think not in terms of years, but in terms of centuries!

With deep respect and affection, I remain, Most Holy Father, ...

Still seeking to clarify the issue, I wrote to Mgr Dell'Acqua to ask for his assistance, knowing full well that he shared our concern. This is the letter I wrote:

Brussels, September 19, 1963

Your Excellency,
As you know, the Coordinating Commission will resume work on the evening of next Wednesday, September 25th. I believe it would be extremely dangerous for the future of our group of four *delegati-moderatores* if we were to take part in these meetings before the Holy Father has clearly defined our exact position with respect to the Commission and with respect to the Council of presidents.

Ideally, the Holy Father should have met with the four of us together by the 25th. However, the earliest flight I can take from Brussels is on the morning of the 25th, since I must remain here for a solemn celebration in honour of John XXIII, at which I must speak after Cardinal Alfrink and Jean Guitton.

Would it be possible for His Holiness to receive the four delegates in the late afternoon of the 25th? I shall be arriving in Rome at about 2 p.m. Such an audience would allow us to receive direct instructions from His Holiness and clearly define our role.

Failing this, we shall be drowned in the Coordinating Commission which is likely to decide *in obliquo et ab extrinseco* [obliquely and for extrinsic reasons] on pastoral matters of vital importance which need to be studied first within the group of four, *in recto et ab intrinseco* [with directness, and according to an inner logic]. Even a simple matter, such as the allocation of seats at the table of the Commission meeting, could give the impression, from the outset, that the Coordinating Commission is a higher body and the group of four merely an off-shoot of the Commission.

Already – and I have heard of this personally – there are those attempting to reduce the role of the group of four in this manner. There is a definite feeling that, from various directions, attempts are being made to pare to the bone the task entrusted to the *delegati*. Any misunderstanding in this direction would in practice lead to a negation of

129

what I understand to be the Holy Father's true intention.

It is not individual sensitivities that are at stake here, but rather the whole problem posed by the need to give the Council the inner cohesion — doctrinal and pastoral — which was lacking.

May I ask you kindly to transmit these reflections to His Holiness?

With best wishes and looking forward to the joy of seeing you soon...

The Dossetti incident

The first time Pope Paul spoke to me of his intention to establish two "legates", we immediately went on to discuss problems concerning the organisation of the Council's work. This task, a much more important one than that of chairing Council meetings, was also the central concern of my two colleagues (Doepfner and Lercaro). This led us very naturally to choose for ourselves — *motu proprio* — an outstanding secretary to assist us in our work. Our choice fell on Don Dossetti, Cardinal Lercaro's vicar-general. Before he entered the priesthood, he had been a leading political figure in Italy, and the principal author of the Italian Constitution after the fall of Fascism.

I had had occasion to appreciate this eminent jurist and serious theologian when he collaborated on the text of my statement concerning the permanent diaconate. I believe that the Council's acceptance of my initiative was due in part to the theological argumentation which he helped to develop.

In his role as secretary to the four moderators, Don Dossetti took part in our first few meetings at the Vatican. However, things became difficult and tense when Mgr Felici, the Council Secretary, demanded to be secretary to the group of moderators as well. He complained to the Pope about our "dualism" until finally, to avoid further tension, Don Dossetti withdrew of his own accord; he did this out of consideration for the Pope and to avoid embarrassing us. In his eyes, this incident was an indication that the Council would evolve in a curial direction, and that the era of John XXIII was at an end. The interested reader can find Cardinal Lercaro's reactions to this episode in his published correspondence.

Our function as moderators had initially been conceived as one of reflection, and orientation of the Council's work; in practice, it was to be reduced to chairing debates and holding a weekly meeting with the Pope.

There were even complaints to the Pope about our speeches at the Council. Cardinal Cicognani asked us to model our conduct on that of the members of the Roman Curia, who had been instructed not to speak at the Council. He told us that our prestige as "moderators" gave far too much weight to our words, which might be construed to reflect official views.

We categorically rejected this invitation to silence, and the suggestion was never repeated. The weekly meetings of the four moderators with the Pope were never questioned; they provided an opportunity for a regular exchange of ideas and opinions.

Preparation of *Lumen Gentium*

By the end of the first session, much of the groundwork had been done; a procedure had been established; a magnificent text on liturgy had been proposed; and Council members had agreed to focus on the Church within itself and in relationship to the world. The most important part of the Council's work would begin with a constitution "on the Church".

The preparation of *Lumen Gentium* included a negative side — the elimination of the draft text prepared by the Curia — and a positive side — the lengthy and demanding task of writing the document that was ultimately adopted.

From the outset it was clear that the original draft text would not be acceptable to the assembly. The verdict of one of the Council Fathers concerning a draft text submitted to Vatican I seemed the most appropriate response to this one: "It should be buried, not discussed."

There was here a confrontation between two different conceptions of the Church. The Holy Office had prepared a draft text inspired by an ecclesiology that was deeply marked by the canonical and institutional aspects of the Church, rather than emphasising and giving priority to the spiritual and evangelical aspects. In our eyes, it was a matter of stepping out of a legalistic ecclesiology and into an ecclesiology of communion, centred on the mystery of the Church in its profound trinitarian dimensions.

To save time (and to the greatest displeasure of Cardinal Ottaviani, who in full plenary session denounced this as a "scandal"), I had asked Mgr Philips to prepare without delay a new schema, even before the old one was rejected. The vote finally took place with the negative results I had anticipated, and the path was cleared for what was to become the constitution *Lumen gentium*.

The man I had chosen for this task − Mgr Philips − had obtained a degree in theology from Rome (he had written a thesis on St Augustine, under Fr de La Taille, SJ), and taught dogmatic theology at Louvain. He personified a kind of *via media* that neither Cardinal Ottaviani nor the Dutch Secretary, Fr Tromp, could find threatening. Moreover, since he was *sénateur coopté* − drafted Senator − in Belgium, he was well versed in parliamentary debate and had considerable diplomatic talent. Members of the Theological Commission still remember the answer he gave to a bishop whose presentation had been very scholarly but rather confused (for the curious, this was the future Cardinal Volk): "I have not understood very well what you have just said...but let me assure you that we will take it fully into account!"

A "Copernican revolution"
In its first outline, the draft text on the Church was divided into three sections − an opening chapter on the mystery of the Church, a second chapter on the hierarchy, and a third one on the people of God.

Mgr Prignon, Rector of the Belgian College and a theologian

by profession, suggested to me one day in conversation, that reversing the order of these chapters would have a salutary effect and wide-ranging consequences. I decided to follow his suggestion, for this would immediately centre the Church on Christians, defined as all those who have received baptism, and, in consequence, on that which is common to all the faithful, and comes before any differentiation of function and vocation. However, the suggestion still had to be submitted for approval to the Pope and to the Council.

At one of the weekly meetings with the Pope, I presented the idea to him, explaining briefly the reasons for such a reversal. Pope Paul made no objections, and his silence led all of us — myself and my three colleagues on the team of moderators — to assume that he had agreed to my proposal.

Upon my return to the Belgian College, I announced the important news to the Belgian bishops. Mgr Charrue, member of the Theological Commission, was delighted. That very evening he was at a meeting of this Commission, and it so happened that its president, Cardinal Ottaviani, strongly emphasised the importance of maintaining the original order of the chapters, placing the hierarchy ahead of the people of God. Mgr Charrue informed him of the conversation I had had with the Pope, and affirmed that the latter had agreed to a reversal of the order. Cardinal Ottaviani forcefully insisted that the Pope agreed with his position, not mine.

The very next day, I went to see Cardinal Ottaviani in the Basilica, to confirm personally what Mgr Charrue had already told him. He vigorously maintained that he was absolutely certain that the Pope agreed with him on this matter. There was nothing we could do except wait for our next weekly audience, at which I immediately broached the subject, stating to the Holy Father that my colleagues and I had definitely understood him to agree to the proposed reversal. He answered as follows: "Personally, I agree with Ottaviani. However, when you pleaded in favour of the reversal, I said nothing, leaving the question open for debate in the Council." And the Pope added: "As a matter of fact, I am not really convinced by the proposed change."

I then suggested that Mgr Philips should put in writing for him the justification for such a reversal of the order. At this point he assumed an attitude of benevolent neutrality, allowing us to proceed.

When my turn next came to preside over the assembly, I took the opportunity to ask the Fathers their opinion concerning this reversal of the chapters. In a moment, by vote, the reversal was adopted, with no problems or objections, by a large majority.

The five crucial points

The second session proceeded uneventfully. Discussions and votes increasingly revealed that the majority wished to see Vatican II redress the imbalance caused by the unfinished work of Vatican I. The earlier Council had emphasised the primacy and infallibility of the Pope, but because of the outbreak of war between France and Prussia in 1870, the Fathers had not been able to go on to the other areas they had intended to deal with, in particular the chapter on bishops. As a result, the Pope's role had been rather simplistically overemphasised – especially in popular understanding – to the point that the bishops were viewed as representatives of the Pope. This led to a misconception of the very significance of the consecration of bishops, and of their true role.

The matter of balance between the two ministries fell within the province of the Theological Commission. However, the latter was dominated by its president, Cardinal Ottaviani, who liked to speak of himself as "the Pope's *carabiniere*". It seemed essential to me that before the end of the session, the Council should be asked to provide precise guidelines to orient the Commission in its work during the interval between sessions; thus the Commission members would know from the outset what direction the majority of Council Fathers wanted them to take.

Such a procedure had not been provided for in the regulations; however, I could find nothing in them that prohibited it. I therefore persuaded my colleagues – including Cardinal Agagianian – that it would be very useful to put some of these questions to the Council before the end of the session. Then I asked a few theologians – Philips, Prignon, Moeller and Congar – to prepare the actual wording of the questions.

Questions in hand, and with no prior warning – especially not to Mgr Felici, who would have blocked this initiative – I calmly announced one day, as I was presiding over the meeting, that a questionnaire was about to be handed out to the Council Fathers; the answers to the five questions would serve as orientation for the work of the Theological Commission.

No sooner had I made the announcement, than Mgr Felici went rushing to the Pope to denounce this "abuse of power". The printing of the questionnaire, which was still under way at the Vatican press, was immediately stopped. Cardinal Ottaviani let it be known, loud and clear, that the Theological Commission – in other words, himself – was alone competent to formulate theological questions, even those intended for a questionnaire.

What followed was indeed a shared Calvary for the moderators, and in particular for me, as the main culprit. We were accused of overstepping our mandate and taking unauthorised initiatives. At our next audience, the Pope seemed puzzled and embarrassed. He finally set up a commission of about twenty cardinals to rule on this matter.

The decisive meeting took place in the vast ceremonial hall of the Vatican, in the offices of the Cardinal Secretary of State. Cardinal Tisserand, as chairman, opened the discussion and – *felix culpa!* – began by criticising our text for its Latin! To my delight, the debate floundered, as three of the four moderators pleaded for the freedom to ask for guidelines and orientations!

At last, the matter was put to the vote. We won by one vote, thanks to an absent-minded cardinal who put his hand up for us even though he had just finished expressing all sorts of doubts. I

135

will never forget the moment when the secretary of the meeting – Mgr Villot, who later became a cardinal – said to me: "Surely Cardinal X is making a mistake!" to which I responded: "Yes, he is definitely absent-minded, but it's neither your job nor mine to point that out to him!" To the day of his death I did not reveal the name of this ultra-conservative cardinal; I kept it as a state secret. His name was Spellman.

The Pope accepted the decision of the arbitration commission, but only at the very last moment. I confided to him that the suspense he had inflicted on me over the preceding two weeks had been for me a painful calvary; he agreed, but then remarked: "I wanted the moderators to take full responsibility for the vote; I did not want to become personally involved."

So it was that the five questions were put to the vote. The purpose of the consultation was to determine whether or not the Council Fathers wanted the text that was to be drafted to make the following points:

1. that consecration to the episcopate constitutes the supreme degree of the sacrament of ordination (2,123 in favour, 34 against);

2. that every legitimately consecrated bishop, in communion with the bishops and the Pope, who is their head and the principle of their unity, is a member of the body of bishops (2,049 in favour, 104 against, 1 void);

3. that the body or college of bishops is the successor to the college of the apostles in the task of evangelisation, sanctification and government; and that this body, in unity with its head the Roman Pontiff – and never without its head, whose primacy over pastors and over the faithful remains unquestioned and whole – enjoys full and supreme power over the Universal Church (1,808 in favour, 336 against, 14 void);

4. that such power belongs by divine right to the college of bishops itself, in unity with its head (1,717 in favour, 408 against, 7 void);

5. that the diaconate must be instituted as a distinct and permanent degree of the holy ministry, in accordance with the needs

of the Church in various parts of the world (1,588 in favour, 525 against, 7 void).

The final vote took place on October 30 and indicated that a definite majority were in favour of an affirmative response to all of these points; in the order in which they are given above, they received respectively 95%, 90%, 85%, 80% and 75% of the vote. It was a triumphant success for the questionnaire.

Every word of each question had been carefully weighed. Professional theologians will be able to discern, in the choice of words, certain nuances that reflect a leaning toward a greater emphasis on the coresponsibility of the bishops, with and under Peter. In times to come, these will be useful for ecumenical dialogue; at that particular moment, they served to bring out and define the shared views of Council members.

This event marked a turning point; we had successfully overcome the first hurdle in the preparatory work of the Commission.

Following this vote, various accusations were made against the moderators at Council meetings, and a number of speakers took us to task. We were reduced to silence, since we had neither terms of reference nor regulations to protect us: these would have clearly defined our function, but no such document had ever been produced. It was quite obvious that the Curia did not welcome our initiative in the least. We could only sit tight and let the storm go by, and thank the Lord for the way the vote had gone.

Claude Troisfontaines, a professor at Louvain-la-Neuve, has written a well-researched and thorough study of the controversy surrounding the five questions and their underlying theological subtleties. It was published in 1989 by the Paul VI Institute in Brescia; the author concludes his study as follows:

> We can now draw certain conclusions from this first episode. At the beginning, we stated that the importance of the consultative vote that took place on October 30 must not be underestimated. The vote came, as we have

seen, as a result of Cardinal Suenens's perseverance. During fourteen days – which have been compared to stations of the cross – the Cardinal pleaded, alone, for the five questions, since the other moderators were quite prepared to abandon the cause *"propter bonum pacis"*.

But the result was well worth the effort. The vote allowed the Council to define clearly the existing balance of power, and led to a major reorganisation of the commissions that would rewrite the documents. Can we then go on to say that the outcome was decided at that moment? The majority were too quick to believe this, while the minority still assumed there was time to rethink the whole thing. Both were mistaken.

What was Pope Paul's attitude at that moment? The Pope ruled in favour of the moderators; but at the same time, he continued to support Mgr Felici, whose role as Secretary General of the Council was further strengthened. Moreover, while he allowed membership in the commissions to be enlarged, Pope Paul made sure, at the same time, that the minority opinion would be heard.

As to the substance of the matter, the Pope, as we have already pointed out, deliberately reserved his final judgement – a point that probably has not been sufficiently emphasised.

(*Pubblicazioni* 7, pp.99-104).

Even posthumously, our status as moderators has never been clear! I am alluding here to a bronze door in St Peter's Basilica on which four cardinals are represented, seated at a table, one of them wearing an eastern head-dress. They are flanked by the two popes of the Council – the one who opened it, John XXIII, and the one who closed it, Paul VI. The *Osservatore Romano* published a photograph of the door, on which the four moderators are vaguely recognisable – the style of the artwork is modern, and the features are only sketched in. One of them resembles Cardinal Agagianian, even though the eastern head-dress is in no way authentic; and the features of the other three can also be more or less imagined. One day, one of the four mysteriously disappeared from the bronze doors: apparently, Cardinal Doepfner had gone missing! There was even a fund-raising campaign in his diocese in Munich, attempting to reinstate him. The official position, which put an end to this Bavarian initiative, was the following: the four figures sitting between the two popes did not in fact represent the four moderators. As for the missing figure, to this day the mystery remains unsolved.

B. PARTICIPATION IN COUNCIL DEBATES

The second session

The permanent diaconate
My main reason for making a statement to the Council concerning this issue was not the shortage of clergy, but rather the intrinsic value of this sacramental order in the Church. It seemed appropriate to re-introduce the permanent diaconate into the Latin Church, and to make it accessible to married men, as it already is in the Catholic Church of Eastern Rite. In my work plan, I had introduced this issue in an appendix to the draft text on the priesthood, to give myself the opportunity to raise the question.

Cardinal Shehan of Baltimore, unaware of my intention, requested and obtained from the Council permission for this question to be eliminated from the draft text on the priesthood. I later explained to him why it had been there, but by then it was too late; meanwhile, I had to find some other way. I asked Mgr Philips, who was then working on the draft of *Lumen Gentium*, to simply mention the diaconate, thus giving me a chance to speak on the question.

This he did, and at a later session, I stressed the theological arguments, assisted by Dossetti as my expert. The diaconate, I said, is part of the sacramental ministerial structure of the Church, and must not be reduced to a simple stage in the transition to priesthood. For psychological reasons, I also insisted on the freedom of each bishop to decide whether or not this practice should be adopted in his diocese. My speech was well received, and I believe it had some favourable influence in ensuring the support of the Council Fathers.

I am happy to note the growing role of permanent deacons in many countries. There are now a fair number in my own diocese, and I have always ordained them personally, in their parishes.

The charisms of the baptised

The mention of charisms during the debate on the draft of *Lumen Gentium* triggered a reaction from Cardinal Ruffini, author of at least one hundred statements. He now asked that this word be suppressed; he felt that charisms were all very well in the primitive Church, but their mention as something that might still be relevant today could easily lead to abuses. I felt, to the contrary, that this mention was necessary, and that the charisms of the Holy Spirit are an integral part of Christian life and of evangelisation.

The Council adopted this point of view, and mention was made of charisms in the Council text, with a wording that was wise and discriminating, but definitely positive. Unwittingly, my remarks had foreshadowed future events, for this text was to come in useful one day to clear the name of the "Charismatic Renewal".

In calling for the recognition of charisms for all the baptized, I had deliberately emphasised that the term "baptized" referred to both men and women. I concluded my call to openness by saying that "unless I am mistaken, women make up half of the human race". To this, on the morrow, a journalist added, on his own initiative, that "women are also responsible...for the other half".

It is hard to believe to what extent such truisms, and their practical applications, were still not obvious in those days. I had to speak personally to Pope Paul to request that the few women who were present as observers at the Council be allowed to receive Communion from his hand. And I was unsuccessful in my attempts to ensure that Barbara Ward — the well-known and remarkable economist from Columbia University — should be allowed to speak at a Council meeting. She wrote a paper which was read by the American observer, Nolan. In later years, she spoke at a post-conciliar synod; many doors have opened since.

A few days after my speech, I read, in the report prepared by the Secretariat for Ecumenical Affairs in Rome, that the Orthodox Bishop representing the Patriarch of Moscow had mentioned my statement concerning charisms; he had affirmed that this could be a starting point for the work toward the unification of the Churches. I believe, indeed, that the full recognition of the role of the Holy Spirit within the Church is essential to any ecumenical dialogue.

A retirement age for bishops

This proposal was one about which I felt particularly strongly. It had been accepted by our Preparatory Commission, with a clause stating that the rule would apply to future bishops. Within the Council itself, my proposal met with a total lack of enthusiasm; this was largely due to the fact that I proposed a specific age-limit, suggesting that the proper age for retirement be set at seventy-five, and that this should apply to all of us, except the Holy Father and the Eastern bishops.

As it turned out, failure at the Council was merely a postponed success. On the day after he was elected Pope, Paul VI told me that such a rule would have made it much easier for him to replace some of the staff of the Roman Curia. A few months later, he introduced it himself, *motu proprio.*

The third session

Mary's place and role in the Church

There was a certain amount of controversy surrounding Mary's place and role within the Church. Some felt that there should be a separate text dealing with this issue; others, that it should be included in the schema on the Church. In my plan for the Council, I had opted for the second solution, and the Council agreed. As far as I was concerned, it was not a matter of minimising or maximising the role of the Blessed Virgin. It was simply a matter of logic; having opted for the Church as focal point of the Council, I felt it was important not to multiply the number of different texts, but rather to attempt to make things converge.

I spoke at the Council during the debate on the proposed text, requesting that it be strengthened. In its original form, the text minimised the role of the Blessed Virgin in the sense that it focused almost entirely on her past role (all of the relevant Scripture texts were quoted); but her spiritual motherhood in the present was not sufficiently brought out. This was my first objection.

I would also have liked the text to show that the spiritual maternity of Mary extends into the role of the Church as mother. At my request, Mgr Philips included in the text a sentence about the relationship between the Holy Spirit and Mary, and about Mary's spiritual maternity. This met with opposition within the Theological Commission, from Mgr Volk (who was later made cardinal).

I insisted so strongly that Mgr Philips managed to work in a few lines; I will quote them here, since this Council text deserves greater attention in view of the "New Evangelisation":

> Hence the Church in her apostolic work also rightly looks to her who brought forth Christ, conceived by the Holy Spirit and born of the Virgin, so that through the Church Christ may be born and grow in the hearts of the faithful also (*Lumen Gentium*, 65).

In an article entitled "Présence de Marie dans la mission de l'Eglise" ("Mary's presence in the Mission of the Church"), Fr Jean Galot has pointed out the fact that Mary's role at the heart of the apostolate was not mentioned in the first drafts of the text. He clearly explains why these lines, which were finally accepted and included, are important.*

Beatifications

My purpose in speaking on this issue was to introduce some form of decentralisation in the whole area of beatifications.** One of the contributors to *Saints d'hier et sainteté d'aujourd'hui* (Saints of Yesterday and Holiness Today) gives an excellent summary of my speech:

> Given the public disenchantment with canonisations, it might be worthwhile to ask whether the proclamation of sainthood must necessarily take place at the level of the Universal Church. During the third session of the Council, Cardinal Suenens suggested in one of his statements that the power to conduct the full process of beatifications should be handed over to episcopal conferences. A commission of priests and laity would be responsible for this process, and the results would be submitted to the Pope for approval. Canonisation by the Holy See would then be reserved to saints who, having already been beatified, are known and venerated beyond the borders of their own country. Saints canonised by Rome would be added to the list of saints of the Universal Church. Those beatified by episcopal conferences would be proposed as models and examples only within their own countries.
>
> Such a procedure would have several advantages: it would renew a practice that was common in the West during the first millennium; it is the same as the procedure still in use in the Orthodox Church, where a distinction is made between ecumenical, national and local canonisations; and above all, it would give communities a chance to play once more their rightful active role in this area.

---

*Jean Galot, SJ, *Omnis terra*, Pontifical Missionary Union, May 1989.
**Speech of September 15, 1964, a summary of which appears in *Documentation catholique*, no.1433, October 4, 1964, c.1242-1243.

> Unless there is such participation, the designation of saints runs the risk of being reduced to a mere formality.*

The same views have recently been expounded in the United States, in a book called *Making Saints*. **

Birth-control

Earlier, I spoke of my interest in the issue of birth-control, and I mentioned the establishment, in association with the University of Louvain, of an International Symposium that meets every year in an attempt to shed some light on problems of bioethics.

At the Council, I was not interested in a public debate on this issue, because the mass media would have sensationalised every statement, and also because the issue was a particularly complex one. When the Pope prohibited all discussion of the subject, I did not see this as an anti-collegial act, but rather as a wise one. My concern was elsewhere: I knew that a very restricted committee, attached to the Holy Office, was studying the question, and I feared a lack of philosophical, theological and scientific openness within this little group. Thus, when I brought up the issue at the Council, I was not motivated by a desire to have it discussed. What I wanted was an increase in the membership of the little group that had been meeting in secret; and I wanted its composition to be made public. In this way, I hoped to increase the chances that any conclusions reached at some future stage would have a certain credibility. I ended my statement with a line which became a catch-phrase: "One Galileo affair should be enough!"

Initially, my suggestion was greeted unfavourably at the highest level. Fortunately, a few months later, the Pope himself opened up the study group to fifty experts. He even asked me for some names of scholars and scientists from my Symposium in Louvain, and he actually used a few of the names I provided.

---

*Saints d'hier et sainteté d'aujourd'hui, article by Philippe Rouillard, in connection with a survey; Centre catholique des intellectuels français, Desclée De Brouwer, Paris, 1966.
**Kenneth Woodward, Schuster, New York, 1990.

The names of those participating in the enlarged study group were to remain secret; the *Osservatore Romano*, however, published a photograph of the group.

The history of this commission and of its debates has been revealed in detail by Robert Blair Kaiser, *New York Times* correspondent during the Council, in a book called *The Encyclical Which Never Was* (published by Sheed and Ward, London, 1987). His facts are historically correct; his book is largely based on the personal papers provided by one of the commission members, Mgr Reuss, Auxiliary Bishop of Mayence.

I discussed this issue with Pope Paul a number of times during the four years he took to reflect upon it; I also sent him papers by Mgr Dondeyne, President of the Institut Supérieur de Philosophie at Louvain; by Fr Haring, the well-known Redemptorist moral theologian who had recently preached the annual retreat at the Vatican; and by Fr Labourdette, Dominican specialist in thomist theology. All of these studies stressed, each from a different perspective, the global and personal aspects of conjugal life, and warned against any position that would miss or ignore its complexity on the pastoral level.

My conversations with the Pope covered all of these crucial points. When the Pope decided to create a commission of fifteen cardinals and bishops to supervise the work of the existing scientific commission, he appointed me to it. In an effort to assist the Holy Father, we drew up a pastoral text, drafted by Mgr Dupuy, which avoided the semantic traps as well as the controversies and polemics that could be expected to arise; it was a draft outline for an encyclical. The Pope, however, adopted instead a text that was prepared by Ottaviani's group.

The fourth session
The fourth session was spent entirely on draft text XIII, which eventually became *Gaudium et Spes*. I made three separate statements in the course of the session. The first one concerned missions; I remarked that this was an excellent schema, but it did not

145

deal sufficiently with the apostolic initiation of missionaries – a subject that should find its place precisely in this document. This gave me the opportunity to insist yet again on the central theme of my book, *The Gospel to Every Creature*. My argument was accepted, and in the final version of *Gaudium et Spes* there is a paragraph dealing with this issue.

My second statement was on the priesthood. The draft text was too abstract and timeless; it was not responsive to the specific questions that our priests were asking. There was, in fact, considerable opposition to this draft text on the part of several groups of bishops; as a result, the text emerged improved, corrected and generally enlivened. But all of this is public knowledge.

Finally, I spoke on marriage, making a number of pastoral and liturgical suggestions.

Thus ended, for me, the final session of the Council.

The use of Latin at the Council

Latin was the official language of the Council – and represented at once a necessity and a handicap. At one point, we attempted to set up a system for simultaneous translation, but the secretarial services insisted that all written statements be handed in five days in advance, which was impossible.

For my own use, I invented a system designed to ensure that I would be understood, despite the Latin. I was truly delighted, one day, when an American bishop said to me "When *you* speak Latin, I always understand what you're saying!" Here is my secret: I wrote my statements in French, and had them translated into good Latin; then I would go over them myself and put them into bad Latin – Cicero, forgive me! – which made them perfectly understandable. A final touch – I always managed to slip in one sentence in French, which would come completely out of the blue, and wake everybody up; in this sentence, I would condense the gist of my entire statement. Here are two examples:

During the discussion on a retirement age for bishops, one objection kept recurring: a bishop is bound to his diocese and must remain faithful to it until death. I think I took care of it by saying, in French, "Never use this objection again; this basilica is full of divorced bishops!" (I meant, of course, that they had changed see.)

And when asked not to set a precise age for retirement (I had suggested seventy-five), I responded in French: "If we do not set a specific age, our document will be nothing more than a sword-thrust in water!"

Outside the council hall

The Council did not involve only public debates. Discussions continued in the city, through press conferences, interviews, and meetings. I remember giving a lecture on "The Church of Tomorrow", on the need to shake off some of the heaviness of the past and put behind us some of the customs of an era long since gone. Alluding to the long train worn by cardinals — Pius XII had already shortened it by two metres! — I invoked the scholastic principle *"In omnibus respice finem"* — respect the finality of all things. I explained that the original and ancient purpose of the train was to cover the back of the cardinal's horse. I then placed before them the following choice: shorten the train, or bring back the horses. This remark delighted the press.

The Council was not merely an endless sequence of speeches delivered in Latin, each one reduced to its allotted eight minutes. It was also an opportunity for many informal meetings among bishops, experts and observers. Before and after the official assembly, they could be found in the cafeterias; these were of vital importance, for they allowed us to refresh our capacity for concentration and possibly continue a discussion while sipping *espresso*. I had established a routine of stopping by for a few minutes, every morning, to get the feel of this atmosphere. The bishops often used this opportunity to ask me, as moderator, to put an end to a debate that had become too lengthy; or to give me instant reactions which I mentally recorded, and which were very valuable to me.

If a vote came up during those few minutes when I was absent, my neighbour at the moderators' table, Cardinal Doepfner, was under instructions to fill in my voting slip and to write *"placet"*, *"non placet"*, or *"placet juxta modum"*, as he saw fit. There was such harmony of views between us that I did not need to tell him what my preference would be.

There was an atmosphere, around the Council, that is difficult to describe to anyone who was not at the meetings. It has become a collection of documents that were discussed, studied with meticulous care, and adopted by a vote that for some of the major texts was practically unanimous. But before that, the Council was above all an event – a breath of the Holy Spirit, a breath of renewal, and, at the same time, a fraternal meeting of bishops from every part of the world. Deep bonds were created there.

Each bishop was very much an individual human being, with his own personality, his own preoccupations, and his own sense of humour. Now and then, a story – often absolutely unfounded, quite fantastic, and of unknown origin – would make the rounds. One of these concerned me, as the author of *The Nun in the World*. This book had been the cause of a certain reticence among some superiors general of women religious, who had banned it from their communities. According to the story, Pope John was talking to the mother general of some order or other (those who told the story never seemed to agree on which order it was), and, having heard of the wonderful deeds of these religious throughout the world, he said to her: "What you are doing is indeed admirable. Is there something I can do for you that would express my profound gratitude?" It is said that the mother general answered "Yes, Holy Father; may I have Cardinal Suenens' head on a silver platter?" I have never been able to find out where this story originated.

The moderators' job was a difficult one, and not only when major issues had to be resolved; on a different level, there were equally thorny problems during the meetings, when we had to cut off some speaker who had taken up more than the eight minutes he was allowed.

An exception was made for dear Cardinal Slipyj, who had just been released from a Russian prison. The first time he took the floor, he spoke for close to half an hour, which was to be expected. The second and the third times his turn came to speak, we ignored the lengthiness of his statements; however, we finally had to give him notice that he was expected to follow the rules. It happened to be my turn to be moderator for the day, and after about ten minutes – this was already very weak on my part – I cut him off. The system was quite radical and drastic: all the moderator had to do was push a button.

This created a certain coolness in our relationship which lasted almost two years. It was particularly awkward since, for alphabetical reasons, our names were next to each other in most lists, and we were frequently neighbours. After the Council, I sent him Christmas cards and New Year's greetings – all in vain. Finally, one day, at a post-conciliar synod, as we were once more seated together, he took from his briefcase a branch of flowering mimosa, which he handed to me. We were reconciled.

He was hard of hearing, and his Latin wasn't very good, so he was always asking me what was going on, especially when we had to vote. He then trustingly copied my vote, which meant I scored twice at every vote!

I have kept a very vivid memory of this great man – a physical and moral giant – on account of his long captivity. I am convinced that when we meet again, up in Heaven, he will hand me a fresh branch of flowering mimosa. Meanwhile, may the Lord bless the Ukrainian Church, of which he was the living and suffering incarnation.

Among the stories picked up by journalists during the Council, there was also the one about the nicknames the bishops used informally in speaking of the moderators. Each had been given the name of an evangelist: Cardinal Agagianian, of the Eastern tradition, was "St John", a little separate from the others, who were in turn described as "the synoptics" because of their concordance. I have to say that we "synoptics" never had the least problem with "St John" and that I have kept an excellent memory of this easygoing colleague.

The Pope knew of this story, and at the end of the Council, he gave each one of us a beautiful bronze bell, very modern in style, on which the four evangelists were represented in bas-relief .

C. AFTER THE COUNCIL – DARKNESS AND LIGHT

The Council – a new springtime for the Church

In the aftermath of the Council, journalists asked me "Are you satisfied with the Council?", and I answered "Yes, it is a new springtime for the Church, but a late-February-early-March springtime; we are still having heavy showers and early morning frosts. But we're moving along."

A few times, I used the analogy of an elevator in a twenty-storey building – when it stops on the tenth floor, it is possible to say, looking up from below, "It's already up there, at the tenth floor; that's great"; if you're looking down, you're likely to say "It's only just reached the tenth floor."

All in all, the Council years were a tremendous grace for the Church; however, we must not lose sight of the wood for the trees.

In my notes for October 15, 1968, I find these words, the result of my own meditations at the time:

> We must beware of extremes: *in medio virtus*. Professor A.Gesché translated this very nicely when he said: "Courage is to be found somewhere between two facile extremes – that of yielding blindly to change, and that of resisting inflexibly. Change must neither fascinate nor frighten."
>
> Therein lies the present call, the sign of the times.
>
> Rahner has warned us that Vatican III is already in

people's minds. "Let us not delude ourselves", he wrote. "The theological style of the Council is far from the language of the future, which is already taking shape — the language in which the man of the twenty-first century thinks and speaks."

And I added:

We must continue tirelessly to probe the future, to listen to its voice, spoken and unspoken. We must pursue the dialogue which began at Vatican II. Professor Debré, famous French doctor and father of the Prime Minister, has proposed that the following words be added to Hippocrates's vow: "I swear to educate myself throughout my life." This is a pressing obligation for all of us.

Some time later, on November 28, 1968, continuing my internal dialogue, I wrote:

Young people already feel themselves to be well beyond Vatican II. A young French bishop, as he listened to his colleagues discussing the days before the Council, commented, "The veterans are talking about Verdun."

We must look at this world of the twenty-first century, which is already dawning, with new eyes, with the eyes of Christ. We must look at it without measuring what is possible or impossible by our own standards; our only points of reference must be his Heart, his Gospel, his Redemptive Death, his Resurrection.

I am reminded of Pascal's familiar words: "Christ has been in agony for twenty centuries. It is no time to be sleeping." Nor can we doze, or do a little superficial whitewashing. What we need is a metamorphosis, a Pentecost, a world created anew in the Spirit.

Poor creatures that we are. The Lord's words stand out, above all else: *"Nolite timere"*. Do not be afraid. Let us exorcise our fears and our caution. Amen.

151

The Council's impact on the times

Vatican II was a turning-point in the history of our times. It put an end to the existing image of an institutional Church and opened the door to an evolution which we must neither minimise nor exaggerate. It was easy to predict that its translation into the daily life of the Church would cause problems. My pastoral letter for the Feast of Pentecost in 1970 dealt with this; here are a few excerpts:

THE CHURCH IN HISTORY

This is a difficult hour for the Church. It is a troubled time, because so many things are being questioned; but it is also a time rich in hopes for the future. There is definitely a crisis, but opinions differ as to the correct diagnosis. Where does it come from, what is its nature, where does it lead?

A correct analysis of the symptoms of a disorder is a necessary prerequisite to any therapy; this applies to us here as well. To find our bearings at sea, we must have a compass, know where we are coming from, study the currents and counter-currents that carry the ship forward or slow it down.

At the present time, the Church is much like a ship, exposed to every wind, tossed about as in some gulf of Gascony. This is in part the result of the external situation — the condition of the sea. The Church exists in and for the world; she is profoundly affected by the extraordinary upheavals that are transforming the world around her. History has accelerated at the end of this twentieth century, and this increase in speed has reached a staggering rate; we move into a new century every five or ten years.

There is also an internal cause, inherent in the ship itself. As a result of the Council, major adjustments and repairs to the ship are being made out at sea, rather than in a dry dock. The Church herself has the appearance of a shipyard in full activity; the crew and the passengers can see and experience day by day to what extent their destiny is identical, and to what extent life on board is a matter which concerns them all.

This too is new. The feeling of the coresponsibility of all Christians has been awakened, but there is still some distance to go before we fully understand the implications of this awakening. The breach has been made, however, and it can only grow and increase. This is the time to remember what Victor Hugo once said: "Nothing is as powerful as an idea whose time has come." Whether we like it or not, a new life-style will develop within the Church.

For a long time — much too long — life in the Church was for many Christians synonymous with passivity, with stagnation, with an unconscious Christianity which was sociological rather than personal. Today we are leaving that era behind.

Instead of accusing Vatican II, as some are doing, of having provoked a torrential thaw, it would be better to wonder where the ice came from which gave rise to this inevitable reaction — and how to prevent new ice-floes from forming in the future.

Certain difficulties are inherent in our times, and they are many and various in nature. One of them springs from the fact that the renewal affects simultaneously every aspect of the life of the Church.

All is in all. All things hold together. Thus, if we want collegiality to be exercised more fully at the supreme level of the Church, logic requires that we re-examine, with the same perspective, the profile of the bishop within the local church, and that of the priest at the heart of the community.

We cannot enhance the priesthood of the faithful without looking with new eyes at the ministerial priesthood, which — though irreplaceable — must be lived differently. The creation of permanent deacons and the conferring of new functions on the laity demand that we qualify our traditional blueprints and introduce a certain pluralism into ecclesial functions.

All things are mutually interactive. We all need to understand in a new way where we stand with respect to one another. These things cannot happen overnight.

What is essential and what is subsidiary

This also presupposes that we know how to distinguish judiciously that which is essential, in the heritage of our past, from that which is subsidiary or obsolete. Our faithful are used to receiving the pure gold of the Gospels interwoven, sometimes indiscriminately, with purely human fabrications; and they have never been trained to distinguish between the two.

It is no easy task to strip clean a gothic cathedral covered with baroque or modern stuccoes, to reveal the original vault. One does not become overnight a renovator of cathedrals in the manner of Viollet-le-Duc.

In a text on ecumenism — the full richness of which has yet to be teased out — the Council has said some excellent things about "the hierarchy of truths". All that is revealed is truth, but not all of it is equally central. This is an important step forward towards any kind of ecumenical dialogue.

It is also an invitation, to all of us, to define that which is at the very heart of Christianity, and to separate it from what is less central. This applies even more to all that theologians, moralists and preachers, over the ages, have added to the deposit of Revelation, on their own initiative, stepping far too lightly over the threshold of mysteries.

Trees benefit from regular pruning; if we cut off sideshoots, the sap can rise and flow to the main branches. But the hand that cuts must be a knowing and firm hand, one that will not slip; and when we look at the strewn dead branches, we need a robust optimism to trust in the coming of spring.

The radicalism of renewal

The current renewal is both difficult to bring about and exhilarating to experience; but it faces yet another major obstacle — the very depth of the "conversion" that is required of us.

If we want to be faithful to the Gospel and all its demands, and at the same time to meet the expectations of the world, we must accept aches, hurts and contradictions. Life is made of tensions, always seeking a balance; the discomforts of the voyage are the price to be paid for the discovery of new horizons. The very depth of the action of the Holy Spirit requires time and patience.

The Church in history

While we wait for the different generations to close the gap which separates them, and for the Holy Spirit to triumph over the sinfulness which stands in his way within each one of us, I feel that we could be of service to Christians today, as they head toward the twenty-first century, if we were to show them that the Church is a reality that has a place in history.

The present hour is easier to understand if we connect it to yesterday and expect to connect it to tomorrow, much as we measure the latitude and the longitude to establish the location of a ship on a map. If we understand where the Church stands in time, we will be better able to see where she stands in our times. There is a great deal to be gained from seeing her inserted, there, at the very heart of history, rather than as an abstract reality, unchanging, untemporal.

We have suffered far too much from a static vision of the Church, defined in terms of a juridically "perfect" society.

Nowadays, thanks be to God, we no longer see the Church in terms of legal categories; rather, we see her as a living reality to which Christ gives breath through his presence and his life, and which is following its path from Easter to the coming of the Lord, moving through time and through history — a pilgrim Church, going forward step by step along her unfinished path.

The story of the Exodus teaches us that God does not like to give his people a large stock of provisions; but he watches over them, and provides them with manna day by day.

We had acquired the habit of accumulating many cumbersome accessories, and of building our houses out of stone and cement, instead of being content with folding tents which would leave us free to move on at any moment.

A Church that is firmly integrated in history is better able to awaken its people, make them aware of the need to be more open and more flexible, and teach them the obligation to be faithful at once to the past, to the present and to the future.

PART III

The Post-Conciliar Years

6

Active Service (1965-1980)

1965-1966

A difficult dialogue between generations

Returning home from the Council, I, like every bishop in the world, experienced the painful turmoil that was spreading through the Church, and in particular through the clergy. In addition to the many defections, what surprised me most was the difficulty of engaging in any real dialogue between generations; I attributed this to the disconcerting phenomenon of the rate at which history seemed to be accelerating.

Suddenly, we realised that we were entering a new century every ten years. There was no common wavelength linking one generation to the next. I remember, in particular, what the rector of a seminary once said to me about the young seminarians I was about to meet: "I must warn you that they do not speak our language, nor do they inhabit our world: they live on a different planet altogether!" We were then on the eve of May '68, in other words at a crossroads; the changing climate was to condition, in part, the pastoral implementation of the Council.

In my own country, there was political tension to contend with as well; it led to a breakdown of unity — a unity that had lasted five centuries — in the University of Louvain.

The tragedy of the Catholic University of Louvain

As soon as they returned from the Council, the Belgian bishops were confronted with the problem of the break-up of the University of Louvain.

As Chancellor of the University, my task was to try to preserve

159

unity of views within the episcopal body – to the extent that this was possible – while also attempting to take into account the contradictory interests that were at stake. Since 1921, the bishops had introduced a two-language system of instruction in Louvain; the particular pressures at work at the time, however, demanded a clear-cut territorial split, since Louvain was on Flemish territory and we were heading towards a political federalisation of the country.

The emotional climate of the time made any compromise impossible. We were even obliged to give up our efforts to preserve the unity of the Department of Theology and of the Institut supérieur de philosophie, both of which concerned us particularly. Three Flemish prelates at the University – Mgr Philips, Mgr Dondeyne, and Mgr Heylen – came to tell me how crucial it was, from a scientific and international standpoint, to preserve the territorial unity of these two academic institutions. Much to our regret, this proved impossible.

The Prime Minister, in an attempt to mediate, proposed that students attending the upper classes should stay where they were, while students in the first years would be sent to French-speaking areas. This proposal also failed. Shortly afterwards, his government collapsed.

For all of us, this was a painful calvary, marked by many stations along the way.

As I write these lines, the linguistic strife has subsided, and a peaceful era of cooperation has dawned between the two Catholic Universities – the one that remained at Leuven (Louvain), and the one in the Walloon part of Brabant (Louvain-la-Neuve). *Deo gratias!*

The fortieth anniversary of the Malines Conversations
In a quiet moment of leisurely retrospection, I look back on the two days of meetings in Malines, held on the occasion of the fortieth anniversary of the Malines Conversations. I would like simply to thank the Lord for this meeting of hearts, for the warmth

of the encounter, for this "victory of hope" for our beloved Cardinal Mercier, up in Heaven.

What a joy, after an interval of forty years, to pick up where he had left off; to add a sixth to the five Conversations of long ago; and to find proof that the unfinished symphony had lost none of its original vitality. The Holy Spirit is a spirit of continuity, but he expects us to wait for his hour, while never remaining inactive. Nothing of what we do for God is ever lost.

A journalist once asked me whether the Malines Conversations had been a failure. I replied: "Not at all. They caused a spring to surge, and for some years, it continued to flow — underground. Then, one day, it welled up again and formed a stream, then a river. At the Council, the river headed out to sea."

Among those present, the major figures were the Anglican bishop who represented Ramsey, and the Catholic bishop representing the English hierarchy. In Paradise, where the funny side of things is easier to appreciate than anywhere else, Cardinal Mercier and Cardinal Bourne must have smiled to see Westminster represented at the meetings!

The Anglican bishop was tactful and charming. The Catholic bishop — a convert from the Anglican Church — was also an outstanding man. He made a few corrections in the article I had written in English for *The Tablet*, and invited me most warmly to visit him.

The Halifax family were there — they were so "old England" that they might have stepped out of engravings of those bygone days which we were commemorating. The portraits of old Lord Halifax and of Cardinal Mercier were hanging at the entrance to the improvised museum. The past was coming alive again. An elderly lady of the Halifax family had a fall while staying at the seminary. As she left for the hospital, she smiled at me and said: "I offer this up for unity."

The ecumenical service in the Cathedral of Saint-Rombaut was a high point of the meeting. Lord Halifax's grandson read the Epistle; after the Gospel, I read a letter from the Holy Father.

Another significant moment was the common prayer service with the Anglicans in the old chapel of the seminary.

Those were for me days of grace, for they witnessed to a brotherly love full of prefigurations and hopes.

Ecumenical meetings with Mgr Bloom, Exarch of the Patriarch of Moscow

Some time later, the Patriarch of Moscow's Exarch for Western countries, Mgr Bloom of London, came to dinner at my residence. He had asked if we could meet "with no specific agenda in mind". We talked for three hours, very openly and honestly. He was an impressive man, very serious, self-assured, not very open to a *rapprochement* with Rome, set in his opinions and judgements, but very charitable in his response to human distress.

I asked him whether the primacy of the Pope would still represent for him an insurmountable obstacle, if the exercise of that primacy were modified. His answer was very firm: "Nothing in the Scriptures authorises the primacy of Peter's successor. The Pope is on the same level as any apostolic bishop. There can be no succession of primacy."

He was more open concerning the "Filioque", and did not see in this an insurmountable obstacle. As for Anglican ordinations, he admitted to a certain perplexity. He did say, however, that the articles in the *Revue de Moscou* (*Moscow Journal*) which I mentioned to him lacked a certain scientific rigour, not because the author was unscholarly, but because the examiners – this was a doctoral dissertation – were not very demanding.

He praised the English Methodists, but remarked that the Church of England was "very poor" from a religious standpoint, and that Anglicanism was more vigorous in the Church of Ireland and in the Commonwealth.

In his view, Ramsey did not measure up to his predecessor, Fisher! He found him more conservative in his ideas, but more liberal when it came to concrete realisations and compromises.

We spoke of the USSR. He was himself the son of the Russian Ambassador to Persia at the time of the Revolution; he had never been to Moscow before 1960. In his opinion, there were still some fifty million practising Christians in the USSR, out of a population of 250 million. According to anti-religious publications, about 65 per cent of the population were in some way involved with the Orthodox faith. Not only the old practised. We should not forget, he said to me, that among the peasants and working classes, old age begins around forty or forty-five. While distributing communion in Moscow churches, he had noticed many a young face under a scarf. In Moscow he had been *persona non grata*, because of sermons he had made preparing the faithful for "the persecutions yet to come". This was his way of strengthening them to deal with the persecutions of the time (eight thousand churches out of twenty-five thousand had been closed down).

A simple untrained worker had nothing to fear if he practised his religion; however, a better-qualified worker ran the risk of losing his job. He told me the strange story of a scientist who had been invited by the police to go to church "somewhere else"; they had even offered him the use of a car, "in order to avoid scandal", they said.

Another strange story he told me involved a customs official who treated him rudely and insulted him as he weighed in his luggage at the airport, but wrote down a ridiculously low weight for his bags.

He was returning to Moscow eight days later, so I gave him a copy of *The Gospel to Every Creature* to take back to the Patriarch of Moscow — it was a way of reaching out, looking for a reaction. He took the book, saying he would be very happy to hand it on, and informed me that I was *persona gratissima* in the Orthodox world because of my attitude during the Council.

Mgr Bloom was critical of our position on mixed marriages, and of the diocesan structures which had remained rigid and unchanged after the Council. We spoke a little more about the conversations on "Orthodoxy and Anglicanism", which had brought together four theologians on each side, and to which he had been invited as observer. He promised to send me an article by Nikodim on his reactions to the Council.

At the end of our meeting, he confided that despite the thirty years he had spent in Western countries, he still found some of our reactions difficult to understand. Clearly, dialogue would be a slow and lengthy process.

I asked him at what level meetings would, in his opinion, be most useful. I remarked that it would be good if we could meet "at the level of our saints", rather than meeting only at the level of "theologians" who tend to intellectualise and protract arguments endlessly. Asked what he thought of meetings "at the level of bishops", he replied, "Our bishops are not theologians, like yours, and in all of Russia I know of only three who can speak French."

We parted on the best of terms. When he came in, he wore a toque on which a cross was emblazoned and from which streamed a long white veil. He removed it at the dinner table; I thought I could detect, in this slight breach of the rules, a sign of friendship and an indication that he felt comfortable and at ease.

He told me that, on Good Friday one year, he noticed an Englishman on a bus looking intently at his pectoral cross. He said to him: "Take your time, and look at it carefully. Today is Good Friday." And the bishop concluded: "It is well worth wearing a cross for fifteen years, if once, on a Good Friday, one person looks at it."

These are just a few sketchy memories. In the end, I was left with an impression of grandeur, of a soaring mind, of great honesty and directness. Yet, at the same time, I had a feeling that the road to visible unity would be a long one, a very long one indeed. Even the best "on the other side" look to the overtures from Rome, and never wonder whether they too might not have to take a few steps to meet us halfway.

This is the terrible ambiguity of ecumenism – Catholics are

expected to become "more Protestant" or "more Orthodox", but there appears to be no openness – or not enough openness – to the action of the Spirit who wants to highlight, in each of these Churches, those elements which are complementary and which are in themselves ecclesial values.

Lord, make us docile to your light and flexible in your hand, that no pride may stand in the way of the action of grace, whether in us or in them! And may Our Lady of Cana, who hastened the hour of her Son's first miracle, obtain for us the grace of hastening the hour of the decisive meeting between the children of the one Father!

* * *

In my notebook, I have found the account of a second meeting with Mgr Bloom, on November 18, 1968; I shall include it here, to complete the story of our first conversation.

Something had changed in his attitude – or so it seemed to me – since our earlier meeting, in 1966; he seemed more relaxed, more "unionist" in his approach.

He told me that, in his London home, he gave shelter to Orthodox criminals who had been freed from jail, and to some people who were mentally ill. However, he had had to stop taking in the mentally ill, because members of his household were afraid of them.

In speaking of the authority of the Russian synod, he told me that, at the time, because of the political regime, practice did not correspond to theory. He too insisted, however, that it is not a matter of a "majority" deciding over and against a "minority". I told him that in my view the most important opinion within a council is that of the holiest person; he remarked that it is much the same in music – the one who has the sharpest ear is better able to recognise the off-key note, though he may be the only one to do so. We were in full agreement: authority within the Church belongs to the realm of the Mystery of God.

Finally, he promised that the four Orthodox bishops who were his auxiliaries would read my book, *Co-responsibility in the Church*, and that they would comment on it, first separately, then as a group.

He complained that the Eastern liturgy was far too long: "We inform God in great detail of things he knows much better than we do." On the other hand, he expressed the hope that the "Jesus prayer" and the "Kyrie eleison" would become more popular, since they bring us face to face with God.

Our meeting was a communion of hope and of faith. It is difficult not to fear that the distances between us and the Orthodox will increase as faith grows dimmer in our ranks. They are "strong in faith", albeit in a faith that is static, frozen, heir to a canonical and ritualistic past that is, like Goliath's armour, too heavy a burden. They need a few daring Davids.

One is left with the impression that "the Spirit speaks to the Churches" with great intensity, these days. If we could only make silence within ourselves, and allow for a deeper listening and a greater receptivity.

* * *

My dear friend Cardinal Bea has just died. It has been said of him that he was the most welcoming of men. May the Lord be for him the Supreme Welcome. May he assist us in our path towards ecumenism. His honesty and his directness made him one of the great figures of the Council. May he deliver us from all human diplomacy and from all manner of bargaining.

* * *

I had a third dialogue with Mgr Anthony Bloom — this time in public, at the Palais des Beaux-Arts in Brussels. The theme of the conference was "The Church of Peter, the Church of John, the Church of Paul". *La Libre Belgique* published an account of the evening:

The crowd in the main hall of the Palais des Beaux-Arts was particularly large and attentive. In the series of Great Catholic Conferences, three key figures were to speak on the problems of the Church: Mgr Suenens, Archbishop Anthony (Exarch of the Patriarchate of Moscow for Western Europe), and Dr W. Visser't Hooft (Honorary President of the Ecumenical Council of Churches).

The speakers were brilliantly introduced by Mr Pierre Harmel, Minister for Foreign Affairs, who pointed out that spiritual ecumenism could only assist in the efforts towards the "social ecumenism" of an enlarged Europe.

The title for the evening's meeting was "The Church of Peter, Paul and John". It was meant to signify that, of the three great founders, Peter appears to be most centrally the father of the Catholic Church; the Reformation emphasises Paul's ideas, and the Orthodox Churches seek above all the mystical spirituality of St John.

The first speaker was Cardinal Suenens. Alluding to the problems of unity, the Cardinal spoke of the progress that has been made in this area since the Malines Conversations, fifty years ago; of the friendship that binds all Christians who seek unity; and of the efforts of those who, in the words of Saint-Exupéry, look together in the same direction.

Archbishop Anthony pointed out that there will never be unity unless and until all Christians become truly and totally Christian. This is what he calls the unity of holiness among the people of God.

Pastor Visser't Hooft, for his part, recalled that all Christian Churches claim descent from Peter, Paul and John. Rather than thinking about what they can give to others, they should be thinking of what they can receive from others. The Reformation admires in the Orthodox Church her endurance, her faithfulness, her marvellous joy in Easter; in the Catholic Church, it admires the sense of visible unity.

Both of the other speakers followed this lead and reviewed their hopes. Archbishop Anthony mentioned his love for the vision of the sovereign Kingdom of God in the Reformed Church; he admired in the Catholic Church her doctrinal daring and her courage to question. Cardinal Suenens said that he has received from the Protestant faith a sense of fraternal community; from the Orthodox Church, he has learned to identify theology and spirituality, which elsewhere are so often separated.

The three men spoke of their views with such sincerity, such eloquence, such fervour and fraternal love, that the audience was deeply moved. The words of these three extraordinary men revealed the road that has been travelled, the road that is still ahead, and a hope that strives to overcome all obstacles. It was indeed a memorable evening.

Turmoil in the media

In my files, I have found an amusing letter from Mgr Prignon, Rector of the Belgian College. A very simple event had been the cause of great turmoil: I had left Rome, but had not returned to Malines.

As it happened, I was taking a few days of rest at the Fraternité Le Rocher, a community in the hills above Nice. Reporters, who had been watching my every move with eagle eyes, had not seen me leave Rome by plane, and were inventing all sorts of wild hypotheses. I had an uncomfortable moment during lunch, one day, when a French television channel showed a photograph of me and announced on the one o'clock news that I was on "secret mission". Luckily, the waiter who was serving my meal, and who did not know who I was, had his back to the television screen!

From Rome, I received Mgr Prignon's letter:

Rome, February 6, 1966

I hope you have had a chance to rest, as you had intended, before going back to face the difficult situation in Belgium.

A few items of news:

Your inconspicuous departure has created unbelievable turmoil and excitement in Rome. For two whole days, every international press agency in town, including such respectable people as Reuter's, has been on the phone to me, asking every imaginable question. We learned that you were in Paris at UNESCO; in Warsaw to negotiate the Pope's visit; at the UN to explain the Pope's appeal to neutral States in favour of peace in Vietnam; in Tokyo headed for Hanoi. The police were questioned at the airport, to find out how and when you had left the country; every airline was interrogated; I received an SOS from the *Osservatore Romano*. Finally, the Secretariat of State was approached. Our representative tells me that the Pope smiled when he read the headlines in the Roman newspapers. Vincent was losing his mind and phoned me at least five times a day. I was obliged to give *some* details to the Ambassador, since it appears that the Government were beginning to express some concern. Instructions were to say, in response to all enquiries, that the Cardinal is working, in seclusion, and is in constant communication with the Archbishop's House; we referred everyone to Malines for further information.

1967

Atlanta

On the last day of the Council, a group of Protestant observers from the United States invited me to a goodbye dinner at their hotel.

They spoke to me about the ecumenical experience that Vatican II had been for them, and invited me to go to the States to talk about the Council in their Lutheran, Episcopalian and Pentecostal churches, and in their universities. I agreed in principle, assuming that this would involve a few lectures over a period of a year or two. As it turned out, it has involved two trips to the US every year, for twenty years! It was the starting-point of an odyssey, with wide ramifications.

Travel was made easy through the kindness, efficiency and generosity of Peter and Margie Grace, who offered me the use of their private plane, sometimes even to cross the Atlantic.

Over the years, and until 1980, my visits followed the pattern of my first trip to Atlanta, with some variations. My first memory of this fifteen-day visit to the States is of a moment of distress, when our pilot announced that the plane was about to land in Montreal, rather than in New York as I had expected, because of unfavourable weather conditions. During our forced stop in Canada, a kindly Belgian couple came to keep me company, and asked me to sign a large number of postcards for their friends back home. At last, the fog lifted over New York and we were able to continue our flight.

The first invitation I had received was from Emory College, a Methodist University in Atlanta. Corson, who had represented the American Methodist Church at the Council, was a friend of Pope John. Emory College wanted to confer degrees *honoris causa* on both the Pope and myself — a distinction that had never before been bestowed upon a Catholic.

The Catholic Archbishop of the diocese, Mgr Hallinan, had been one of the great figures of the Council. He had presided over the Liturgical Commission of American Bishops. There was great harmony between us; he insisted that I should accept this offer, and invited me to stay with him.

And so I arrived in Atlanta, at Emory College, where I received a very friendly welcome. This was my first experience of a typically Methodist environment; I was struck by the seriousness and by the pietist tone.

The first lecture I was scheduled to give was on "Ecumenical Dialogue". My task was made easy by the presence at my side of several highly qualified men, each one prepared to answer questions from the audience about his particular field. This kind of panel discussion has certain advantages; you can pass the ball, much as in soccer, to the next person on your team, rather than having to come up with an instant answer to every possible question. In addition to the outgoing President of the Methodist World Council of Churches, the panel included Archbishop Hallinan, and Dean Cannon (later appointed bishop) of the Department of Theology.

The questions were many and intense, but the atmosphere was relaxed. Both Corson and Cannon declared that the Methodist Church is closer to Rome than to any other Protestant denomination. A Lutheran in the audience asked me, point-blank, whether the Holy Spirit had inspired the Reformation. A silence followed his question, and there were a few amused smiles here and there. I barely had time to invoke the Holy Spirit before replying: "Yes, inasmuch as the Reformation was a challenge to the Church and an invitation to reject all manner of abuse. No, inasmuch as the Reformation led to a break and to separation, for the Holy Spirit is a Spirit of union and of unity."

There was also a very large crowd to hear me speak at my second lecture, and the audience was particularly attentive. Clearly, our Methodist friends appreciated the fraternal presence of a cardinal among them. For my part, I learned what a strong hold pietist Methodism has on its followers; in many parishes, up to 40 per cent of the faithful gave several hours a week to some form of apostolate.

On the last day, we received our doctorates in theology, *honoris causa*. In my final thank-you speech, I called for all to "look together in the same direction" and to react together against the theology of the death of God, which at the time was quite popular. Altizer, one of the proponents of this theology, was present; he was introduced to me at the end of the ceremony, but there was too much confusion, at that stage, for us to have a proper conversation.

The high point of my stay in Atlanta was the end-of-session ecumenical service. In the sacristy, Corson asked me to improvise an opening prayer, and handed me his own stole to wear over my vestments. Then he preached, with profound emotion, a sermon on Wesley's famous sentence: "If your heart is like mine, give me

171

your hand." It was pious, serious, sincere. In the evening, there was a banquet for the alumni – perhaps a little on the pompous side, but pleasant in its fraternal simplicity.

After Methodist Atlanta, I went on to Catholic Atlanta. Two whole days were spent with Archbishop Hallinan and his Auxiliary, Mgr Bernardin, who has since become cardinal. I thoroughly enjoyed the atmosphere of friendship, communion of ideas, and deep sharing. I could tell that the Archbishop was one of the leaders of the American Church – I later heard Fr Abbot describe him as "the" leader. He was a man of daring, willing to assume responsibilities. He suggested that a good model for us might be that of the insistent intruder of the Gospels, who wakes people in the night and seizes what he came for. He recommended this kind of perseverance with respect to some of the decrees issued by Rome which cannot be implemented in the United States.

He was attentive and kind to those around him, showing tremendous respect for each person, including those "hard-liners" in the clergy with whom recent elections in the presbyterial senate had burdened him. I found him to be an intellectual of great standing, an academic man, charming in his modesty.

Here is the letter which he wrote to thank me, and in which the pastoral harmony between us is very obvious:

February 2, 1967

Dear Cardinal Suenens,
Your visit to Atlanta will be remembered by our priests, our religious and our faithful for many years to come.

Your sharp sense of evangelisation and the skill with which you lead others to share in it, your friendly kindness and the instinctive contact you establish with all those you meet – these qualities, and many others, have won our hearts.

Dean Cannon, and others at the University, have telephoned or written to tell us that your visit has greatly encouraged the ecumenical spirit which we occasionally breathe — sometimes precariously — in our Southern regions.

The most significant aspect of your visit was the fact that a leader of your standing, of world fame, known for his zeal, his spirit and his wide horizons, accepted to come to our archdiocese, where Catholics are few in number. In this area we have no great universities, seminaries or cultural centres; yet I feel that the words you spoke to us were as significant and forceful as they would have been had you been speaking to the Council or to the United Nations.

I shall not forget you, and in future, if I may, I shall turn to you for advice, and from time to time send you a few diocesan articles about our pastoral efforts.

Austin

The next day, I gave a lecture at the State University in Austin. The tower overlooking the campus had recently been the scene of a horrific massacre; a mad student had shot fifteen people from the tower-top.

The meeting that evening was organised by the Newman Club. My lecture was very well received, and was followed by a great many questions. The audience had the kindness to applaud each one of my answers, including my refusal to answer a question concerning Vietnam.

Boston

Next came a quick stop in Boston, where I had dinner with Cardinal Cushing; he was in great form. I have kept a rather comical memory of that encounter. Every so often, during the meal, the Cardinal would grab my right arm and hold on to it, so that I hardly managed to eat at all. The kindly and charming Cardinal never noticed a thing: each time I tried to take a bite, he grasped my forearm to make sure I was paying attention to his words. The only conclusion I could possibly draw was to resolve that if I ever dined with him again, I should choose to sit where my arm would have *carte blanche!*

A curious country, America; a place of great contrasts. In private, they have a manner that is direct and simple. In public, however, ceremonies have a precision and a decorum which are somehow unexpected.

A curious country, where cities often resemble vast commercial fairs where all is new and shiny and brightly coloured; lacking sheen, or mystery, or surprises; no oasis, no greenery. Their cities have not grown out of conglomerates of villages or overgrown villages, as ours have. There, practicality triumphs, and one goes straight to one's goal along roads that do not follow the contours of the land and do not respect any heritage. A curious country, plunging into the future with such *élan*, dragging the world behind it.

Back at home, I discovered in myself a new respect for our old cathedrals, our antique furniture and our ancestral traditions.

* * *

On the evening of May 2, 1968, when I had just learned of the death of my friend, Archbishop Hallinan — who, of all the American bishops, had been closest to me — I wrote down something he had once said. Someone had been suggesting that he should be more cautious in his public pronouncements concerning the Vietnam war; he knew at the time that he was to die before long, and he replied: "You know, where I am going, the only problem will be — did I speak clearly enough?"

Munich
The Council also created bonds of friendship among bishops, especially between those who had experienced it in the same way, from the "inside". Thus I owe to the Council my friendship with Cardinal Doepfner, Archbishop of Munich, who was, like me, one

174

of the four moderators. Here, dated March 1967, are my comments on my first visit to Munich.

In response to an invitation from Cardinal Doepfner, I went to Munich for a jubilee conference, on the occasion of the tenth anniversary of the foundation of the Catholic Academy of Bavaria. After the conference, we discussed, in private, the post-conciliar Church.

We discussed some of the current anti-establishment "protesters", and Cardinal Doepfner commented: " 'Prophets' today are not what they used to be; in the old days, they had a sense of the Church and a deeply rooted faith." He mentioned Karl Adam and Guardini, who, though they had their trials and tribulations, were men of strong and resilient faith. I added a few names to the list, names such as Mercier, Dom Lambert, Lebbe and de Lubac.

In the evening, the German experts I had met at the Council gathered around the dinner table. It was a joy to talk to Rahner, and to Tilmann ("author" of the German catechism). Rahner stressed the fundamental truths in which we must believe, and affirmed that the existence of angels belongs to the deposit of faith. I listened to him with great joy.

That night, I had a rather unusual adventure. I woke up, got out of bed, washed, shaved, and dressed, thinking it was seven o'clock in the morning. When I was quite ready to celebrate the Eucharist — I only had to put my wristwatch on — I noticed that it was 1:30 a.m. and that I had been looking at my watch upside down! It is a very strange sensation — one feels stupid rather than guilty, half asleep and already half involved in the day's activities — it is not at all like sleepwalking. Such a feeling of stupidity does not invite humour. I slowly realised that there was really only one way out of my predicament: to go back to the starting point — in other words, back to bed.

The following day, I had dinner with Doepfner's assistants. They were a group of excellent people, but to hear them speak, one would never have suspected that a Council had actually taken place, or that pastoral ministry was in crisis, or even that a certain amount of questioning was going on. They were firmly rooted in Vatican I – the Cardinal must have been in some ways a prisoner of his own rearguard!

A procession of cars, flags flying from their front bonnets, delivered us to the Museum, where I was scheduled to speak on "The Church in the World". I was inwardly relaxed, but grammatically tense, since I had to respect the peculiarities of a language which I do not know well. Here and there, I felt that I was skating on thin ice, so to speak, but on the whole I think I managed quite well.

The really painful part, however, was the reception that followed. Hundreds of people were introduced to me. It was a very strange experience to hear so many people say so many things, most of which I only half understood; I only occasionally ventured a yes or a no, and threw in a sibilant exclamation here and there! I concluded that, back home, I would have to take an intensive course in German!

The flight back to Brussels brings back memories of dishes and cutlery clattering all over the plane as a record storm tossed us about. Eventually things settled down, however, and we reached our destination safely.

Sotto il Monte

After giving a lecture in Brescia, I went to pray at Sotto il Monte, in the house that belonged to Pope John's family. I was very surprised to find so many pilgrims there; the parish priest told me that on a Sunday there can be as many as twelve thousand, and on weekdays between five and six thousand. Holiness is something the people recognise instinctively; of itself it commands their veneration.

Lost in the crowd, I listened to the very simple words of an old priest to the passing pilgrims. Suddenly, much to my surprise, the priest handed me the crucifix that had belonged to Pope John – the very one he had sent to his dying mother – and I blessed the pilgrims with the cross "on behalf of Papa Giovanni". At that moment, I felt very close to Pope John, and I saw in this little episode one of those *fioretti* of which he had the secret – his own special way of thanking me for my visit!

There is in the town an excellent bronze statue of Pope John, smiling and giving his blessing. So many people have kissed his hands that they shine like living gold.

I also met the Pope's brother, Zaverio Roncalli, with whom I had a simple and friendly talk. He explained to all who came on pilgrimage that it is not enough to have a holy brother; we must all have an up-to-date passport if we want to go to Heaven.

London

Archbishop Ramsey of Canterbury invited me to visit him, and I went to Lambeth Palace in May 1967. The Archbishop, clothed in purple, met me at the door of his imposing palace – the Vatican of Anglicanism – and welcomed me very warmly. Mrs Ramsey, in a green silk dress, stood a few steps behind, with the secretaries. Together, we walked up the main stairway.

To my great joy and surprise, an icon of Mary greeted us in the entrance hall. Beneath it was a magnificent bouquet of flowers; above it, a tapestry had been arranged in such a manner that there seemed to be a crown on the Virgin's head. In his room, my secretary found another portrait of Our Lady, bedecked with flowers.

I was led to the guest room, which was spacious and airy, and which opened onto an impeccable lawn of a soft shade of green. In its perfection, the park showed many centuries of loving care.

We changed into our liturgical vestments for Evensong – Vespers – in the Lambeth chapel. About one hundred guests were present; a choir of young people sang, supported by a few strong voices; all in all, a grand ceremony.

We were already in the chapel when my secretary pointed to a line in the printed programme which announced that after the *Magnificat*, the Archbishop would make a speech of welcome, to which I was to respond. This came as a total surprise! Nobody had warned me that I was to give a speech, and so I was obliged to improvise, with the assistance of the Holy Spirit. I did my best, and said a few words about Cardinal Mercier and the Malines Conversations.

There were about thirty of us at dinner that evening. When it came time to make a toast, I told of my first interview with Cardinal Mercier, which had taken place when I was seventeen years old. I also spoke of Pope John, and I quoted one Council observer who had expressed the hope that we would never canonise him, "so that we can venerate him together"!

It was a very relaxed meeting, friendly and warm. I was given the Lambeth Cross, and in return I presented the Archbishop with two prints of the cathedral in Malines, from the inside and from the outside.

The following day was the eve of Pentecost. I concelebrated Mass with my two companions, Dessain and Servotte, in a room facing the chapel. Dr Ramsey was present, kneeling at a very low prie-dieu, almost level with the ground. His wife and other members of the household were there as well. At the sign of peace, during the Mass, I went over to him with open arms, in a gesture of communion. After Mass, I gave thanks in the chapel, where Dr Ramsey celebrated later. I was deeply moved to hear him mention my name at the canon, and pray for those who, on the following day, were to inaugurate the new cathedral in Liverpool. At the sign of peace, he crossed the nave to give me a liturgical embrace. It was a very intense moment, so rich in hope, like a snowdrop at the threshold of spring.

A very relaxed Archbishop showed me, at lunchtime, a collection of caricatures of himself. Later, we moved to his private office to discuss ecumenical matters. The office was spacious. I immediately noticed, on the mantelpiece, a portrait of Pope John and one of Cardinal Bea.

Our conversation covered a vast range of subjects. At the end of this meeting, I was able to draw the following conclusions: the

Marian dogmas (the Immaculate Conception and the Assumption) are only obstacles inasmuch as the Catholic Church imposes them as dogmas. Dr Ramsey was quite prepared to accept them as theological opinions.

As for Paul VI, whom we also discussed, Dr Ramsey saw him as a man whose strong desire for openness was blocked by his own theology.

We talked about mixed marriages, and about birth-control. He asked me to explain my own views in detail. There were no indiscreet questions, simply an atmosphere of easy, comfortable friendship. He suggested that we should find one area of spirituality in which theological oppositions could fade away; he felt that we needed to reach deeper, in order to eliminate surface oppositions. This was, certainly, the most striking of his remarks, the one that carried most promise for the future.

He assured me that the Thirty-nine Articles of the Anglican Creed would be revised and corrected in a way that would make them more acceptable. He also announced that a doctrinal statement would be issued in 1968, when the next Lambeth conference was scheduled to take place. Briefly, he complained of the Eastern Churches' reluctance to change, but also expressed his appreciation for their doctrinal input. He told me he was planning to write a book in response to Bultmann. At the time, he envisioned it as a book about the Eucharist – a book very close to us. He was not planning to publish it before his retirement. From an ecumenical standpoint, he confided, he regretted the Pope's pilgrimage to Fatima. He could see no signs yet of a visible union; he hoped, however, that we would see great changes, and that these would be stepping-stones towards such unity.

We parted at the door of the palace where, for the first time since the Reformation, a cardinal had spent the night. The last Catholic to live there was Cardinal Pole, in the sixteenth century. As we walked down the gallery, we paused for a moment in front of his portrait.

This visit was a memorable event for me: I could feel Cardinal

Mercier and Pope John smiling down from Heaven, and I could just glimpse the outlines of a bridge, arching from one shore to the other, slowly taking shape. May the Lord find us always faithful and available, receptive to his powerful plans, as we await his hour!

A few days after I had given Dr Ramsey the two prints of the cathedral in Malines, I received a letter telling me that he had searched for a good place to hang them in his main living-room; finally, he had decided to place them "right under the big portrait of Cardinal Pole, so he will no longer feel quite so lonely".

Liverpool

We left, headed for Manchester and Liverpool.

On Saturday evening we were invited to an official dinner at the Lord Mayor's. On Pentecost Sunday, I spent the morning in conversation with Dom Butler and Bishop Wheeler of Leeds, both converted Anglicans and renowned academics. Dom Butler gave us a very enriching review of the theological situation. "As I listened to theologians at the Council", he told me, "I was very glad that they are not in charge of the Church. I am struck by the charism that is peculiar to bishops; even when they are not intellectuals, there is in them a pastoral wisdom, a sense of responsibility, that is often lacking in theologians." I found this to be quite an astonishing remark, coming from a theologian of his standing; and I am sure that his opinion has not changed since he was made bishop.

The consecration of the altar and the inauguration of the Catholic cathedral in Liverpool took place on the afternoon of Pentecost. This cathedral is connected to the Anglican cathedral in the same city by a street called Hope Street — what a splendid symbol!

Dinner that evening was made excruciating by countless toasts and speeches. I was seated, however, next to the Speaker of the House of Lords, and we had an interesting conversation. I briefly met with Mr Heath, the opposition leader; he appeared to be an intelligent man, of great personal worth.

Monday morning had been set aside for a private meeting with Mgr Cardinale, Apostolic Delegate to England. For three hours, we exchanged confidences and shared serious and profound ideas, all of this delightfully sprinkled with humour and wit. He is indeed a priest of great distinction, one of the best in Italy, in the same mould as Tucci and Dossetti — perhaps somewhat less intellectual, but more pastoral in his approach. This true servant of the Church held much promise for Rome — provided his wings were not clipped too short. He later became nuncio in Brussels and was a faithful and courageous friend to me. In 1982, the Lord called him back to himself — where he is closer to us than ever before.

Toronto

Of the many friendships that I made during the Council, those with the English-speaking Canadian bishops deserve a special mention. During Council sessions, I often spent an evening with them — partly to answer questions on the progress of the Council, but also simply because we enjoyed each others' company. Alex Carter, Bishop of Sault-Sainte-Marie (North Bay, Ontario) and President of the Canadian Bishops' Conference, became a close friend; and naturally, this friendship extended to include his brother, who later became Cardinal Emmett Carter.

The group of Canadians had asked me to visit them in their homeland after the Council. I had answered "Yes — but you must find a good reason to justify my trip!" Soon after the Council, they invited me to participate in the National Theological Congress, organised by the bishops in Toronto in August 1967. The theme for the Congress was "The Theology of Renewal in the Church". I thus had the opportunity to call for the establishment of an international theological commission with a view to broadening the horizons of the Curia. The text of my statement is included in chapter 6 of my book, *Co-responsibility in the Church* ("Co-responsiblity at the level of the bishops"). In time, the idea was accepted in Rome.

A visit to Belgian priests in Brazil

That same year, in response to an invitation from my friend Dom Helder Câmara, I decided to visit our Belgian priests working in Brazil as *Fidei donum* priests, and in particular those who came from my own diocese. This took me across the country, from north to south, with stops in both Recife and Sao Paulo.

It was a strange experience, to be followed by the police wherever I went, even into the presbytery room where I met with the Belgian priests! Finally I said to them: "For heaven's sake, let's speak Flemish", just to annoy the "eavesdroppers". I have never really understood why those policemen kept such a close watch on us.

The indescribable poverty of the *favelas,* in Rio and elsewhere, left a profound impression on me. The images have never left me; they are like a thorn in my flesh. How can people be reduced to such an inhuman situation — a situation that cries out to Heaven for vengeance?

I remember a Sunday Mass in the poorest parish of the diocese of Recife. Dom Helder had brought me there so that I might see for myself their poverty, but also their faith. Together we assisted as the parish priest celebrated Mass. At the offertory, I watched as a procession of poor people, dressed in rags, advanced through the church; one carried a banana, another a bottle of Coca-Cola; others brought gifts that were even more humble. It was impossible not to think of the widow's mite; impossible not to feel challenged.

After that, Dom Helder took me to visit a family in their home, where a child was dying. Later, we went to a secret meeting of poor people who were trying to set up a sort of workers' union, in an attempt to resist expropriation and to save the tiny plots of land they owned.

Brazil was a unique experience for me because of the contrast I saw between the unbelievable poverty of the many, and the wealth of a few individuals. It was a live illustration of *Populorum progressio*, a cry of distress that must be made to resound throughout the world. Vivid images are engraved in my memory — of Dom Helder Câmara, the very incarnation of courage, and of a people astonishingly young, sensitive and proud, on whom rests, to such a large degree, the future of the Church of tomorrow*.

The 1967 Synod and the International Theological Commission
At the Synod of October 1967, I concentrated all my efforts on my earlier proposal for the establishment of an international theological commission. I defended the idea in the presence of the Holy Father, after responding, also in his presence, to Cardinal Siri's objections. Cardinal Seper arranged to have me selected president of the theological sub-commission, whose task it was to put in writing the wishes of the members. Thus I was able to draft the text of the proposal for the establishment of a theological commission, which was then put to the vote, and adopted by 127 votes to 14.

In the course of a private audience, the Pope said to me that it was a mistake to set up such a commission, because "all our ills today are caused by the theologians." I answered that all the ills were caused by third-rate theologians; we needed good theologians to counteract these. Apparently my arguments did not convince him, however, for that very evening I heard from Cardinal Veuillot that Pope Paul told five French cardinals — who met with him just after I left — that he had informed me of his objections. On the following day, a strong majority supported me, and the Pope concurred.

---

*Fr Schooyans, who was with me on this trip to Brazil, gave a detailed account of it, which was published in French, Dutch and German in the *Bulletin du Collège de l'Amérique latine*, a periodical published by Louvain University for our friends in Latin America.

Two personal memories

In my journal for this year, I find two other memorable episodes, both of which occurred "at home". Here are my unedited notes, in all their spontaneity:

The First Communion of the Crown Prince

Little Prince Philip received his first communion with his class-mates, in a private ceremony at the church of Saint-Michel. It was a simple and limpid event.

It came naturally to me to stress, in my homily, the significance of this occasion and the primacy of the child in the Gospel. It was tempting to bring in *The Little Prince*, and to tell the grown-ups how much they still need to discover. I said something to that effect – not quite as poetically as Saint-Exupéry – indicating that God is very simple in the eyes of a child: we are the ones who make things complicated, who make life complicated. Children step easily and whole-heartedly into the world of the invisible; they play with angels as they play with their peers. While Jesus explained how much easier it is for children to enter the Kingdom of God, the apostles argued over matters of precedence.

After the Eucharist, lunch was served at the Belvedere. Before sitting down to the meal, Prince Albert handed the child a letter from his uncle, the King. The prince was shy and hesitant, and it was his father who read it out loud, while we listened in respectful silence. There were tears in the eyes of his mother, Princess Paola. The letter was a marvel of faith and of loving kindness. In it, the King explained to the little prince what it means to encounter God, and told him that this encounter, and nothing else, is what matters in life. He concluded by inviting the child to seek Jesus by following the royal path – in other words, by way of his Mother.

What beautiful, crystal-clear faith! The theme of my homily found here its perfect illustration, made transparent for all to see, in the life of the King – a stained-glass window through which God's love shone unhindered.

I thank you, Lord, for introducing, along my path, a few of these special people whom you and you alone create, solely to prove your existence. I thank you also for those solutions that choose the simplest way, for that grandeur attained through humility, for that majesty placed entirely at your service. Amen.

A Visit to the "Salon des Vacances" with the Minister for Tourism

Because of my involvement in pastoral services for tourists, I visited the "Salon des Vacances" (a commercial fair on the theme of holidays and travel), where an official dinner had been planned. On my left at the dinner table was the Minister for Tourism, Mr Piers, whom I had known when he was a student in Louvain. He reminded me that I had once given him a copy of a little book by Carnegie, called *How to Make Friends: the Art of Success*. I remarked that he had certainly made good use of the book. Then he told me that he used to have a great gift of prophecy. "As a matter of fact", he said to me, "back in 1941, when you were only a canon, I predicted that you would in turn become prelate, bishop, archbishop, cardinal..."; then he lowered his voice and whispered in my ear his final prediction.

He assured me that his fellow students knew of these predictions and telephoned him every time another one came true. Now he was waiting for the final proof of his charism. I fervently urged him to keep his mind on tourism and rest on his laurels.

We finished our dinner and went off together to admire the landscapes, sailboats, canoes and camping equipment on show in the various pavilions. Along the way we paused to fish for trout in a pond – with instant success – while amused onlookers smiled their encouragement.

* * *

185

1968

A troubled year

On a public level, 1968 was a year marked by the events of May and by the turmoil they produced, particularly in universities. For complicated reasons, this had a kind of backlash effect on the ecclesial level. We experienced a religious upheaval which resulted in the painful departure of many priests and religious, and which further accentuated the generation gap.

Not long before these events, in February 1968, I wrote the following comments in my journal:

> We must resolutely look at what is lacking in us, at what is narrow, at the ways in which we turn inwards on ourselves, if we want to understand the immense clamour that is shaking the world and the Church — the piercing cry for breathing space, for air.
>
> Violent rebellion is spreading throughout the world; the young are challenging today's society, condemning it for its emptiness, its lack of soul, its lack of ideals, the absence of spiritual oxygen.
>
> It may be that the young are still stammering, searching for words in which to proclaim their dreams; nevertheless, we must take very seriously what they say as they criticise the world of yesterday and of today. The Church is on their side, since from them will come the necessary "supplement of soul" for which Bergson called; in them is the hope of those who want to be human beings rather than robots. The Church has no choice; she must opt for the future, as they do.

Lectures in the US — from Berkeley to Hollywood

I had agreed to give a series of ecumenical lectures in Berkeley during the week known as "Pastors' Week", when about one thousand ministers, representing all Christian denominations, gathered in one place. The programme featured question-and-answer sessions "with a cardinal of the Roman Church", which came as a surprise both to them and to me.

We were living in a post-conciliar atmosphere. A Protestant pastor walking by called out to me "The sun is shining through your words."

I was deeply touched by the final ovation they gave me, because I could feel how powerful was their yearning for unity. Back home, I received a letter from a Methodist pastor, thanking me "for being, during these days, a pastor to all of us".

In Berkeley, we also had an extensive dialogue in the First Presbyterian Church. Once again, there were honest, straightforward questions, and a strong desire for visible unity.

One evening, I had dinner with the Episcopalian Bishop Meyers, the very one who had caused such a sensation by asking that the Pope be recognised as the universal pastor of all Christians, and who had offered his cathedral to the Catholic Archbishop of San Francisco when the Catholic cathedral burned down. He gave me a letter, on the subject of birth-control, to take back to the Pope; I faithfully delivered this by hand.

As I think about Berkeley — the birthplace of the students' revolutionary movement known in Europe simply as "May '68" — I remember a meeting I had with these very same students, the instigators of the revolution. The university chaplains at the Newman Club had insisted that I should speak to them, but had also warned me that there might be some trouble of the sort that was by then common at the University. These meetings were generally held outdoors, with the students sitting cross-legged in a circle, or on the terrace of their cafeteria. Later I learned that throughout that meeting, a nun had walked round and round the area, praying the Rosary for the speaker.

As an opening, I said to them:

"My friends, they tell me that you are revolutionaries. Nothing could be more normal at the age of twenty or twenty-five. If you were not revolutionaries, it would mean that something was wrong with your hormones, and that you needed to see a doctor!

"So there is nothing remarkable in the fact that you are revolutionaries. What I am interested in is what you will be at the age of forty or fifty, when you have settled down into bourgeois, middle-class life...[here I gave a description]. What matters is that you should still be revolutionaries then; that you should not have allowed yourselves to become bourgeois."

Based on these premises, I spoke of their social responsibilities. All went well, and later on I thanked the nun for the support she had given me through her prayers.

This episode reminds me of another curious event – this time in Hollywood, where I was asked to give a lecture. I was not very popular in some Catholic circles there, as I was considered a modernist and a leftist.

A group of exactly thirty-five protesters walked around the conference hall carrying a poster, and reciting the Rosary for my conversion. Meanwhile, inside the hall, I was speaking of how essential Mary is to Christian life. Quite a misunderstanding! I gladly forgive them, and thank them for their prayers!

An audience and a letter to Paul VI

In March, I travelled to Rome; I had been invited by the military chaplaincy to give a lecture as part of a religious cycle intended for Italian officers. The subject they had chosen was a dry one: "The Theology of the Death of God", which enjoyed great popularity at the time, especially on the other side of the Atlantic.

In fact, this lightning trip to Rome was a pretext to meet with the Holy Father; Cardinal Villot had insistently been asking Cardinal Doepfner, myself, and probably others as well, to go and see the Pope – in order, he said, "to offset the local influences, which tended to point in a counter-conciliar direction".

Pope Paul was deeply influenced by the personality of Pius XII. Moreover, he was caught between a desire for openness and a desire to avoid antagonising those who were there before him. This was the source of his well-known hesitations and of the difficulties he encountered.

The Holy Father spoke to me of his fear that my insistence on collegiality would be abused to "democratise" the Church. It is quite true that in stressing co-responsibility, one always runs the risk of being misinterpreted in this way. I would like to say again, loud and clear, that the Church is a community in the Holy Spirit, and that the faithful who are best able to grasp what "the Spirit is saying to the Churches" are those who are most closely at one with God. As far as I am concerned, the Council — and in its wake, the Renewal in the Holy Spirit — have emphasised the democratisation of holiness, which has nothing whatsoever to do with universal suffrage. Some truths are so obvious that they don't seem worth repeating; and yet it is sometimes just as well to say them plainly.

Pope Paul was not "collegial" by instinct; he was more concerned with preserving the pontifical prerogatives he had inherited. Moreover, each time a reform was enacted, he was criticised by some for being far too revolutionary, and by others for not being revolutionary enough. In an interview with a Roman newspaper, Pope Paul had even tried to explain — contrary to custom — the reasons for his decisions.

I have provided this psychological background to help the reader understand my conversation with the Pope, and the letter that followed.

At the audience, I brought up the matter of birth-control, which was still at an impasse. However, I did not have a chance to express my thoughts in full. Since the atmosphere of our meeting was excellent, I felt free to follow up our conversation with a letter, pleading vigorously for collegial dialogue on this issue:

March 19, Feast of Saint Joseph

Most Holy Father,
Now that I am back in Belgium, it is a duty and a joy for me to thank Your Holiness with all my heart for the affectionate and encouraging welcome I received. I remember your words with gratitude and emotion.

These feelings prompt me to continue our conversation in writing, and to reveal openly, in a spirit of complete filial loyalty, my thoughts concerning what I believe to be the crucial problem of our times with respect to the papacy.

Having prayed very intensely, I would like to put this problem before you, Holy Father, in the presence of Our Lord; for I believe that what is at stake here is the manner in which pontifical primacy is exercised — and thus the very future of the Church.

The sense of unease which surrounds this problem can be felt throughout the world. It arises with particular intensity in the context of two burning issues: that of birth-control, which affects countless couples; and that of optional celibacy in the Latin Church, which continues to trouble the clergy — and this despite the encyclical which should have brought it to an end.

In both these cases — and I have chosen them simply as examples — what is foremost in my mind is not the issue in itself, and I am not at present pleading for any particular solution. My intent is respectfully to call your attention to a more basic question. The feeling of general unease, in my opinion, does not stem from any specific issue *per se*, but rather from the fact that Your Holiness has reserved for yourself the right to choose the appropriate solution, whatever it may be — thus foregoing the possibility of any collegial input or analysis by the bishops. As a result, discussion of certain issues was forbidden at the Council, and again at the recent Synod.

If I may be allowed to say so, Most Holy Father, the psychological and theological drama of our times lies here.

The Council has given the Church a new awareness of collegiality; everything that promotes such collegiality in turn promotes pontifical primacy, enhancing its role as the heart and head of collegiality in action. All that misunderstands, or, in practice, ignores episcopal collegiality is felt to be, at present, a danger for the Church; it makes obedience more difficult, both for the faithful and for the clergy; and it sets back any progress we may have made in the area of ecumenism, for our separated brethren are extremely sensitive on this point, seeing in it a test of fidelity to Vatican II.

The good of the Church would be dramatically endangered, in my opinion, if the Holy Father were seen to take upon himself the role of sole defender and guardian of the faith and of moral standards — if he were to stand before the world alone, cut off from the college of bishops, from the clergy, and from the faithful.

We know full well that Your Holiness has engaged, and continues to engage, in private and secret consultations. Far from dispelling the unease, this type of consultation feeds it. It is felt that these controversial issues need to be studied openly and thoroughly by qualified theologians and experts who are recognised as such, and that the results of their work should then be submitted to the bishops for discussion. As long as there is no such open debate, it will be impossible to create the receptive climate essential to any authority. To take one example among many, the issue of birth-control was not well understood by the bishops before the Council, since the Holy Office had forbidden all publications that did not conform to traditional thinking, and all discussion of the issue. The opinion of an uninformed bishop could have no real value. Today, however, it should be possible to consult the bishops — after providing them with the necessary information, or explaining to them the arguments both for and against — and thus to obtain an informed opinion.

In our world today, it is essential to pay special attention to the preconditions for obedience. The central fact, which we cannot ignore in today's Church, is that adhesion to any decision is dependent, not on the uncontested legal authority of the one who makes the decision, but on the "credibility" of the authority itself, which must show that all the "pre-conditions" to the decision have been met and respected, and that the interested parties themselves — be they the clergy or the faithful — have been properly consulted, if the decision concerns their lives.

Against the background of these general observations, may I suggest, Most Holy Father, in all humility and kneeling before you, that the two major issues of our time — birth-control for the laity, and the image of the priest in all of its contemporary dimensions — be included on the agenda of the special synod that Your Holiness is about to convene.

The mere announcement that these issues will be discussed and dealt with at that time, and that the members of the synod will have a chance to study them thoroughly in advance, would be enough to allow us to hope for maximum acceptance on the part of the faithful and of the clergy. If Your Holiness were to decide on these matters in isolation, there would be an immense danger of inner refusal. Theologians would claim that, *in casu*, the decision would not be infallible, due — among other reasons — to the absence not of "consensus" but of "communion" with the episcopate of the world; they would cite the dogma of the Assumption, which was proclaimed after extensive consultation.

The bishops have been sensitised by the Council to the collegial and communitarian aspects of the Church; they would be painfully torn in their conscience as pastors, for they would be jointly bound by a decision for which they would in no way have been jointly responsible, at their own level, and which many would not consider valid.

The faithful, well aware of this situation, would find it difficult to obey in the circumstances. The authority of the magisterium would thus be gravely impaired.

A French politician recently said that the decision-making process is more important than the decision itself. There is some truth, I believe, to this paradox, which is based on human psychology. This is confirmed, on the supernatural level, by everything in the very nature of the Church, which calls for communion and for the cooperation of all.

If the Council had, from its outset, such a tremendous impact on the world, was it not precisely because we were

Jeanne Suenens, née *Jannsens*

Jean-Baptiste Suenens

Leon-Joseph, aged three...

... and in his army uniform

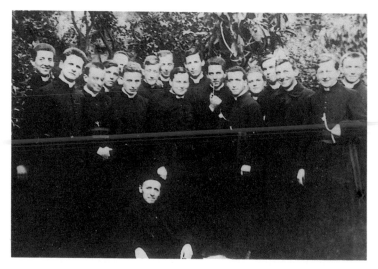

Students of the Belgian College Rome, 1927, with Fr Lebbe at the front

Fr Suenens during his ten-year term (1930-1940) as Professor of Philosophy at the minor seminary in Malines

Fr Suenens with his mother in 1943

With General Eisenhower in 1945. The general was conferred with the degree of doctor honoris causa *by Lourvain University.*

The new Cardinal, 1962

The Cardinal with Pope John XXIII

Cardinal Suenens addressing the UN, on the encyclical Pacem in Terris, *at the request of Pope John, 1962*

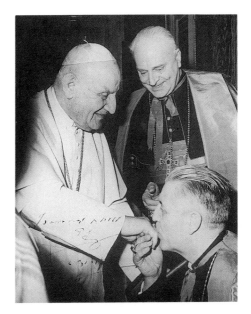

With Pope John

Delivering the eulogy in memory of Pope John at the opening of the second session of Vatican II, October 28, 1963

With Pope Paul VI, 1963

In discussion with Cardinal Ottaviani

With Frank Duff, founder of the Legion of Mary, and Bishop Kowalski immediately before the beginning of the opening session of Vatican II

Lourdes, 1972

Lourdes, 1972

Speaking With Monsignor Cardinale, papal nuncio in Brussels, 1970

With Dom Helder Câmara in Malines, during a visit in 1972

Receiving the Templeton Prize from the Duke of Edinburgh in 1976. Also in the picture are Mr and Mrs Templeton.

With Pope John Paul I, 1978

With Pope John Paul II

With the Archbishop of Canterbury, Dr Ramsey, in 1967

With Fr Walter Burghardt, SJ, in 1972

The Cardinal in relaxed mood in 1972

The Cardinal in his study in Malines

Cardinal Suenens speaking at the golden jubilee of his ordination in 1977

able to show that freedom of expression is real, and taken very seriously, within the Church? Even though the media distorted some of the debates, can we not say that, overall, the openness, and the confrontation of different ideas, have been beneficial?

One could hope that, *mutatis mutandis*, the same would be true if there were freedom of research, freedom of enquiry, of study, of discussion, on the two issues mentioned above. The synod could serve both the Church and the papacy by showing that Vatican II has indeed introduced a new style, and that the Church has no fear of raising questions that can lead to better answers and to their fuller acceptance.

These words, Holy Father, are inspired by the intense love I have for the Church and for the papacy; by a profound filial affection for Your Person; and by the gratitude I feel for all that you have already done for the Church. Papal primacy is a priceless good, and all that reinforces its exercise is of inestimable value in my eyes. In pleading for a collegial approach to the exercise of papal primacy, in the context of the major pastoral problems of our day, my sole desire is to increase its radiance throughout our troubled world. I felt this to be, moreover, a duty in fidelity to the Master who entrusted his Church to Peter and to the Eleven — in different ways, but indissolubly united by a double bond: the bond that joins the Eleven to Peter, and the bond that joins Peter to the Eleven and to the people of God.

With the deepest devotedness, I remain, Your Holiness, more than ever,

Your humble and obedient son,
L.J. Cardinal Suenens

I sent a copy of this letter to Cardinal Villot. In reading the biography of the Cardinal by Fr Wenger, I notice that the Cardinal informed him of the contents of my letter;* Here is the letter that Cardinal Villot sent me in response; it reveals a great deal about the atmosphere in Rome, and about the extent to which our views were similar.

Bogota, August 23, 1968

Dear Eminence,
I have received the copy you sent me of your letter to the Holy Father, and I am deeply touched by this sign of your trust. Your letter followed me to France; I had left Rome for a few days' rest at home, on my way to Colombia, where I am to spend three weeks.

From a Roman perspective, the situation is complex. On the one hand, there is the isolation of the Holy Father; I know that I am not the only one, among those in charge of various dicasteries, to be aware of the painful aspects of this isolation. There is also, however, the absence of sustained communication and trusting dialogue with the bishops' conferences. Personally, I believe that a synod that would bring together the presidents of these conferences would allow a new style of cooperation to develop.

Here I have seen many priests, in five different dioceses, and I have gathered much useful information. There are still a few bishops whose attitudes are "pre-conciliar", and who need to reflect on co-responsibility! On the whole, however, Colombia represents a hope for the Church of Latin America. The Pope's visit has been greeted with tremendous popular enthusiasm.

After the congress, I will go for a few days to CELAM, and then back to Rome on August 31.

May these words bring you the expression of my deep and respectful affection.

Jean, Cardinal Villot

---

* See Antoine Wenger, *Le Cardinal Villot (1904-1979)*, Desclée De Brouwer, 1989.

In confidence, I shared this letter with Mgr Prignon, who reacted with the following words, which went straight to my heart: "This letter will go down in history. Had you done nothing else, this letter alone would give worth to your primacy of Belgium."

Where are we going?

In this post-conciliar era, the Church strides forward, into the future. Ahead is the mysterious third millenium which is on everyone's lips, and whose outlines we can barely glimpse through the fog.

Where are we going? My hope is that we are moving towards a Church that is closer to Pentecost than to canon law. We need to rediscover the royal priesthood of the faithful; to develop a deeper sense of commitment to co-responsibility at all levels; and to build a lifestyle that is responsive to these new perspectives.

We need priests who are happy to have chosen celibacy and who live it out as a charism. And there is no doubt that one day we shall need mature, married men who will take on the responsibilities of the diaconate and of the priesthood of tomorrow.

We need true Christians, messengers of the Good News, who live with pride a faith that is focused on that which is of essence and is source of life.

Lord, I do not yet know what it is that you expect of me in this final stage of my life. Forgive me for that which in me is me, and thank you – immensely – for all that in me has been and still is You. May Our Lady of the Annunciation open our hearts to a tomorrow that is unknown and rich in hopes because rich in the love of God, who is unfailingly faithful. There is nothing more that I need to know. Amen.

An incident at the palace

There was a great commotion at the palace that week. At a dinner in honour of the King of Denmark, I had turned up wearing clericals, with a touch of red at the neck and my episcopal ring on my finger. This was viewed by some highly-placed individuals as a scandalous disregard for the solemnity of the occasion. Our King and Queen, however, had been warned in advance, and had not only agreed to my decision, but had actually welcomed it.

The King of Denmark, Protestant though he was, remarked to the King that this abandonment of the splendours of the cardinalate was lamentable; that the Church was following a dangerous path with all these breaks from tradition.

General Cumont protested to the King against the wearing of battledress at Court. The King replied that he thought this was quite normal in a Church that preaches poverty and service to the poor; the General went away saying "You are very fond of the Cardinal."

Two ladies of the aristocracy decided to have it out with me face to face, and asked me why I had turned up like that – in battledress. I admired their familiarity with military jargon, unaware at the time that they had probably borrowed it from the General. I quietly replied that we were living in post-Vatican II days, and that this was one of the consequences of the Council.

The ladies immediately rushed off to the nuncio to denounce this monstrous outrage and to ask him whether Vatican II had truly decreed such indignities. The nuncio was quick to reassure them: nothing of the sort had been decreed, and it was indeed a terrible abuse on my part to hide behind Vatican II. Besides, all they had to do was look at him: was he not dressed in full scarlet splendour – the only attire worthy of the Church and of the furnishings surrounding him?

So much for all the hullabaloo.

There were consoling remarks as well, and these made all the commotion well worthwhile. Someone asked the King's Chief of Cabinet what he thought of my outfit, and received this answer: "It is the only one that makes sense in today's Church; all this fuss is ridiculous."

The second comment is very revealing indeed. The socialist secretary of the King's Cabinet, with whom I had a long conversation on the famous evening, was asked the same question. "Well", he replied, "it's the first time I've ever had the courage to sit down next to a cardinal and talk with him, man to man. If he'd been wearing all his finery, I'd never have dared!"

All of *Gaudium et Spes* is summarised right there. Amen.

The first priest leaves

This was the climate in which a particularly painful meeting took place, when a dedicated priest and friend suddenly announced his departure.

It was an unexpected and moving encounter with A.S., who had just told me that he was giving up the priesthood, the Church, Christ, and the faith. It was long and sorrowful. Once I understood that his decision was irrevocable, my only concern was to be for him the one who spoke in the name of the Lord.

Shortly thereafter, he wrote me a letter: "How can I thank you for the way you welcomed me this morning and again this afternoon? You were so simple, so human, so fatherly and brotherly at the same time, and so evangelical. Thank you for all that you said to me, thank you for all that you respected, thank you for all that you asked me, and thank you for all that you silenced in yourself so that you could really listen to me..."

I embraced him and held him for a long time before I let him go, and I hardly heard or understood his words of thanks, because we were both so deeply moved. He told me that he had just spent an hour in the chapel where he had been ordained twenty years before; he had prostrated himself, once again, as he had on that day.

We must not bring judgment. "I did not come for that", Jesus said. Nonetheless, the elements of a defection are very mysterious indeed. Who can say whether it was a sorrowful love affair, or a process of reflection, that brought faith to an end? I asked him, despite everything, to believe in the personal love of Someone for him; I wanted to save what is essential. He left, and it is all in God's hands.

A meeting with Lambilliotte

Days come and go, and no two are quite the same. Today, a socialist writer, Lambilliotte, came to see me; he is the editor of a magazine called *Synthèse*. I would have liked very much for the priest who was with me yesterday to hear this "unbeliever" – a Christian who does not know he is one – talking with me about the Holy Trinity with so much openness and receptivity.

I quoted these very simple words of a working man speaking of the Holy Spirit: "In my home, love is something so real that I have no trouble believing that, in God, love is Someone equally real."

My visitor's sense of communion was very moving. I don't know why his implicit Christianity did not burst forth into the light. More than Nicodemus, he was already in the sanctuary, even though he did not know it. He had come to ask for my support in requesting the assistance of the Cardinal of Vienna for a European congress which he was organising, and which was to bring together a number of well-known personalities from both Eastern and Western Europe. He was essentially a builder of bridges, in the style of U Thant, but on a level that was more spiritual, literary and mystical.

Such strange contrasts between souls – yesterday's priest who had read so many books and who was walking out, and this unbeliever who knew nothing and understood everything. The difference lay in one thing: a humility that brought tears to one's eyes, in this man who had been touched by grace and knew nothing of it. The Lord's own *fioretti*, scattered here and there along the way...

A meeting with Léo Moulin

It was a great joy, last Saturday, to hear Léo Moulin talk about the Council and about Pope John. He told me of a meeting he had had with a well-known man, a socialist of good standing, at the time of the death of Pope John. This man had spoken to Moulin in confidence, and had told him something never to be repeated to the members of his party: "I don't dare to admit this," the man had said, "but when Pope John died, I wept." Léo Moulin, himself an agnostic, had answered: "So did I..."

This is an illustration of the impact which the Council had outside the Church. It would do some Catholics a lot of good to hear comments of this sort!

Léo Moulin went on to say to me: "The Council is the only case, in my experience, of a reform from within that actually worked. Nothing of the sort has ever been done in a political party; it's not natural." And he added: "If Vatican I had been Vatican II, the face of Europe would have been transformed."

He asked me to write an article about the organisation of the Council, for his magazine, *Res Publica*. I told him that I would be glad to let him have a copy of the rules of procedure, but that I would find it difficult to sing the praises of a document that had a great many shortcomings. I did admit, however, that it was quite an accomplishment to arrange for over two thousand people to talk and deliberate together.

Léo Moulin left with these parting words: "Pope John made me uncomfortable in my disbelief."

A day off

For the first time in ever so long, a holiday! A blank page in my calendar: nothing planned, no meetings scheduled, no telephone calls, no mail. A whole day where nothing leads inexorably to anything else. A day where one is free to come and go, to wander aimlessly, to write, to put the pen down and wander some more.

How strange it is, in this hyper-stressed world of ours, to be a bird on a branch, a seagull on a wave, landing where one pleases, only to fly off again. Freedom is such a curious thing! It has the taste of a ripe peach that one bites into eagerly; it smells of lilac, and feels like a soft spring breeze at dawn.

Memories and Hopes

It is good to have nothing urgent or specific to do – to be able to step back for a moment from things, from people, from oneself; to be able to situate oneself in time and in the world; and to understand with a new heart what this "Kingdom of God that is to come" is all about, this Kingdom that will make all things clear and understandable.

The encyclical *Humanae vitae*

In the Pope's mind, this encyclical was meant, above all, to reinstate the true meaning of love, and to highlight its elements.

We live in a world where the word "love" has become trite and has lost its sacred meaning. It has become a synonym for boundless and unregulated sexual pleasure. Increasingly, it is disfigured and desecrated. We no longer remember that true love, between married people, implies a communion of spirits, of hearts, and of bodies, and that it has its source in God who is Love. This is perhaps the one area in which the mass-media has had the most deleterious effect; "love" has become an ambiguous word, full of snares and pitfalls.

I attempted to react against this profanation of love, in a book called *Love and control*,* chapter 3 of which is, from beginning to end, an effort to shed some light on this basic misunderstanding.

Given the existing climate, the encyclical had little chance of being understood. Many took it to be an intrusion in an area that should be exempt from any kind of moralising; for many Christians, it appeared to contain guidelines that were far removed from the context of their own lives and from their personal motivations.

It was the task of the Belgian bishops – as of all other bishops in the world – to make known to the faithful the content of the encyclical *Humanae Vitae*: a delicate task, in support of which I requested prayers and sacrifices from all the convents of our land.

*Desclée De Brouwer, 1960, and Burns and Oates, London.

The text of our statement was worded by Mgr Philips – author of *Lumen Gentium* – in collaboration with the moral theologians of the University of Louvain.

Just as we were about to adopt our text, I was called to the telephone; Cardinal Doepfner of Munich wanted to inform me of the contents of the statement that the German bishops were proposing to adopt. Their document was almost identical to ours. They too had called on their moral theologians for assistance – in particular on Fr Fuchs, Professor of Ethics at the Gregorian University in Rome, who, like me, had been a member of the Study Commission set up by Pope Paul.

Our common purpose was to place the encyclical within a pastoral perspective, and to relate it to the duly enlightened consciences of married couples, reminding them of the traditional doctrine in this area.

Future shock

In November 1968, I read an article entitled "Thirty-five professionals of the future tell us about the dawning of the 21st century". It is quite hair-raising. Here are a few samples of what they said.

It will take twenty minutes to get from Paris to "Boswash" – in other words, to the huge urban unit into which Boston and Washington will have merged. Other similar conglomerates – such as "Chippits" (Chicago-Pittsburgh), for example – are expected to form. Anyone can play this game, trying to imagine what form the human antheap will have in the year 2000. But that's just the outer structure: computer sciences are still capable of endless surprises; biology will make it possible to remodel human beings from top to toe, and to transform death into a sort of hibernation. All of this is very strange, yet it appears to be inevitable.

We shall have to tell anew the eternal meaning of life to these men and women of the future. For no matter how we learn to modify life, to knead it, mix it, suspend it and prolong it, we will always need to give it a meaning, an ultimate meaning.

This vast human mass – what will it reach out for, as it crowds into the airplanes of the future to fly to the moon? Where will all this racing around lead? What will be the end result of all these discoveries? Humans play such strange games.

It will be possible to reduce working days to 137 per year, leaving 228 non-working days. Will we know how to fill so much leisure time, how to take full advantage of it in ways that indeed make us more human?

The year 2000 will offer us as much silence as we can wish for – possibilities for meditation, for prayer, for contemplation, for art and for beauty. I would like to add "for human kindness and fraternal love"; but how are we to guarantee these, and how can we put an end to nuclear and other explosions?

How can we, in the new world of the future, increase unity among people, increase true love? It is all so very much a part of a different order of reality... No matter how fast I fly from Paris to New York, I shall still be the same person when I get there. Speed in itself has never brought a smile or a moment of self-forgetfulness. This brave new world will indeed require a huge supplement of soul, as – thanks to the new possibilities of electromechanics – it lives its almost totally mechanised life, while most of the world's population continues to live in utter destitution and in the greatest of misery.

Chinese wisdom

An old friend – Carlo Van Melchebeke, a missionary bishop who lives in Singapore – came to visit me. He is, delightfully, at once Chinese and Belgian – an explosive mixture! He showed me a quote from Confucius, which he had had engraved on a platter:

> At twenty, we study.
> At thirty, we know ourselves.
> At forty, we occupy our rightful place in the world.

At fifty, we know the Ways of Heaven (Providence).
At sixty, we may follow our intuition.
At seventy, we may follow our hearts and not be afraid of making mistakes.

These words invite me to meditate on each stage of my life.

I thank you, Lord, for being so near, your light so bright in the darkness, your presence "a starry sky" in the night.

We are at a strange moment in the history of the Church; at a collective level, the Church is experiencing the dark night of which St John of the Cross spoke.

Perhaps what we need is a touch of Chinese wisdom!

A conversation with an old shepherd

A friend, returning from a trip to Morocco, told me of a conversation he had with an old shepherd by a roadside. "What do you think about all day?" my friend asked him. "I think of God and of my sheep," the shepherd replied. "What will you eat tonight? " "First I must know whether I will still be alive tonight; there will be time enough then to think about food." A whole world is in those words! Secularism has become a real disease in our societies; for us, only the sheep matter, and the evening meal. We have no perspective, no horizons; the sky is low and heavy over our heads, like a ceiling; all is flat, catalogued, labelled. We run the risk of becoming claustrophobic.

Confronted with such overwhelming materialism, we must preserve the vision of the One Absolute that gives meaning to our lives. We must also have a sense of the greatness of God, which is not a greatness that crushes. We must live Christianity profoundly, in all its fullness, with and in God.

The story of the shepherd inspired me to read again the masterpiece of spirituality, *Abandonment of Divine Providence,* by Fr J.-P. de Caussade, SJ, in which he invites us to be in constant communion, moment by moment, with the loving will of God over each one of us.

Memories and Hopes

A visit from Mgr Butler

In September 1968, the eminent theologian Mgr Butler, who was one of Cardinal Hume's auxiliary bishops in London, came to spend three days with me in Brussels.

In long, friendly conversations, we exchanged our views and impressions — which were, I may add, strikingly similar — concerning the evolution of the Council and the outlook for the future. His book, *The Theology of the Council*, has a great deal in common with my *Co-responsibility in the Church*.

Since then, we have met in England on a number of occasions. I remember with great affection his complete loyalty, and the honesty that guaranteed his absolute credibility. His insights as a convert from the Anglican faith were particularly valuable, and his Anglican friends continued to listen to him even after his conversion.

1969

The seeds of ecumenism

I spent a weekend in London from January 18 to 22, 1969. My programme included a homily at Westminster; a meeting with Archbishop Ramsey and the Apostolic Delegate, Mgr Cardinale; a lecture at Oxford and one at Heythrop; a press conference at the Challoner Club; and a television show on the following day.

Articles in both the *Times* and the *Guardian* had created a welcoming atmosphere that made it easy to plant the seeds of ecumenism.

The journey to ecumenical unity is a long one. Each one of us must pick up the pilgrim's rod and walk unseeingly ahead, inspired by the story of the Magi. Their story tells of a star that disappears over Jerusalem, no one knows why, and reappears where Mary and the Child are to be found — a sign to guide us.

The first permanent deacons

On the eve of February 2, the feast of Light, I celebrated a Mass in the course of which I received the first commitment of the first five permanent deacons of our diocese.

They were called one by one; their professions, and the number of children each one had, were mentioned. This made the ceremony very real and human. I was very moved to learn that two of the five deacons belonged to the Legion of Mary; I saw in this a smiling sign from Our Lady.

For the seeds of grace to sprout, for snowdrops to break through, a great deal of suffering is required. Perhaps these first deacons are the early signs of a new springtime for the Church. This day of the dawning of the diaconate was for me a particularly joyful one.

Moreover, the Lord granted on this occasion two wonderful graces — two conversions. At the end of the ceremony, one of the new deacons said to me, profoundly moved and with tears in his eyes, "My brother-in-law, who had not received communion in forty years, and his son, both came to the ceremony; they received communion together, and they said to me: 'This is our gift to you for your diaconate'".

These were *fioretti* for this Christian family, to whom the Lord had given such a visible sign of grace. I said to them: "The Lord is spoiling you, giving you sweets and cakes to help you get off to a good start." They agreed that this was a memory to cherish, to keep for grey and cold days to come.

"The Man from la Mancha"

That year included a memorable day trip to Paris. I went, with friends, to see and hear "L'Homme de la Mancha", a delightful and beautiful show: through his dreams and idealisations, Don Quixote single-mindedly pursues his vision, his vocation to be an awakener of others.

Is he mad, or are the others? Where does truth lie — in appearances, or in the reality beyond? To love is to enable. There is such pathos in his appeal to Dulcinea to believe in what is best in others, to believe in it so strongly that it will come alive in proportion to hope itself.

Jacques Brel was sublime in his intransigence, his courage, his commitment to truth. The message was clear to everyone: dare to believe in the impossible; though you may be alone and misunderstood, continue to seek the "unreachable star".

I found the following words in the libretto from the show: "Nothing is ever your own, nothing but your soul. Of your present, love only what is already in the future. Do not take pleasure, for it may take you... And when in doubt, remember that we are owed nothing, since all we have is only on loan. And live in that vision which aims for what is great."

The show was a joy; Jacques Brel's intense voice, and that unforgettable song "To dream the impossible dream...", made my thoughts turn to Jesus, who looks at us, poor men and women, with eyes that transform, that bring light and transparency to all that is opaque.

The poet is more true than the man who is content with the surface of things. The poet is a prophet, for he sees far ahead, and in the present he loves "that which belongs to the future". A passing breeze, a breath of spring.

Jacques Brel's song found in my heart a lasting echo:

> To dream the impossible dream
> To bear the pain of partings
> To burn with an impossible fever
> To go where no-one goes
> To be torn by love
> To love — even too much, even wrongly —
> To try, with no strength and no armour,
> To reach the unreachable star...

Meetings in England

My ecumenical meetings in England took place forty years after the Malines Conversations. Cardinal Mercier once wrote: "When the hour of the harvest comes — that blessed hour — another will have taken my place." I was to be that other. I went where he had opened the way, and in spirit he was present at our meetings.

My visit to Mirfield was unforgettable. The Archbishop of Canterbury, who had come from London expressly to mark his solidarity, welcomed me very cordially. He asked me to bless, by myself, the people gathered in the Church of the Congregation of the Resurrection; then he introduced me to the audience with the following words: "No one is more welcome or more loved in this country." I could tell that these were not mere words. The question-and-answer period which followed was a very lively one indeed!

Later I had a private conversation with Ramsey, and we agreed to meet again in March, in the United States, to continue our joint ecumenical efforts.

Then on to York, where I had a long and friendly private meeting with Archbishop Coggan. I had been warned that he was "Low Church" and therefore more distant from us than was Ramsey, who was "High Church"; but in fact he was much easier to talk to, more cordial, less academic.

That evening, I had dinner at the Halifaxes. Among the guests was Mr Wood, a handicapped man of rare courage, with a flower in his buttonhole. As he had done once before, in Malines, he read out the Epistle for the day.

The following morning, at the Cathedral, I said a few words commenting on the scene in the Gospels where some strangers approach the Apostle Philip, saying: "We would like to see Jesus." After the ceremony, Archbishop Coggan said to me with great simplicity, by way of thanking me, "They will see Jesus."

In the sacristy, I was shown the chalice into which had been set the ring Cardinal Mercier had given Lord Halifax on the eve of his death. This gesture had inspired Pope Paul to give Archbishop Ramsey an episcopal ring, saying, "This is not yet a wedding ring, but it is already an engagement ring."

All of this past history was deeply engraved on my mind and on my heart. It was present, too, in the homily I gave. It was natural that this homily should be a commentary on a saying I am particularly fond of, which makes the following distinction between the difficult and the impossible: "What is difficult, we can do right away; the impossible will take a little longer."

A transparent Church
The words "We want to see Jesus" remained very present to me. I find their echo in these lines, in which I attempted to describe what a transparent Church should be like.

"We want to see Jesus." This request, put to the Apostles long ago, is still valid today.

God wants to see Jesus in us.

The world wants to see Jesus in us.

And the final criterion of the last judgment once more echoes these same words; God will ask us whether we have loved Jesus in our neighbours. And our neighbours will want to know whether we have loved them truly, with that love which we claimed to make known to them – the love of Jesus Christ.

To evangelise the world is not merely to speak and to tell; it also involves assuming the human condition, as Jesus did – making it our own, with all that it contains of pain and crucifixion. It is always a mystery of Incarnation at the human level, within the hearts of human beings.

Jesus chose the horizontal dimension of Incarnation to introduce the vertical dimension of the "Our Father, who art in Heaven."

A book and an interview on collegiality
Once the Council was over, I decided that it would be useful to define and explain some of the underlying logic in the areas of coresponsibility and decentralisation in the Church; for it is here that the future of ecumenism will be played out. It is unthinkable

that non-Roman Christian Churches will ever accept uniformisa-
tion. Pope Paul himself repeated, on a number of occasions, that
unity does not mean uniformity; he even quoted the expression
which Dom Lambert Beauduin, in his famous Memorandum for
the Malines Conversations, coined in speaking of the Anglican
Church — "united, not absorbed." It seemed to me that it would
be useful to underline anything that would point in this direc-
tion.This was my purpose in writing *Co-responsibility in the
Church*, a book which I considered to be a fruit of Vatican II.

Pope Paul expressed some anxiety — which was not, however,
shared by those around him. In a letter dated June 26, 1968, Cardinal Villot wrote to me as follows:

> Your beautiful book on *Co-responsibility in the Church*
> arrived here last week. I started reading it immediately and
> eagerly. Without waiting to finish, and although I cannot
> as yet give you the comments for which you asked me, I
> would like to express my deep gratitude.
>
> This is an extremely invigorating book, so clear-sighted
> that it should help us all to move forward, at a time when
> fear might perhaps paralyze all efforts of renewal.

The dangers he mentions came from certain groups within the
Curia, which were gaining influence with the Pope, and which
wished to restrain and arrest the efforts toward renewal.

In this same letter, Cardinal Villot urged me to write to the
Holy Father concerning a message to priests which was being
prepared. He gave me his reasons for this request: "The Holy
Father is increasingly isolated, difficult to reach, frequently in
pain. I have realised that what comes from you is received with
attention and carries weight."

At a later stage, I reformulated the central thesis of my book
on coresponsibility, in an article intended for a wider public; this
was published by *Informations catholiques* in various countries,
simultaneously, with the title "The unity of the Church in the

209

perspective of Vatican II". The article caused a tremendous commotion.

Let me draw an analogy that will explain how I felt at the time. This article was for me the equivalent of the statement made to the Council by the Superior General of the Bavarian Benedictines, whose vigorous appeal for the restoration of patriarchates in the Church ended with these words: *"Dixi et salvavi animam meam"* ("I have spoken, and I have saved my soul"). I liked this ending; it meant that his eyes and his mind were set not on tomorrow but on the day after tomorrow, while all the while he attempted to clear a path through the impossibilities of today.

My intention was to help remove the obstacles that stood in the way of post-conciliar renewal.

The key passage of the article, with respect to the relationship between the Pope and the episcopal college, was the following:

> For ecumenical reasons, as well as for theological reasons, we must avoid presenting the role of the Pope in a way that would isolate him from the college of bishops, whose head he is. When it is pointed out that the Pope has the right to act and to speak "alone", this word "alone" never means "separately" or "in isolation". Even when the Pope acts without the formal collaboration of the episcopal body — as he is indeed legally entitled to do — he always acts as its head.

As we all know, this issue was at the very heart of the Council. Mgr Philips, the official interpreter of *Lumen Gentium*, has stressed the need to avoid all simplistic interpretations in this area. Recognising that we lack the proper words to express the underlying reality, he adds: "We can never sufficiently insist on the fact that the comparison is not between the Pope and the other bishops, but rather between the Pope and the episcopal college of which he is himself a part." Further on, he writes: "Those theologians who would like to see the Council become a regular institution are making a mistake. By its very nature, the

Council is an event rather than an institution, and, in some ways, it belongs to the charismatic aspect of the Church."

We are faced with the Mystery of the Church. Here, as in the case of the Holy Trinity, we are called upon to harmonise a plural unity and a single plurality. Fr Congar speaks in this context of "mutual interiority".

The whole problem of the relationship between the universal Church and particular Churches is also part of this issue. To quote Cardinal de Lubac:*

> The Universal Church is not the result — in a second "stage" — of a sum of particular Churches, or of their federation; no more than these particular Churches should be seen as resulting from a subdivision of the Universal Church which would have preceded them. They all proceed from the first concrete particular Church, the Church of Jerusalem, from which they emerged through a process of propagation, by cuttings that were planted.

I stressed the fact that Christ entrusted his Church to Peter and to the Eleven, indissolubly, though in different ways; they are united by a double bond — the bond that links the Eleven to Peter, the bond that links Peter to the Eleven and to the people of God. I am struck by this verse from the Acts of the Apostles: "Then Peter, standing with the Eleven, lifted up his voice and addressed them" (Acts 2:14).

A great many people wrote letters and articles in response to my interview. Most of the reactions were favourable, but a few of my colleagues expressed reservations; some agreed on the substance of what I had said, but not on the advisability of making it public. A few of my colleagues expressed very negative feelings; the "spontaneity" of their reactions intrigued me.

Only one colleague publicly defended me, and this was Cardinal Pellegrino, Professor at the University of Turin. Pope Paul

---

*See *Les Eglises particulières dans l'Eglise universelle*, Aubier-Montaigne, coll. '*Intelligence de la foi*', Paris, pp.53-54.

had appointed him archbishop just in time for him to participate at the last session of the Council and to make a remarkable statement concerning scientific freedom.

His name brings back a pleasant post-conciliar memory. I had been invited to a Youth Congress in Turin — "Il Pomeriggio della Speranza" (The afternoon of hope) — for which nearly three thousand young people had gathered. They had chosen the speakers themselves, and had chosen three old men: their Bishop, Pellegrino; Carlo Carretto, former leader of the Italian Catholic Action, who had left to become a hermit; and myself. This paradoxical choice of speakers indicated at least one thing: these young people were not afraid of appearing old-fashioned! During my talk, I happened to say that bishops naturally tend to be cautious people. I interrupted my sentence with a smile, as if to go back on my words, and then added, "Of course, your bishop is an exception!" This made them all laugh heartily, and they gave Pellegrino a tremendous ovation. But back to my story!

Although Cardinal Pellegrino was the only one who spoke up publicly in support of my interview, I received, privately, a number of endorsements and words of appreciation. The most moving was a letter from Cardinal Malula, Archbishop of Kinshasa, dated January 13, 1970:

Your Eminence:

I wish you happiness and peace in the coming year.

Through your ideas, which flow logically from Vatican II, you contribute greatly to the progress of the Church in the path of *aggiornamento*. We are not unaware that to speak aloud what many others think, but do not say, often requires great courage on your part. Only your profound love for the Church can be the motive and the secret of such great courage.

May the Holy Spirit fill you with his strength and with his light, so that you may continue for many years to play your role of light-bearer – I was about to say, of prophet – and of pastor.

Joseph Albert, Cardinal Malula,
Archbishop of Kinshasa

There was no lack of enthusiastic support from theologians such as Rahner, Laurentin, Thils and Philips. However, because critics presented me as a challenger of pontifical prerogatives, I was obliged to reaffirm, loud and clear, my total allegiance to Peter's See.*

This I did in the Cathedral in Brussels; I then went on to recall Pope Paul's own words, addressed to the Roman Curia on September 21, 1963, by which he invited members of the Curia "to receive criticism with humility, reflection, and even gratitude." "Rome", he had added, "does not need to defend itself by turning a deaf ear to suggestions from honest voices, especially from the voices of friends and brothers." My words received a friendly ovation, and the new nuncio, Mgr Cardinale – who had only just arrived in Belgium – publicly supported me there in the Cathedral.

Reactions to the interview, and comments from a Belgian writer
Jules Jacques, a Belgian writer and a priest, wrote his memoirs, which were published under the title *Ce siècle que j'ai vécu.* The past which he evokes coincides with my own.

His account of the interview of May 15 has a few more details concerning public reactions. He describes the overall feelings of the clergy quite accurately, I believe, although I might have chosen milder terms, or qualified them somewhat.

---

*The author of the incriminating interview – José de Broucker – gathered together in one volume all the articles that were written in response, both for and against. They were published by Editions Universitaires, under the title *The Suenens Dossier.* An American publisher did the same in the US, and called his collection *A Case for Collegiality;* it includes some responses that do not appear in the French book. In an article for *The Month* of London – August 1970 – Peter Hebblethwaite clearly defines the theological implications of this debate.

On May 15, 1969, *Informations catholiques internationales* published an interview with Cardinal Suenens. This was greeted by many as a major event, and I sincerely believe that it has rendered a very great service to the Church, a service of historical import.

The title of the interview was "L'Unité de l'Eglise dans la logique de Vatican II" ("Unity of the Church in the Perspective of Vatican II"). The interview itself is clear, judicious, respectful; true to the Gospel, to the Council, and to *Co-responsibility in the Church*, the book published by the Cardinal a year earlier, which made an impression but caused no uproar.

Three French curial cardinals have made public their disavowal. The first asked the Cardinal to retract his words, which he did not do; the third said that it was regrettable that the Cardinal should have made his views known to the general public.

This appeal to public opinion is easily explained. The general tone of the interview is much the same as that of the book, which was published in 1968. We all know that during the Council, the Curia vigorously opposed the concept of collegiality – in other words, of coresponsibility at the level of the episcopate – and that certain Roman groups have been intent, ever since, on recapturing lost territory. In his commendable desire to be effective, the Cardinal had no choice except to turn to more explosive means. He himself later compared his statement to an alarm bell, "which is always somewhat loud and strident". There would have been no point in sending a report that would simply have been buried in the Vatican archives. By bringing the debate out into the open, he set off an alarm loud enough to be heard around the world. In our times, this is the way to spread ideas, and give them their only chance of realisation.

It is perhaps not surprising that this unusual initiative was not appreciated in high places; indeed, it is unusual only because most bishops have yet to rediscover the "glorious freedom" that St Paul claimed for all Christians (Rm 8:21).

It is painful, however, to see Cardinal Suenens' ideas distorted and misrepresented in these same circles. In an article in the *Osservatore Romano*, Mgr Felici claims that Cardinal Suenens wants the Pope's primacy "to be subject to the control and approval of the bishops". Cardinal Suenens explicitly stated the very opposite in his interview. Cardinal Siri, Archbishop of Genoa, wrote the following: "Christ did not intend the Church to be a democracy." Co-responsibility does not mean democracy. Christ did not intend his Church to be an autocracy either, nor did he want it to be a bureaucracy, or a gerontocracy – or, indeed, any kind of –cracy (from the Greek *kratia*, meaning power, dominion); yet, over the ages, all of these have been added onto Peter's humble mission, which was to watch over the unity of his flock, and to support, if necessary, his brothers in times of weakness. "Among pagans it is the kings who lord it over them; this must not happen with you" (Lk 22:25).

Cardinal Pellegrino, Archbishop of Turin, was more objective in his reactions. He regretted that most commentators did not see "the main point" of the interview, which was to "note the fact that the principle of collegiality proclaimed by the Council has yet to be applied in practice, in ways that concretely influence the life of the Church". Essentially, it was no more than a statement of non-implementation.

Those who defend an autocratic papacy insist that "the body is nothing without the head". This is only true to the extent that we accept the converse statement that "the head is nothing without the body". The head is the top of the body, it is a part of the body; but, as Cardinal Suenens said, it is not "above" the body.

Nobody questions the fact that the bishops must be in communion with the Pope. However, this does not mean that the Pope must direct every diocese in the world. The Church was entrusted to "the Twelve" with Peter. Nowhere in the Gospels is the Church presented as an autocracy, coupled with a centralising and absolutist bureaucracy. No doubt primacy, as it was defined by Vatican I, has the legal right to be such an autocracy. Whether this is the best way to use such authority, however, is a different matter. Moreover, Pope Paul does not claim anything of the sort; he knows full well that government of the Church is *sui generis*. It would seem, however, that his offices are incapable of placing any trust in the freedom of the children of God, or of admitting that the Spirit breathes wherever He pleases. Yet the two are closely related: "Where the Spirit of the Lord is, there is freedom." (2 Co 3:17)*

Helder Câmara

Dom Helder Câmara, Archbishop of Recife, expressed his support for my statements with a uniquely Brazilian enthusiasm. His letter, written on "the eve of Sts Peter and Paul", begins with these words:

I know by heart practically every word of your courageous and timely interview. I can think of no better way of celebrating the feast of St Peter and St Paul than to go over it with you, and to say to you – in God's name, continue! The Holy Spirit inspires you! It is from the Spirit that you have received the gift of intelligence and the gift of strength.

He then went over the interview, giving detailed comments, paragraph by paragraph, and ending with a few concrete examples, taken from situations in his own country, which were illustrations of the thesis expounded in the interview.

Thinking of Dom Helder Câmara brings back many fond memories. Our friendship goes back to the very early days of the Council. Although he never once took the floor in the Council assembly, he played a very significant role behind the scenes. Together with Canon Etchegaray – who was then the secretary of the French bishops – he animated a discussion group, which was regularly attended by about twenty European and South-American bishops. This resulted, more than once, in landslide votes in favour of our proposals. After the Council, I met with

---

*pp.502-503

Dom Helder on a number of occasions, and we wrote a book together: *Renewal in the Spirit and the Service of Mankind* (number 3 of the Malines Documents).

I remember one rather amusing event, which occurred in Belgium. A French television station had asked Dom Helder for an interview, and had suggested that this should take the form of a dialogue between the two of us, to be recorded in Brussels and later broadcast from Paris. We went together to the Belgian TV studios, expecting to find a French journalist ready to interview us. Much to our surprise, we were told that no interviewer was expected – they would simply record a conversation between the two of us! We took a few moments on our own to decide on a subject for our conversation. I suggested that Dom Helder should speak of the importance of prayer, while I would emphasise that prayer must always lead to social action. And we improvised from there. Our conversation lasted an hour, and was recorded in the presence of about fifty people who had been invited by the executives of the TV station.

At the end, the audience was invited to ask us a few questions. The first one was, "Could you tell us why Dom Helder is not yet a cardinal?" which made everyone laugh. Dom Helder's answer came quick as lightning: "Ah, but I have 'my cardinal'!" He always referred to me as "his" cardinal! I had to add something to that, so I said, "And you must know that between us, all things are held in common."

A day in Coire
Close to one hundred European bishops gathered in Coire, Switzerland, for a meeting that turned out to be quite turbulent – not in itself, but as a result of another meeting held nearby: a large group of "protesting" priests met in the same town and demanded the right to talk to the assembled bishops. This request was not granted. A few individual bishops met with them, but the atmosphere remained tense and filled with ambiguity.

This was the background to the speech I gave at the end of the Congress. In it I attempted to build bridges — without, however, endorsing all the demands made by the priests; they were admitted to this final session, and warmly applauded my closing speech.

The international press gave great importance to these events. The *Figaro* correspondent, Fr R. Laurentin, later wrote me a letter commenting on my final statement in Coire:

> Your concluding remarks saved this European symposium, which had lost face in the eyes of the media by appearing to sidestep problems. Your conclusions, and the freedom of spirit in which you expressed them, created a climate that was practically one of unanimity. For this, I am grateful to you.

The 1969 Synod on collegiality

The main task of the 1969 Synod was to define the relationship between the centre and the periphery — in other words, to harmonise primacy and collegiality. This question was at the very heart of all that I said in the interview for *Informations catholiques*. What would be the bishops' reactions to it at the Synod, in the presence of the Holy Father?

From the very first moments of the Synod, I was under attack. The first accusations came from dear Cardinal Heenan, always unpredictable and combative. He stated that we had the right and the obligation to criticise the Pope — but only within the Synod, never in interviews. This was confusing primacy, which was not being questioned, with the manner of its implementation by the Curia, which varies from age to age.

I must admit that in giving my rebuttal, the following day, I was at an advantage: the *Sunday Times* had published an article, personally authorised by Cardinal Heenan, in which he openly criticised the Vatican and demanded the right to public expression of opinions and ideas.

An African archbishop also spoke against me during the Synod; he stated that in his country, when the chief speaks, everyone obeys and no questions are asked. At the end of the meeting, we happened to be in the elevator together, and I explained that he had misinterpreted my words; by the time the elevator reached our stop, we had become the very best of friends.

Outside the official meetings of the Synod, I was warmly praised by many, and in particular by the bishops and archbishops of the Eastern rite. Some of my own statements were inspired, in fact, by the speeches they had made at Council meetings, which had been published in a volume entitled *L'Eglise melchite au Concile*.

In my statement, made in the presence of the Holy Father, I said that the draft text submitted for our discussion was not sufficiently collegial in its approach. I added:

> Unilateral insistence of this sort leads in practice to a denial of collegiality. The concept of *"cum Petro"* is eclipsed by that of *"sub Petro"*. This approach is a very dangerous one, within which the hopes awakened by Vatican II are doomed to failure.
>
> We must openly recognise that there is unease within the Church concerning this issue; this is an obvious fact, one that is publicly known and discussed among the people of God. Only recently, Cardinal Heenan wrote an excellent article, published in the *Sunday Times*, concerning the need, within the Church, for public expression of opinions and ideas.
>
> We must therefore be willing to recognise, with serenity and in a spirit of clarity, the tension that exists, within a common faith, between a tendency that is known as "monarchic" and one that is known as "collegial". Underlying this tension are two different theologies of the Church. There is also a difference in approach, as well as a difference in sensitivity to the signs of the times, in a world in

which participation in decision-making (rather than "deci-sion-taking") is increasingly viewed as a normal exercise of coresponsibility and as the *sine qua non* condition for the correct use of authority, whatever its nature.

As we examine these questions, we must at all costs avoid mutual suspicions and excommunications. It would be far too easy to attempt to outdo one another in respect for the sovereign pontiff; all of us here, each with equal fidelity and conviction, profess our will to be respectful and obedient. We must have the courage, however, clearly to recognise our differences, in order to avoid becoming trapped in ambiguities.

As I read the *schema* submitted to the Synod for discussion, I cannot help noting that its underlying theology exalts primacy to such an extent that bishops appear to be reduced to little more than attendants to the pontifical throne.

The draft document was widely criticised by many participants. Other speakers after me – for example, Mgr Perraudin and Cardinal Willebrands – stressed the collegial aspect, and the majority of the Synod Fathers expressed similar views. Finally the draft was replaced by a new Roman text – a definite improvement on the first.

After the plenary sessions, the Synod set to work in language groups (*circuli minores*). I was elected president of my French-speaking group. Mgr Philips was appointed rapporteur for the group, and a canon lawyer was officially assigned to work with us: Mgr Onclin, a Belgian of traditional views, who was highly regarded in Rome. Thus, the only three Belgians in the group held all the key positions. We submitted twenty proposals, all of which were adopted unanimously by our commission (even Cardinal Staffa, of the Curia, voted for them); these were later referred to the plenary assembly, in the form of requests addressed to the Holy Father.

I noted that Mgr Onclin's specific input consisted of the following: he suggested an amendment to the draft text which we had been given, concerning the bishops' obligations with respect to documents emanating from the Holy Father. The draft text stated that in such cases, bishops were under the obligation to present and comment on the text *"ad mentem Summi Pontificis"*. This meant that they were to present each document in accordance with the personal thinking of the Pope, which they would simply echo. By contrast, the expression *"una mente cum Summo Pontifice"* invited the bishops to "a communion of thought" which was not purely passive, and which involved more than mere repetition.

On that day, I came to the conclusion that canon lawyers have a place in the Church after all!

1970

Two ecumenical visits

I received a visit from von Allmen, a Swiss Calvinist theologian, author of a book called *La primauté de l'Eglise de Pierre et de Paul (Primacy in the Church of Peter and Paul)*, in which he makes a laudable effort at a *rapprochement*. He is remarkably open to dialogue. As we discussed the May 15 interview, he told me how happy his elderly father had been, seeing in this a hope for reconciliation.

That year, I also received an ecumenical visit from my friend Jerald Brauer, Dean of the Department of Protestant Theology at the University of Chicago, who had been an observer at the Council. After the Council, he had invited me to Chicago, in an attempt to hasten the establishment within the University of a chair of Catholic theology; this has since been accomplished. For me, his friendship prolonged the ecumenical atmosphere of the Council. When my book *Co-responsibility in the Church* appeared, he wrote and published a long article in which he described the book as "a tract for our times" and called for a continuation of the dialogue which had begun during the Council.

We shared memories. I had not forgotten a lunch we had had with faculty members of the theology department. We were seated at small tables, in groups of four or five. During the meal, I found myself talking with my neighbours about John XXIII, and telling them a few anecdotes. As a result, there was more and more loud laughter from my table. Suddenly, a professor at the other end of the room stood up and said: "We can't imagine what is going on at your table, but we'd love to be part of the conversation!" And that is how, to avoid causing jealousy, I had to stand up halfway through a meal and launch into a full talk on Pope John. It was an excellent opportunity, in this Protestant context, to sketch the image of a pope who had exploded every stereotype of traditional authoritarianism.

May Pope John be blessed for the image he gave to the world – an image of a spiritual father for all men and women, and of a papacy that caused every heart to open wide – through his total self-forgetfulness and supernatural transparence.

New York

The first item on my busy New York schedule was a television interview. I had been asked to stay at the Westbury Hotel the night before the show, so that I would be near the studios at dawn the following morning. The interview took the form of an exchange with Newmann, the well-known reporter on the *Today Show*, who turned out to be a true gentleman. I had been told that everyone in the United States watches this morning show, and that this would be the ideal means of getting a message across. And indeed, wherever I went from then on, I kept meeting people who had seen the show.

Next came another television show; this one was a dialogue with Archbishop Ramsey, President of the Anglican Communion. About thirty reporters bombarded us with questions – mostly insidious ones – basically with one purpose in mind: to get us to say something as sensational and as heretical as possible. All we could do was attempt to neutralise these attacks as best we could. The following morning, a big headline in the *Daily News* announced "Christians beat Lions", presenting us both as Christians who had escaped alive from the lions' den!

Such was the prelude to three days of theological and pastoral renewal, organised by the Trinity Institute for the benefit of eighty-four participating Episcopalian bishops. This turned out to be a friendly, fraternal session, where questions – designed not to embarrass the speaker, but rather to prolong our exchange and to seek points of contact – flew around in a relaxed atmosphere.

In the mornings, Archbishop Ramsey gave a talk and answered questions; in the afternoons, I took his place. Often, the meetings stretched out to become friendly conversations, occasionally interrupted by one or other of the bishops taking pictures or asking for autographs.

At noon every day, there was a eucharistic celebration, admirable both for its style and its atmosphere of contemplative reverence. All of us suffered visibly from being unable, as yet, to receive communion together. On the last day, Ramsey and I blessed the bishops, after invoking the Holy Spirit and reciting the Lord's Prayer together.

Finally, I spent the whole of Friday with four Episcopalian bishops, specialists in ecumenical dialogue. They had arranged for us the use of an apartment on the thirty-fourth floor of the Waldorf Tower, placed at our disposal by a family named Schism – surely a predestined name!

Our discussion took the form of a friendly review of differences – in fourteen points! At the end of the day, they presented me with a pectoral cross, and one of them wrote a letter to the Holy Father expressing their hopes for a future *rapprochement*. As we were getting ready to leave, the four bishops knelt and asked for my blessing; in turn, I asked for theirs.

In addition to the busy programme at the Trinity Institute, Ramsey and I were scheduled to give a public lecture at the Riverside Church and to receive doctorates, *honoris causa*, from the Jesuit Department of Theology at Woodstock (which has since moved to Washington).

I received another honorary degree from the Anglicans; a magnificent document – beautifully written out in classical Latin! – was presented to me in the course of a liturgical ceremony. That evening, the Anglican President of Union Theological Seminary hosted a dinner. In the course of the meal, he told me with amusement about his twelve-year-old granddaughter's reaction to the joint lecture at Riverside Church. She had attended the event with her parents; when her father later asked which of the two talks she had liked best, Ramsey's or mine, she had replied that, in her opinion, "the Cardinal's lecture was much more interesting to children"!

A debate on *The Nun in the World*

On the occasion of the fifth anniversary of the publication of my book, a congress entitled "The Nun in the World Debate" was held in the United States. About six hundred women religious gathered at St Mary's College for the event. I had been asked insistently to participate; I could not refuse.

I was welcomed very warmly, and the discussions were open and frank. I took the opportunity to stress, once again, the true message of my book; it is an invitation to religious in active orders and congregations to become more deeply involved in the evangelisation of the world, without letting the world take over their lives. I also pleaded vigorously for a rediscovery of the place of the Most Holy Virgin, in these days when there is an icy coldness towards her. Once more, the response was all that I could have hoped for.

Detroit, and Cardinal Dearden

On that same trip, I gave a lecture to several thousand people in the Ford Auditorium in Detroit, at a meeting chaired by Cardinal Dearden.

The time I spent in private with the Cardinal allowed me to appreciate even more the many qualities of this great Archbishop. He is a quiet man, by temperament, and avoids giving his opinion unless he is invited to do so with some insistence. I discovered this on a number of occasions, in particular in Rome during the meetings of the Commission on Birth-Control, to which we both belonged and where we held similar views.

His sense of humour was discreet and reserved — like so much about him — but never far away. He told me, for example, that he had recently informed the lay people of his diocese that a bishop's job used to be a good job before Vatican II; since then, what with all this co-responsibility business, it had become a much less enviable "profession", neither secure nor comfortable. I could only agree with him!

The interview of May 12, 1970

At the Council, the debate on collegiality had raised questions, concerning not pontifical primacy — about which no one there had any misgivings — but rather the ways in which it should be exercised.

This, in turn, raised the question of freedom of debate within the Church, especially on matters concerning the future of the Church itself, such as recruitment to the priesthood. The 1971 Synod was being prepared, and the problems of the clergy were to make up a large part of its agenda. Moreover, the bishops of the Netherlands had openly requested that married men should have access to the priesthood.

This was the background to the interview I gave, on May 12, 1970, to the French newspaper *Le Monde*. In essence, it was a plea that during the upcoming Synod, Rome should allow open and free debate.

The article did not argue in favour of any particular solution, but only pleaded for the right to free debate, the "right to the penultimate word"; it never contested that the last word belongs to the Pope. I simply appealed to the philosophy of the Council.

As could have been predicted, reactions to the interview were varied and contradictory. Mgr Butler, future Auxiliary Bishop to Cardinal Hume, defended me vigorously in *The Tablet* of May 23, 1970. Bishop A. Carter, who had been President of the Canadian Episcopal Conference during the Council, also supported me; he wrote to me in the following terms:

> I read your interview with the greatest care. You will not be surprised to learn that I am fully in agreement with you concerning the need to discuss the question of celibacy in a collegial manner. Like you, I do not take a stand on what the outcome of such a debate should be. But we cannot refuse a public debate without giving the impression either that we are unable to justify our current practice of celibacy, or that we are refusing to heed the requests of our priests and our lay people, who want a joint study of the problem. In any case, to continue the present policy is simply to increase the credibility gap and to weaken even further the authority of the magisterium and of the Church.

The letter ends on a more personal note:

> My support for the position you have taken is deepened by the awareness I have of the pain and suffering you must endure at this moment. On a more modest scale, I too have experienced the painful price one pays for loyal and honest statements made for the good of the Church, and, in the final analysis, to strengthen the position of the Pope himself.

Father Rahner, for his part, published a very strong article entitled "The duty to discuss: in defense of Cardinal Suenens" (*Publiek*, no. 24, 1970).

My own spiritual conclusions are reflected in these words, which I wrote at the time: "We must obey the Lord, when we believe that it is his will and not our own. Beyond that, we must leave things to the Lord. He alone is master of the storms and of the winds. It is enough to know that he is there, in the boat with us, even though he may appear to be sleeping."

Reading the signs
"If you believe, you will see the glory of God."

These startling words, spoken by Jesus, open up infinite horizons. They invite us to ask ourselves: how can we give to non-believers a glimpse of this mysterious faith that opens the doors to unknown kingdoms?

We must try to make them see it by analogy, through signs that can be read and understood. Faith is an instrument which allows us to tune in to unknown wavelengths, in order to discover the God who is hidden at the very heart of the story of our lives.

God is present, not in distant clouds, but at the very heart of my heart; he is the soul of my soul, the life of my life, the breath of my breath. But he does not interfere at the level that is my level; God is not on the same wavelength, he does not compete with the world. The level at which he acts is far too deep for that.

And yet, his actions betray him; by the thousands of clues that point to his presence, God beckons to us. Intermittently, in flashes, God reveals his presence, like a volcano which periodically shows signs of the fire that is burning within. The volcano may appear to be extinct, and its ashes may have cooled. The theologians of the death of God have tried to make us believe that God is an extinct volcano; but all they have achieved is their own death.

God beckons to us from time to time. As we gradually learn to read the signs he gives us, we are dazzled by his many-faceted presence. He knows us, follows us, loves us in the smallest details of our lives. Nathaniel under the fig tree, and the man with the jug leading the disciples to the Cenacle, remain to this day living images of this attentive love.

God habitually hides, like a sun that only occasionally breaks through the clouds. We must be very attentive to the signs; we must learn to read between the lines of the book he is writing with us.

The believer is the one who captures this beyond, this God who is at the heart of our existence. God was here, and we did not know him; it will be the ultimate surprise to discover one day, in the full brightness of light, the glory of God revealed, this shining love that envelops us, loving us in a way that is so impossible for us to grasp.

Faith is like a sixth sense, a science of clues. There is something similar in detective stories. To appreciate what is going on, we must be alert and attentive, and have a certain flair. Starting from a clue, an abandoned glove or an open window, we can find and follow a trail. The science of clues is a vital skill to the hunter and to the soldier at war; it plays an equally important role in human psychology. The gift of reading the hearts of others is what we call intuition, or even second sight. A person, a book, a play, can all be understood at so many different levels. The messages to be decoded are many, and so are the codes that are available to us.

Faith is like a key, or a code. When we use it, we are filled with wonder at all that it opens up for us. God's code consists of one single word – love.

Try to use this code; you will find immediately that the door creaks on its hinges, for some of the locks are tough – if God is love, how to explain all the suffering in the world? I cannot explain the mystery of evil, yet I do not, because of this, give up using the key. One bright ray is enough to reveal the sun, even if clouds surround it and hailstones are falling. I know it is there. Why is it that the sun in God is not a triumphant sun, and the world is not always a bright and sunny Mediterranean beach? I don't know. Something must have happened. I have no explanation. I do know one thing, however, and that is that I do not have the right to doubt good because of evil. And where goodness is, there God is, at the heart of all that is light, truth and love. This suffices to my faith; more would be a beatific vision.

I do not have to understand everything, but I do have to be open to all that betrays God's presence. Faith signals to me that he is there, in that chance event, that meeting, that friend, that word, that coincidence, that loss, that drawback, that perfectly timed joy. He weaves our lives, each strand of our lives, and his hand knows why the threads go off in all directions.

Faith is this: an openness, a listening, a receiving. If only the non-believer could pierce the sound barrier and hear the voice of the Lord; if he could pierce the dark night and see the stars!

The World Congress of Theologians in Brussels

The first striking fact about this Congress was the extraordinary number of participants – there were close to one thousand. I was also struck by the diversity of views represented, which in no way disrupted the atmosphere; only later, after 1970, was there a parting of ways, as theologians regrouped themselves around two competing publications, *Concilium* and *Communio*.

During those days, in Brussels, it was possible to see Fr Dhanis of the Holy Office sitting at a small restaurant table, engaged in private conversation with Hans Küng. I was struck by something Fr Congar said to me: "I am a man of the '40s, and here I am in a new world. While the Pope is busy implementing the *aggiornamento* of Vatican II, the world has gone far beyond it."

In my closing remarks, I spoke of my ecumenical dream: a return, together, to a second Jerusalem. The following day I received a telegram from Mr Chouraqui, assistant to the Mayor of Jerusalem, extending a warm and enthusiastic invitation! In thanking him for his kind gesture, I had to beg him to be patient a while longer.

Memories and Hopes

A Jewish evening

On Wednesday September 23, I spent a moving evening with Freddy Herrmann, President of B'nai B'rith in Brussels. With us were the chief rabbi and his wife; the Ambassador of Israel; and Minister Scheyven.

We had a very friendly dinner. Skull-caps were brought in for the gentlemen. I felt that I was in a foreign world, very distant from ours. The connotations attached to every word are so different; and yet, at our roots, we are joined.

The lecture that evening was organised by the Jewish Arts Association, and was a very moving event. I was thanked profusely for my presence and for my friendliness. Many of the Jews attending the lecture owed their lives to Christians who had hidden them during the war; this too contributed to the climate of the evening. I had the feeling of a people stepping out from the catacombs into the open air and, perhaps for the first time ever, feeling understood and loved by someone who for them represented and incarnated our Church. It is difficult for us now even to imagine the contempt and the hardship to which Christians subjected them for so many centuries.

At the end of the lecture, I was presented with a gift, to remind me of this evening: a seven-branched candlestick, symbol of the Jewish feast of Light; it is customary to light candles every day during the period of preparation for the feast. The Jewish people are waiting for the light; they know they have a mission to accomplish, and with these lighted candles they are saying that the Spirit is stronger than the forces of darkness, that it continues to be a light in the night.

I have kept this candlestick carefully. It will always say to me that we are all children of the light, and that we do not have the right to keep the light hidden beneath a bushel. It will invite me to pray with our fathers in faith, the patriarchs and the prophets — *"donec veniat"* — until the Kingdom of God comes in all its triumphant visibility.

230

A smile from Pope John

This was the year of the twenty-fifth anniversary of my consecration as bishop. A major liturgical ceremony took place in the national basilica, in the presence of the King and Queen, members of the Government, the Belgian bishops, and the clergy. However, this ceremony took place at a time when my relationship with my fellow bishops was strained.

The reason for this tension was a statement I had made to the 1969 Synod. I had publicly expressed the hope that the question of a double clergy – one celibate, the other married – would be examined, and that under certain conditions, to be determined at a later stage, it would be possible for the episcopal conference of a missionary nation, for example, to explore this path further if it so wished.

I had taken care to state that none of this applied to our own national conference, within which there was complete unanimity on this point. However, I felt that the question needed to be studied at the universal level. I had also specified that I was speaking in this case in my name alone; moreover, I had used only three of the eight minutes allotted to me by the rules to express my feelings concerning this particular matter.

Nevertheless, this was a point of contention and disagreement within our Episcopal Conference, where it was felt that the President of the Conference should do no more than transmit proposals which had been unanimously adopted by his Conference – that he should act simply as a "liaison officer".

Since then, lay national councils in various countries have been demanding the same thing, and this certainly raises problems for the future, concerning the precise nature of a synod and that of an episcopal conference. In the year 2000, the institutional Church will still have a lot to do. However, memoirs are not the place to talk about the future.

So much for the background; and now, I hasten back to the brighter side of that darkened anniversary.

That morning, as I was leaving for the ceremony, a book

slipped out of a shelf in my library and fell to the ground; no doubt it had not been put away properly. I picked it up automatically, intending to replace it, only to notice, with surprise, that it was Pope John's *Journal of a Soul*. With the book in my hand, I addressed a brief prayer to Pope John, reminding him of how kind he had always been to me down here, and wondering whether, on the occasion of this anniversary, he might not have something to say to me, to encourage me with my problem. I told him what my dilemma was — should I mention delicate issues, or should I leave them be? I then opened the book randomly, and this is what I read:

> On the day of my consecration as bishop, the Church commanded me very particularly to love truth: "May he love humility and truth, and may he never abandon these, letting himself be overcome by praise or by fear. May he never mistake light for darkness, nor darkness for light. Let him never call evil what is good, nor good what is evil.."
>
> I thank the Lord who has granted me a particular aptitude to speak the truth always, in all circumstances, in the presence of all people — with good grace and courtesy, of course, but also calmly and fearlessly.
>
> Because I am growing old, I now want to be particularly careful to speak the truth. "May the Lord help me in this" — how often I have repeated these words, swearing on the Gospel.

Thank you, dear Pope John, for being so caring, and for sharing this with me at precisely the moment when it gave me most comfort!

A visit to the BBC in London

The most vivid memory I have of the four days I spent in London on this occasion is of an hour-long interview for a BBC programme called *Analysis*. The agnostic reporter who questioned me had introduced himself as a former Anglican. He told me at the outset that he would not be trying to ask me any "trick questions", but rather to give me the opportunity to express my views, in depth and with clarity, for a non-Christian audience.

What followed was a dialogue where each question gave new scope and opened new perspectives. The reporter had spread out before him a wide selection of filing-cards, on which he had written out questions; he had them organised in such a way that he could follow up with further questions, depending on my answers, which thus became the guiding thread from one question to the next.

At the end, he thanked me profusely, and added that even though he saw only symbols where I saw realities, perhaps beyond the symbols, and through them, he too was seeking to express the divine.

I also remember that at the end of the lecture I gave at the London School of Economics, the Orthodox Archbishop Athénagoras of London remarked to our Ambassador: "There are no theological differences between the Cardinal and myself."

Next came an excellent radio broadcast, intended for Ireland and Australia; both reporters were anxious to correct the image of the "rebel cardinal" and to replace it with that of "the cardinal — a man of faith". Next came an interview with a Polish reporter, and he too had the same purpose in mind: to correct an image.

It is a charitable act to discredit myths. But why is it necessary to keep on repeating self-evident things? Poor humanity, caught and bedazzled by the distortions of the mass media, jostled along its painful and sorrowful journey.

1971

A second trip to Canada

As I stepped off the plane in Canada, I was met by a reporter, microphone in hand, who wanted to know what I thought of

Canada and what I thought of the Council! My first impulse was not to answer, but he obstinately followed me through the terminal, saying "Just one word! Surely you won't refuse to say one word!" Finally I asked: "What word is that?" He replied, "Is the Church, after Vatican II, in evolution or in revolution?" I barely had time to call on the Holy Spirit before saying "Evolution is too weak. Revolution is too strong. Goodbye!" He seemed satisfied, but you never know what a journalist, or a headline, will later claim you said.

Vatican II was still a matter of lively interest in Canada; and the National Theological Congress, whose documents were later published, was an event of some importance. On my first visit to Canada, in 1967, I had pleaded for the establishment of an international theological commission in Rome; I had hoped, in this way, to break out of the monopoly exercised by consultors too narrowly hand-picked by the Holy Office, and thus to broaden the information input into doctrinal statements from Rome, and to increase their credibility. The text of my speech was published along with other Congress documents; it also appears as the final chapter of my book, *Co-responsibility in the Church*. The suggestion followed its course, and has since become a reality. Such an international body now exists, and has already produced important and valuable studies.

I undertook this second journey to Canada at the invitation of my friend Alex Carter, who at the time of the Council was President of the Canadian Episcopal Conference. He had finally convinced me to spend some time with him, to rest and relax.

However, my holidays turned into a series of lectures. Several Canadian bishops – including my friend's own brother, Emmett Carter, who has since become Cardinal and before that was Archbishop of Toronto – asked me, as a very special favour, to speak to their clergy and their faithful; how could I refuse, and how could I avoid a snowball effect?

During this "supernaturally" relaxing stay, I felt very much on the same wavelength with the Canadian bishops. Their manner was so straightforward, their style so simple and direct, that the welcome they gave me was truly fraternal. Alex Carter offered to drive me wherever I needed to go, and to come with me on my airplane flights.

My travels took me to Montreal, Toronto, North Bay, Seedbury, Windsor-London, Ottawa, Winnipeg, and Regina.

My friend went so far as personally to choose a title for my lectures, and found one which announced my "colours" and guaranteed my orthodoxy: "The Church of the extreme centre". This title echoes a remark made by John Murray, the American theologian who played a very important role at the Council in the debates on freedom of religion. He had been asked "Are you a man of the right or a man of the left?" and had replied, "I am a man of the extreme centre!"

In my notes, dated January 30, 1971, I find a few brief reflections of my own on this choice; they bring back the climate of those days and explain the title. I wrote:

"The Church of the Extreme Centre": an original title, and an apt one, suggested by Alex Carter for my Canadian lectures — an excellent flag to fly over the stormy waters of protest on which we sail these days.

Conservatives have to be told that the world is not a stagnant and unwrinkled sea, a flat surface reflecting blue skies, like a lake; that the Church exists in a world in evolution; that evolution is an integral part of our historical existence — a part that is situated and "contexted"; that, to quote Bergson, "we shall never again have the soul we have tonight". Nor will we have the same bodies we once had, since they are renewed every seven years. All of this is simply to underline that history has a meaning and that we must discover it.

Liberals, on the other hand, can only see the turbulent waves of a stormy ocean, the constant movement of one breaker after the other; they need to be told that the ocean is always the ocean, deep down beneath the waves, and that it has a life of its own. This echoed Paul Valéry's words: "What matters to me is not the foam of the wave, but the sea itself."

Despite all of this, Alex Carter had not forgotten that his original invitation had been to "come for a rest". So he planned for us a day of real relaxation, in his private cabin by the sea, to meet some of his friends and to go out on snow-mobiles across the frozen waters. And this is where things became difficult. I had never ridden a motorcycle, and I had no idea how snow-mobiles work. Our little group took off on the ice; Alex Carter's vicar general was to accompany me and keep an eye on me. Suddenly, way out in the middle of the sea of ice, I realised that the vicar general was nowhere in sight.

For about fifteen minutes, I was completely alone. I had managed to stop the snow-mobile — without turning off the motor, since I had no idea how to turn it on again. For fifteen minutes, I felt abandoned by heaven and by earth. The rest of the group were miles away, and my guide and guardian angel was nowhere to be seen! At long last he reappeared — he had had an accident and had stopped on a little island along the way. As long as I live, I shall never forget those fifteen minutes!

Later Alex asked me "What did you think about during this adventure?" I answered, "I thought about eternity — it felt very imminent!"

In her book, *Cardinal Suenens, a Portrait* (London, Hodderand Stoughton, 1975), Elizabeth Hamilton has dwelt at length on my friendship with Alex Carter. From him, she obtained all the details of my snow-mobile adventure. I therefore refer the interested reader to chapter 14 of her book.

After a brief stop in North Bay, I met with Archbishop Pocock; we shared dreams and plans for the future synod on the clergy.

Next, I headed for Windsor, where Cardinal Dearden had come to meet me, across the nearby border, to refresh some of our memories of the Council.

After that I went to Toronto, where Archbishop Emmett Carter had asked me to give a public lecture. Although he had already introduced me at the beginning of the lecture, he had the kindness to step back up on to the stage at the end; he told the audience that now that he had heard me speak, he was even more puzzled by the reputation, which some members of the press had given me, of being "on the fringe" of the Church.

Back in Ottawa, I was warmly welcomed by Archbishop Plourde. I went to an official dinner with the pro-nuncio. I also paid a protocol visit to the representative of the British Crown, Lord Kitchener, and his wife; they were a charming couple, very "Old England" — he was an admirer of Jacques Maritain, and much of our conversation centred on him.

Next I flew from Ottawa to Winnipeg, where I had a delightful meeting with Archbishop Flahiff (who later became Cardinal, and who died in 1989). He was a man overflowing with kindness and humility. He volunteered to be my driver; he wore a basque beret, and was most kind and considerate. In my notebook I find the following remark: "Were he not so gentle, I could see him on St Peter's throne; it would be somewhat like the days of Pope John, in a more elegant and distinguished style; essentially, he is in the same spiritual class. I know he is an authority on Joachim de Flore" — an interest he shared with Cardinal de Lubac.

From Winnipeg I was taken to Regina, where a Congress of priests was in full swing; the purpose of the meeting was to make the clergy's wishes clear to Alex Carter, who was to be the delegate of the Canadian Episcopal Conference to the upcoming Roman synod.

Then I went back to Sault-Sainte-Marie, my host's second residence, where another ecumenical meeting took place with the former Anglican primate of Canada. Finally, we had a goodbye dinner for Carter and his secretaries; they were a lively group, very fond of their boss. On the following day, Alex Carter took me back, safe and sound, to Toronto, where I boarded my flight for New York and Brussels.

* * *

237

Memories and Hopes

My impression of Canada is one of immense spaces, of peace, of a unique cleanliness of the air. And of snow — endless snow; I saw enough snow to last me till the end of my days! The country exudes a feeling of robustness, of tranquil serenity in the face of rising snowdrifts and howling winds.

The distances there are overwhelming to us. There are two cathedrals in the diocese of Sault-Sainte-Marie, for example, as far from each other as Amsterdam is from Paris. The plane trip from Toronto to Vancouver, all of it over Canadian territory, is longer than the flight from Brussels to Toronto.

As for my friend Alex, he is for me the gentleman bishop, the loyal friend who would defy the winds and the seas if it were necessary. He has a remarkable store of common sense, of courage and fair play. He loves truth more than he loves himself — a rare virtue indeed — and he is willing to pay the price.

He reacted vigorously and publicly in the Canadian press when the editor of the *Canadian Register* attacked me because of something I had said (which he had misinterpreted) at the Theological Congress in Brussels; I had spoken of a "Second Jerusalem" as of a distant dream. In his response, Alex Carter recalled Newman's words and applied them to me: "Good is never accomplished except at the cost of those who do it; truth never breaks through except through the sacrifice of those who spread it." Newman spoke from his own experience, and it is good to remember his words, and to live by them.

One last memory of Canada

This happened in Quebec, on a later visit to Canada. I was there to give a lecture, following which I had lunch in the refectory of Laval University. It was an intimate meal, and the group was a small one; there were a few Canadians — Cardinal Roy of Quebec and the university chaplain — and with me were Margie Grace and Veronica O'Brien.

Veronica O'Brien had also arranged to invite Jean Vanier; she

238

had known him in Paris, during her years with the Legion of Mary, and he had become for her a loyal and grateful friend. Since he was late, we decided to start lunch without him. He appeared very late, with an unknown and rather strange-looking person whom he did not introduce. He sat with him at the far end of the table and spoke with him in whispers throughout the meal. We were somewhat taken aback by this friendly and intimate private conversation. As soon as the meal was over, Jean Vanier and his guest left in a great rush, without giving us any explanation. Vanier was our friend, however, and we were biased in his favour; so we gave him the benefit of the doubt for this breach of good manners.

It wasn't until later that evening that he gave us the key to this riddle. The strange intruder was a common law prisoner, released from jail that very morning, thanks to Vanier; he had brought him along to our luncheon because he had yet to find him a place to stay. As we were sitting down to lunch with Cardinal Roy, a violent demonstration against the Cardinal had broken out in the streets of the city; demonstrators claimed that a decision which he had made, concerning Catholic schools, had been unfair to a staff member. Our mysterious guest had read the newspapers, and had become enraged with this "clerical cardinal"; in his private conversation with Jean Vanier, he had threatened several times, "If I ever meet this cardinal, I'll kill him!" Since he had never seen him before, he didn't realise that he was having lunch with the Cardinal, who was sitting across the table from him.

Nothing ever seems to surprise Jean Vanier, who calmly continued his conversation with his prisoner – a past and potentially a future murderer – with enough charity and warmth to melt an icicle. He did, however, hurry off, taking his protégé with him, and foregoing dessert in the cause of safety.

Dear Jean Vanier, thank you for revealing God's compassion and tenderness to the world!

The Congress of the Marian Ecumenical Society in London
This Ecumenical Society was founded in London, in 1967, by a layman, Martin Gillet; he had been an Anglican originally, but later converted to Catholicism. He was a warmhearted, honest and sincere person, a discreet Nicodemus.

He was a friend of Mgr Cardinale at the time when the latter was pro-nuncio in England; when Mgr Cardinale was appointed nuncio to Belgium, Martin Gillet often visited him there. In Malines, on the occasion of the anniversary of the Malines Conversations, he met Veronica O'Brien; this meeting was for him a source of valuable inspiration. She encouraged him to speak to me, during the reception, about his project, and I in turn suggested that he should get in touch with Cardinal Heenan. There, his project was received with the greatest enthusiasm, and he was offered the use of an office at the Archbishop's house. His health was failing, and twice he called me to his sick-bed to read me the story of the origins of his plan, and to share with me his supreme hope: that Mary, Mother of the Church, will reunite her dispersed children and bring them home to their common hearth. It is an open path towards ecumenical communion, and I believe it to be rich in promise for the future, provided it is given the opportunities and the support it needs.

The Society has three Presidents — Cardinal Hume for the Catholic Church, Archbishop Runcie for the Anglican Church, and the Orthodox Archbishop of London for the Orthodox Church — and four "protectors", of whom I am one.

I was present when the Society was created, in Washington, and one day I celebrated the Eucharist for the small American group, at the National Marian Shrine. At the offertory, I watched as two professors from the Episcopalian University of Virginia carried a pitcher of wine and a pitcher of water to the altar. One was Professor Dawe, an eminent theologian and an authority on Hinduism; the other was Professor Ross Mackenzie, author of a book on Mary for which he asked me to write a preface.

At the 1971 Congress of the Marian Ecumenical Society, in

London, the atmosphere was, as always, relaxed, friendly, and prayerful. I opened the proceedings with a lecture on the Holy Spirit and Mary. I mentioned that I had once asked Rahner why trendy Christians are so indifferent to Mary, and I quoted his reply: "For too many people, Christianity has become another 'ism', an ideology, an abstraction – and abstractions have no need of mothers."

I included two improvised prayers. Just before leaving, and in conclusion to my speech, I attempted to redress the biblical minimalism of the Dean of York and the theological minimalism of a Catholic speaker; the latter, in my opinion, had been far too anxious to show that Vatican II had eliminated our exaggerations, without then taking the trouble to show all that Mary does mean to us. In response to a question concerning Lourdes, he had asserted that, in his opinion, Mary plays no role in the transmission of sacramental grace. To this I added: "Indeed, Mary does not 'interfere' in absolution; however, in Lourdes she gently urges the pilgrims to go to confession and to receive communion." I also spoke in defence of Louis-Marie Grignion de Monfort: "Let us abandon the casket, but keep the rare and precious pearl – Mary's secret."

Seven Catholic bishops and a few Anglican bishops attended the Congress. I had very useful talks with all of them.

A woman in the audience later said to me, with a moving sincerity: "I am Protestant, and Mary had always been for me a closed door. You have opened this door for me, and I have understood. I have come to thank you." I also had a very good meeting with an influential Methodist pastor, who obviously found me very "Methodist" because of my improvised prayers. I signed the book which he held out to me, and he asked me to mention, beneath my name, the Doctorate *honoris causa* awarded to me by the [Methodist] University of Emory, in the United States.

* * *

In London, I had lunch with Archbishop Ramsey. I have always left Lambeth with the same impression of welcome and warmth and openness – and nothing precise with respect to the future.

Ramsey confided to me, "I have met here with Welles, the Episcopalian bishop from the United States. He read me your "instructions" concerning his visit to the Pope, and told me that you had advised him to "mention neither Suenens nor collegiality"" – he found this amusing. Then Ramsey told me again of his own hope to meet once more with the Pope, but he added "I am waiting for some sign of a new springtime, perhaps in the next year or two – something positively ecumenical around which I can focus my visit." And then he added, "You can be sure, at any rate, that I will mention both Suenens and collegiality!"

Of Cardinal Heenan he said, in passing, "His heart is ecumenical, but not his mind."

He presented me with a copy of the book we had written together, *The Future of the Christian Church*, in its English edition. It is definitely an improvement on the American edition.

At about 5 p.m. I arrived at Cardinal Heenan's country house; this used to belong to Mgr H. Benson, who is buried in the chapel. It was all very English.

I received a very friendly welcome. The Cardinal had recently finished writing the first volume of his autobiography, *Not All the Truth*. A newspaper had just offered him ten thousand pounds for the right to publish some excerpts.

He admitted that in the old days, when he was Bishop of Liverpool, he had been quite authoritarian. People spoke then of "the cruel see of Liverpool".

In his reactions, Heenan is very spontaneous, but equally humble and direct. I have the impression that he does not really follow a conversation – he talks in spurts, with witty remarks and unexpected comments. However, he received me as a friend, and certainly had no prejudice against me.

At one point we were discussing the press, commenting on how often our words had been twisted out of shape, and he declared: "I believe I have never once been quoted correctly by the press." This was very painful to him. He had just received a letter from the nuncio, asking what exactly he had said a few days before, in Ireland. He had actually said something very sensible; but quoted out of context, his words were a little strange, to say the least.

This is the eternal problem; we must speak up and accept the risk of being misunderstood. What is truly distressing is that the Roman Curia is quick to believe what it reads in the papers, and to worry about it. I remember saying to the Holy Father, on one occasion, "If I were to read in the newspapers that Koenig, in Vienna, has declared that there are four persons in the Holy Trinity, I would not allow anyone to write and ask him whether this is true." What I meant was very clear: "This is the way your offices should be dealing with all of us."

Butler — who lived a few miles away, at St Edmond's Seminary — joined us for dinner. In the course of a lively conversation, Heenan told us that after he became Archbishop of Westminster, he had arbitrarily taken back the vice-presidency of the "Jewish-Christian" group. He had decided to do this against the express will of Cardinal Ottaviani, who had barred Catholics from the association. He had said to Ottaviani, "You will never change; so I shall simply present you with the *fait accompli.*" And to further impress him, he had added that this was a case of *"graviter onerata conscientia"* ("serious obligation of conscience"). The issue of interdiction never came up again.

President Pompidou's visit to Brussels
The programme for President Pompidou's visit included a dinner which he hosted at the Palais du Cinquantenaire, in the presence of the King and Queen. At table, I had a chance to talk with him. He is a charming man, reserved, humorous, self-assured. He comes from Auvergne, with a basic honesty and a seriousness which inspire confidence. He gives the impression of a solid man,

a man of heart; yet he is ruled by his mind, and perhaps because of this, in his relations with others he comes across as a great intellectual rather than as a warm human being. He is always Pompidou — it would be nice to think that now and then he takes a little time off! But I suppose he may be hiding his real self.

I told him my favourite story about husband-wife relationships. A man was asked what was the secret of his blissful marriage. He replied: "It's really very simple: my wife makes all of the minor decisions, and I reserve the right to make all major decisions." "Could you give an example?" he was asked. "Of course!" he said. "Which school should the children go to; where should we spend our holidays; should we build a new house — these are things my wife decides." "What would be a major decision that you would make?" "Well, for example, should China be admitted to the United Nations? That's for me to decide!"

In turn, President Pompidou told this story to his wife, and the following day, on the train to Liège, he told it to our Minister Harmel. This must surely mean something!

During the dinner, I also asked him, "Mr President, if you had to take a stand at the Synod concerning assistance to the Third World, what areas would you focus on?" "Agriculture," he replied. "The first priority is to feed the people. Next, encourage small-scale industry. And only in the last stage, develop large-scale industry: we must not put the cart before the horse." He spoke for some time on the subject, commenting on the evolution of the USSR in the area of political development, which had been determined by military preoccupations — a priority, he noted, that should not be transferred to other countries.

A funny episode comes to mind: after dinner, we moved to a private living-room; on the way, we paused before a beautiful bronze vase, a valuable item. Someone asked: "What period is it from?" President Pompidou instantly gave the exact date. We all looked amazed and admiring at such erudition — until the President admitted, with a smile, "I looked at the inscription on my way in!"

The Faith and Order Conference in Louvain
The Faith and Order World Conference met in Louvain from
August 2 to 8. Those were valuable and enriching days for me. In
the opening speech, I went immediately to the heart of our
theme: "Unity of the Church and Unity of the World". Most
importantly, the Conference gave me the opportunity to meet
some of the main figures of the ecumenical movement among the
Orthdox, Meyendorff and Borovoy from Saint-Serge in Paris; Meliton, representative of Athénagoras in Geneva; and many others.

A long conversation with Meyendorff helped me better to
understand the concern of the Orthodox about any change that
challenges tradition. They have to contend with their own version
of "old Catholics", who keep a watchful eye on them, and who
always have a tendency to canonise the past. Meyendorff spoke to
me of his fear that, without being aware of it, Catholics may at
this point be leaning a little too far toward Protestantism. In all
that he said, however, I was unable clearly to distinguish his personal opinions from those of others whom he may have been
quoting. He is an outstanding theologian – there can be no
doubt about that; his paper on "Unity of the Church and Unity of
the World" is remarkable, and deserves to be read with the greatest care.

I also met with representatives of the reformed Church. I had a
good talk with von Allmen, who argued that unity among the
Churches should begin at the level of local Churches.

I also talked with W.A. Visser 't Hooft, Secretary General of
the World Council of Churches in Geneva. He explained to me
both the advantages and the disadvantages of a potential decision, on the part of the Catholic Church, to join the World Council of Churches; he was clearly in favour of such a step. I remain
uncertain on this point. I consider close cooperation, at every
level, with the various sectors of the World Council of Churches,
very desirable – but I fear that fusion could be a source of conflicts and ambiguities. Moreover, I do not think that the collaboration of our ten theologians with members of Faith and Order

has been particularly successful.

I took the opportunity to invite Visser 't Hooft to Brussels, to speak with me and Archbishop Bloom of London on the theme "The Church of Peter, Paul and John". He accepted, and mentioned the famous page in Russian literature on this subject. He recommended that I read the Russian novelists, whose works are so deeply imbued with the spirit of Christianity.

Visser 't Hooft has been identified with the World Council of Churches for a great many years. I felt him to be a man of wide experience and vast culture; however, he is very Protestant on the issue of ministries within the Church. He told me that he completely accepts Küng, and shares his position. He has great faith in Willebrands, and an indulgent smile for the human race.

A brief conversation with David du Plessis, the world leader of Pentecostalism, left me with an image of a rather paternalistic man, but a man of great warmth – as is only to be expected from a pentecostal.

I also briefly met with, among others, Nelson, from Boston, and with the director of the Institute for Ecumenical Studies in Jerusalem (the first director of which was Mgr Charles Moeller).

The Conference ended on a Sunday. Mass was concelebrated at 10 a.m. in the presence of all the delegates of Faith and Order. A rumour had spread in the media that non-Catholics would be receiving communion. To avoid misunderstandings, I had included a printed notice in the documents distributed to the participants, stating that, alas, in the present circumstances, we could not sit at the same table, and that we should all offer this common suffering for the cause of unity. Max Thurian told me later that he had seen three Protestants receiving communion; a professor from Louvain had counted ten. To avoid the possibility that this would be used against me in Rome, I deliberately did not distribute communion.

The Mass was magnificent, both in the music and in the prayerful atmosphere. Everyone joined in singing familiar hymns, and our own Gregorian chants in Latin were beautifully integrated into the whole. I gave the homily, in which I spoke of the Holy Spirit – the link that binds the past to the present and to the future.

During Mass I offered the sign of peace to the Orthodox and the Anglican bishops, all of whom were deeply moved; Borovoy was actually weeping. After Mass, Meyendorff privately said to me that it had all been very "Orthodox" and very "fraternal". Borovoy, a Russian archpriest who had been observer at the Council and who later became bishop, came to thank me: he was so deeply moved that he could not finish his sentence, and could only shake my hand with deep emotion. I said to him: "Thank you; I understand all that you want to say to me."

This was a very important moment for me, something like the day I gave the eulogy for Pope John before the Council. Here we were living anticipatory eschatological moments – a foretaste of the Second Jerusalem that is still in gestation. I ended my homily with a few profoundly moving lines from Eliot – a call to a future meeting at the Cenacle in Jerusalem:

> We shall not cease from exploration
> And the end of all our exploring
> Will be to arrive where we started
> And know the place for the first time.

Zagreb

From August 11 to 16, I presided over the World Conference of Mariology, which meets every four years in a different place. Pope Paul had appointed me President of these conferences, probably because of my involvement with the Legion of Mary.

This time, the Conference took place in Yugoslavia, in the city of Zagreb. Holding a meeting of this sort in a communist country posed some problems. All the Yugoslav bishops had experienced severe hardships and trials, often including prison.

One evening, we were invited to an official reception by the President of the Croatian Republic. Every one of the bishops present that evening had been sentenced to two, ten, or even fifteen years in prison as a result of his savage indictments. On the surface, there was nothing unusual about the atmosphere of the official gathering; but the underlying tensions were there and could be felt.

The Pope had sent Cardinal Seper, former Archbishop of Zagreb, as pontifical legate to the Conference. Much to my astonishment, in his homily to the crowd of about two hundred thousand pilgrims who had gathered there, he broke out into a heartfelt attack against the publisher who had printed in Croatian my interview of May 15, 1969, and who had described it as "an attack against the Pope".

Since I do not understand Croatian, it was only at the end of the pontifical Mass that I was informed of the incident, as a number of journalists and professors from the Seminary came to express their regrets and their warm feelings of cordiality.

While I was there, I gave an interview to the Yugoslav magazine, *Vus*, "The Wednesday Weekly". When I saw the translation, provided by the Belgian Embassy in Belgrade, I discovered that my presence had been the cause of some turmoil. The last part of the article began as follows: "Careful observers were able to see just how vigilant conservatives are." There were then a few further details concerning the rather cool reception I had received. The last sentence stated: "The facts are proof of the vehement 'dialogue' which has arisen, since the Council, between the two 'currents' in the Church; they are also an indication of the tone which those who distrust all innovations are attempting to give to this 'dialogue'."

A princely wedding in Brussels
I was asked to celebrate the wedding of Prince Philippe of Licht-

enstein and Isabelle de l'Arbre. At the end of the wedding Mass, we were all suddenly transported to the eighteenth century! This impression was heightened by our surroundings, since the wedding reception was held at the château of Grand-Bigard. All of pre-Napoleonic Europe was present: Princes of Liechstenstein, of Lowenstein, Habsburgs...

Everybody was very charming indeed. I was seated next to the bride's aunt, who was delightfully original, provocatively conservative; she was sufficiently witty, however, that we managed to cross swords with velvet gloves. Everything appeared to distress her – "There is no more respect", she complained. She was just about to criticise the absence of any distinctive episcopal signs in my outfit, when, halfway through her sentence, she noticed the ring on my finger and the touch of red at my collar. She made a rapid recovery, and adjusted her aim.

Two different worlds were face to face, but I am sure that friendliness won the day. She asked me – as is proper in polite conversation – who would be the next pope. I told her that if it were to be a non-Italian, her own Cardinal in Vienna was the most likely choice. She cried out in indignation that if this should happen, she would become Orthodox. I was quick to recommend Uniate Orthodoxy, and we laughed together.

My most amusing memory of the day is of my brief encounter with the bride and groom, to whom I had given a copy of *Christian Life Day by Day* and a copy of my pastoral letter on fidelity. Isabelle came towards me and exclaimed: "I am very cross indeed..." "And why, may I ask?" "I was expecting everyone to rush over to me and tell me that my gown is absolutely ravishing, and instead, everyone is telling me that your homily was absolutely marvelous. It's quite infuriating!" I consoled her as best I could, and assured her that her gown, glittering with sequins – I think that's what made it glitter; I'm afraid I didn't look too carefully! – was very becoming. I concluded from this that the hierarchy of values is a very relative thing.

Memories and Hopes

The debate on pontifical infallibility
My *credo* on this issue consists of three points:

1. I believe in the infallibility of the Church;
2. I believe in the infallibility of the pope *within* the Church;
3. I do not believe in the infallibility of the Holy Office *on the subject of* the Church.

And my *spero* can be summarised as follows:

1. I hope that the word and the concept of infallibility will be studied further, for the purpose of clarification;
2. With Mgr Weber — former Bishop of Strasburg and eminent biblicist — I hope that the questions of biblical inerrance and conciliar and pontifical infallibility will be examined together;
3. I hope that, while we await clarifications and greater precision, we will all behave as "non-infallible" seekers.

Rome — the 1971 Synod
This Synod dealt, in part, with the priesthood. I made several statements, the most important of which was a request that those episcopal conferences that might wish to do so — and this was not the case in my own country — should be allowed to open the priesthood to married men, in circumstances which would have to be defined. What I was seeking was in fact to open up the possibility of a double clergy, the one celibate and the other married — such as we now have in the Catholic Church of Eastern Rite, and such as existed several centuries ago.

This was not a problem concerning natural rights, nor was it a "trendy" liberal demand. The crux of the problem lies elsewhere, I believe — as is clearly stated in a letter I received from a very spiritual Christian couple: "The People of God have an absolute right to be nourished with the body and the blood and the word of Christ; because of the decreasing number of priests, more and more men and women are starved of these; it is precisely by multiplying eucharistic centres that we can increase the number of vocations."

The Synod proved that such a possibility is not yet accepted within the Church of Latin Rite. A majority of the bishops (107) voted against this idea; however, a substantial minority (87) were favourable to it, under certain conditions. All agreed that the final decision, concerning both the appropriateness of such an option and its practical applications, should rest with the Pope. Pope Paul did not want to go in this direction; nor does the current Pope, John Paul II.

If the union of the Christian Churches were to become a reality, this problem would necessarily have to be dealt with; however, things have not yet reached that stage.

The future will tell "what the Spirit is saying to the Churches".

1972

A conference in Liège

Where are we? Where are we going?" This was the title of a conference concerning the future of the Church, which took place at the Palais des Congrès in Liège. The hall was magnificently decorated, and the audience was very attentive.

During the meal that preceded the conference, the liberal Minister Rey had very comically confessed that he had been an anticlerical student – had taken part in demonstrations and shouted anticlerical slogans. One confession calls for another, and so I told him that I had once put up electoral posters on the walls and on the door of Foucart's house, when he was the liberal mayor of Schaerbeek.

Then the Minister publicly saluted me as "one of the great instigators of change in our time". I believe he was speaking sincerely; and his private reaction, at the end of the lecture, was quite extraordinary.

Memories and Hopes

I spoke both of the institutional aspect of the Church and of its charismatic dimensions. I said that the time had come to move forward on both those levels at once – on the visible, institutional level, but also on the spiritual level, in continuity with the Incarnation and with Pentecost. We must give the Holy Spirit a chance to be both the Faithful One *par excellence* and the Revolutionary whose breath is new life.

A pontifical audience

As I came in, the Pope embraced me very cordially, and immediately told me that it was a great joy to see me and to have a chance to talk with me about how to make progress in the field of ecumenism. He was well aware of my interest in this area, and in particular of my desire to promote "Marian" ecumenism. He told me that he had spoken with Cardinal Willebrands about possible ways to coordinate my efforts, but that they could find no way of doing this within the framework of the Secretariat for Unity – a view I agreed with completely.

I was anxious not to appear to be free lancing in the ecumenical field. I described to the Pope my meetings with the Patriarch of Rumania, with Visser 't Hooft, with Archbishop Bloom, with Ramsey, and with others, and told him about all that was being planned. I pointed out to him the impact that the Council had had on all of this. We then went on to talk about the two major obstacles: Mary, for the Protestants; and pontifical primacy, for everyone.

Then the Pope spoke to me in great detail of his own personal difficulties with regard to the Ukrainian Church (Slipyj) and to the Romanian question. We discussed some other unresolved matters, and he remarked, "To continue our conversation comfortably, we need a garden and some trees." I laughed and said that all he needed to do was invite me to Castel Gandolfo.

In conclusion, the Holy Father gave me two gifts. The first was a book by Mgr Batiffol, *L'Eglise naissante et le catholicisme (The*

New Church and Catholicism). Pope Paul had acquired the copyright to this book; he had had it reprinted, and translated into Italian, at his own expense. The text was unchanged; it was still identical to the first edition which had appeared in 1909. No doubt this represented a subtle and discreet invitation to go back and study the relationship between primacy and collegiality from its earliest origins.

The second gift was a Japanese print of the Virgin, on beautiful silk — "as a symbol", he told me, "of our meeting today, around Mary".

A thank-you letter after the audience
The day after the audience, I wrote a letter to the Holy Father to thank him. This letter marks a turning-point in our relationship, since the problems of the Council were from here onwards increasingly replaced by new concerns. These were to include, in particular, preparations to receive the Charismatic Renewal Movement, which was then at its earliest stages in Catholic groups in the United States.

Here is the full text of my letter:

Holy Thursday, 1972

Most Holy Father,

On this Holy Thursday, my thoughts turn spontaneously to you, and I send my warmest wishes for the Feast of Easter to you and to the Church.

I was very moved by your warm and loving welcome, and I fully intend to find or create some reason to visit you again in the course of the year. I am also very grateful for the welcome you gave to Miss V. O'Brien, who fully appreciated its importance and its significance. I know she has shared her joy with Chiara, whom I look forward to seeing again before long.

I would have liked to send you a few comments on my recent trip to the United States. I was there during the first two weeks of March, to give a series of lectures and to preside over ecumenical debates; all of this was the result of invitations I received from various universities, bishops, and apostolic organisations. I had no time to keep you informed along the way. During the Easter holidays, I hope to have time to put my impressions in writing; I will give my report to Mgr Benelli at some later meeting.

My lectures focused on the following general theme: during the sixties, the Church concentrated on a revision of her "institutional" aspects; in the seventies, we must stress the spiritual, "pneumatic" aspect of the Church. This allowed me to set aside the structural problems, and to move on to a concern which seems to be pervasive in the United States: a thirst for prayer, for the discovery of Jesus as a person, and of the Holy Spirit.

It would be easy to write pages and pages about the "charismatic" movement in the American Church, with the reserve and the caution that are essential in this area; on the whole, however, my impression is a positive one.

I simply wanted to share with you the joy of this discovery, in a country that is otherwise horribly torn by crime, drugs, racial strife and war.

I had meetings with several bishops, including Cardinal Cooke and Cardinal Krol, in whose residence I stayed. I asked both of them, on behalf of the Belgian bishops, to appeal to the US Government for assistance to Cardinal Malula of the Church of the Congo. Both have promised to do so. I was also able to ask this of some of my American friends who are very close to President Nixon. In addition, I had the opportunity, through a Canadian bishop, to make the same request of the Canadian Prime Minister. I hope that the current crisis in this unfortunate country will soon be over. Despite everything, the people there still need religious peace and the help of our missionaries in order to face the future.

Once again, Most Holy Father, with respectful affection

may I convey my sincerest good wishes for a blessed East-
ertide.

L.J. Cardinal Suenens

* * *

The fundamentalist press was quick to criticise me during this
trip to the US. They had portrayed me as a "rebel" cardinal; now
Walter Burghardt, SJ – an eminent and respected theologian, and
a member of the Roman Theological Commission – introduced
me to a large New York audience in the following words, for the
eloquent originality of which he must take full responsibility!

Today's speaker does need an introduction: he is *not* all
you have heard. He is not an enemy of Pope Paul; but he
has written with bold accuracy: the greatest day in the life
of a pope is not his coronation but his baptism, his mission
"to live the Christian life in obedience to the gospel".

He is not turning the Church into a democracy; but he
does insist that ministry is the task of *all* Christians, that
today's Christian need is *co*-responsibility.

You may indeed call him a radical, but only if you realise
that this man, who will tell you that "in a few years history
will have relativised us all", holds lovingly to all the Christian past that genuinely links Catholicism with Christ.

He is hardly indifferent to the differences between
churches; but he does agonise over the sobering words of
Jesus: only by our oneness will the world know that Christ
has come and that God loves.

He is a cardinal, yes; but he has transformed the meaning of cardinal from "prince of the Church" to "servant of
man".

It gives me uncommon pleasure to present "Tomorrow's
Church" as envisioned by a scholar whose learning enrich-
es us all, by a priest whose parish is the world, by a very
human person whose life is love: Léon-Joseph Cardinal Suenens.

Ecumenical lunch and dinner in London

London was in darkness as the result of a strike. In the evening, I had dinner at the Belgian Embassy, with Tom Burns and Norman St John Stevas. The following day, I had lunch with the Ramseys; it was an intimate meal, with no other guests. As usual, I was welcomed with great warmth; and as usual, there was a concise quality to all they said, each sentence putting an end to a particular subject. With some perseverance, however, I kept the conversation going till 2:45.

The Archbishop remarked pleasantly that he was planning to go to Rome in 1973, "to congratulate the Pope if he does something good between now and then, or to protest if he does something ecumenically not-so-good!"

We discussed the American "Jesus Movement", concerning which he had four questions:

— Is the Jesus to whom these young people lay claim an open door to the Father and to the Kingdom of God?

— Is this Jesus truly food for the spirit, and not only for the heart?

— Is he truly incarnated, and not merely a "docetist" Jesus who only appears to be human?

— Does the Gospel of Jesus, as they proclaim it, have the essential social dimensions?

The Archbishop has given two lectures in New York on this subject, and he intends to publish them.

The evening was excellent as well; I had dinner at the Anglo-Belgian Union, with the Archbishop of York, Mgr Coggan. He was planning to publish a letter at Easter, together with the Catholics and the Free Churches, as a joint witness to the Gospel before the world; it would then be up to the various Churches to develop the message, each in its own way.

Mgr Coggan struck me as a warm and direct person; he is more pleasant to talk to than is Ramsey. His speech at the banquet was very friendly to me. When my turn came to speak, I set aside the prepared text and decided to improvise, since the atmosphere called for something light and easily absorbed. I spoke on the theme "Who is Jesus Christ for us and for the world?" And I believe that we "confessed the Lord".

Once again I saw that the words by which we witness personally to our experience of God in our own lives are the words that carry weight.

An unexpected conference in Philadelphia

I went to Philadelphia, invited by Cardinal Krol, to participate in an ecumenical meeting at the city's university. At the same time, a COCU Conference was being held; this was an organisation that had been working for a number of years towards the reunification of the Christian Churches – among themselves, not with Rome.

In the evening, after a day of debates and discussions, the participants in this Conference came to hear my lecture at the university. At about 10 p.m., as they were heading back to their hotel – where I was also staying – their secretary general asked me if I would be willing to preside over their meeting on the following day. I accepted this somewhat paradoxical request.

On the following morning, we had breakfast with the participants. After that, discussions resumed under the chairmanship of a cardinal of the Roman Catholic Church – somewhat unexpected, to say the least! I asked them why it was that despite their efforts over a period of years, they still had not achieved the desired integration. Immediately, and with complete openness, they explained the reasons for their differences.

For a long time, I listened carefully; towards the end of the morning, I told them, very honestly, that I felt that their efforts consisted disproportionately of practical debates among themselves, on a very pragmatic level; unity of Christians, however, must come about first through looking together in the same direction, toward Jesus Christ, our common Master.

And so I left, profoundly moved by the sincerity of these Christians. Later I received a very friendly letter from their organisers, thanking me for the time I had spent with them.

As I write these lines, I see in the newspaper that after twenty-five years of discussions, nine Churches belonging to this group have successfully merged; their common name is now "Christ of Church Uniting".

The Orthodox Patriarch of Romania visits Malines

Patriarch Justinian arrived in Malines on May 3 and stayed until May 10; he was accompanied by Archbishop Nicolas, Bishop Anthony, a university professor, a secretary, and a deacon. My guests were also planning to visit the Bishops of Gand, Bruges and Namur, as well as a few monasteries. This was a week of intense but complex ecumenism.

My final impression was that they were far, I might even say very far, from accepting the primacy of Rome. In their view, the pope would have to denounce and retract Vatican I, repudiate *Ecclesiam Suam*, and announce: "I am not your chief, but your brother." On this basis they would be willing to recognise him as first among equals.

I attempted to interest them in the new perspectives and possibilities opened up by Vatican II, but at the mere hint of a step toward Rome, their fear of being "absorbed" verged on panic. This explains Justinian's policy of approaching various national Churches one after the other, never explicitly stating his goal.

They spoke frequently of the situation of the Uniates, who have been forcibly integrated into Romanian Orthodoxy. They have their own way of telling this story.

On leaving, they expressed satisfaction at having found a Church that is "ecumenically open", as well as monasteries that are welcoming and fervent in prayer.

Since I could visualise no immediate practical follow-up to this meeting, I tried to point the conversation towards the future. My feeling was of a Church still deeply entrenched in hierarchism, where protocol and custom have an importance that we cannot understand. I had sent a secretary to Bucharest, beforehand, to make practical arrangements in preparation for their visit; he spent six hours in meetings in Bucharest, discussing every detail of dress and protocol.

After his visit to King Baudouin, the Patriarch first compared it with his visit to the Queen of England from the standpoint of protocol; it was his secretary who spoke of the spiritual aura that emanates from the King. The Patriarch then agreed with him, and commented on the directness of the King's questions and on his simplicity.

It is difficult for me to reach any conclusions concerning the Patriarch; the need to communicate through interpreters creates a kind of filter, often screening out subtle nuances. He seemed astute, skilful and political, believing that he holds the definitive truth and has nothing more to seek. I had a feeling that he was close to the dictator Ceaucescu, whom he had sheltered during the War, when the latter was trying to persuade his countrymen to rise up against Hitler.

Not once did he raise a theological question; these all came from me. The Patriarch seemed pleased to have established contact; he is no doubt an excellent administrator. He seemed to appreciate the spirituality of our monks, and to be somewhat opposed to the narrow-mindedness of the Greek monks on Mount Athos.

Metropolitan Nicolas, who was with him, was a different kind of man altogether. However, his self-effacing manner in the presence of the Patriarch made it impossible to engage in serious dialogue with him on any substantive matter.

As for Bishop Anthony — the patriarchal bishop — he was a theologian of great integrity, a staunch defender of Orthodoxy, intelligent and not without a sense of humour. He was a novelist, and had had a book, *Three Days in Hell*, published. Ten thousand copies were printed, and sold out in one week; Italian and German translations were in preparation. Tenacious and self-assured in theological arguments, he is nevertheless made likeable by his honesty.

Three men of good will, in other words, but prisoners nonetheless – just as we are, of course – of many centuries of history; journeying, in their own way, towards unity along a federal model. Together we reviewed the various hypotheses of a step-by-step *rapprochement.*

Their Eastern world is very different from ours. Even their lifestyle reflects this: the Patriarch rose each morning at 5 a.m., no doubt to pray.

Only once did they celebrate their liturgy, on a Sunday in Brussels. I was present at the ceremony. I was worried for a moment when, after the consecration, they offered me bread and wine. I asked the monk from Chevetogne who was with me whether this bread and wine were consecrated, and whether this would create misunderstandings concerning intercommunion. He assured me that this was merely a gesture "to break the fast" and that the bread and the wine had not been consecrated.

If we were to try to penetrate to the very soul of their liturgical life, we would discover a whole new world. I could sense a richness that we could usefully transpose; we could give them, in exchange, a breath of new life.

At the end of their visit, we reviewed all the possible approaches at various levels – those of bishops, theologians, people – and I mentioned the idea of Marian ecumenism. This is when I discovered that Bishop Anthony knew Martin Gillet of the Marian Ecumenical Society of London. There are possibilities of an opening there. Our Lady, "door to Heaven and to unity", pray for your pilgrims of unity. The journey ahead of us is still very long.

The conversations were to resume in Bucharest in September. This would give us time to breathe, to reflect, and to allow the Spirit to breathe on us. For the Spirit alone can overcome barriers and move mountains. The Carpathians are not the sort of little mountains or hills you can climb with ease.

In the end, I was unable to visit them as planned, since I could not go there without meeting with the Catholic bishops who were being held prisoners by the government; the authorisation for such a meeting, however, was not forthcoming.

I received the following letter of thanks from Archbishop Nicolas of Timisoara — a place that has become sadly famous. The letter reveals his inner state, and the receptivity hidden beneath his discretion. It filled me with joy.

Mitropolia Banatului
Cabinetul Mitropolitului   Timisoara, May 14, 1972

Your Eminence:

The days in Belgium made such a deep impression on me that once again today, my thoughts go back to that visit. Especially — and I want you to know this — I shall never forget the long conversations at which I was present, your deep understanding and your enlightened vision of the unity of the Church, the evangelical simplicity which characterises you, the love and the sincerity which can be felt in your every word and gesture. I shall always remember the warm welcome we received from the bishops, the professors, the priests, the monks, the religious, the faithful, the public authorities, and in particular His Majesty the King.

Allow me therefore to thank you for all that you have done for us, and for me personally; I pray God that he may bless your work, and bless you.

With the deepest respect, I remain, Your Eminence, sincerely yours,

Nicolas, Metropolitan of Banat

The Protestant Synod in Brussels
In June 1972, I was invited to the Protestant Synod in Brussels by Dr Pieters, president of the Synod. He publicly stated that I

had helped him to a better discovery of Jesus. Be that as it may, it was said with touching humility.

My contact with the audience was brief, but very warm. I wanted merely to love them, without entering into any controversial issues — to make the ice melt in the warmth of the love that envelops us all. The tone was somewhat sedate and solemn; it would have been unseemly, at the beginning, to try to make them smile. However, the ice did melt, and the rest is in God's hands.

The current changes are very obviously a source of difficulty for many of the faithful. They too feel the weight of a conservatism that is made up largely of sociology and history. A continued openness to the beckoning call of the future is indeed a prodigious gift of the Holy Spirit.

A Roman document mentions that one of the many qualities essential to a bishop is an ability to read the signs of the times. This is now more essential than ever.

A lightning visit from Dom Helder Câmara

On June 24, I received a very brief visit from Dom Helder Camâra. He arrived from Munich, with a formidable German bible which had been given to him and which he in turn offered to me. He left the very same evening to deliver a lecture in Liverpool. He got off one plane at 10:45 and onto another at 1:15, but in the little time we had, we were able to commune once again.

"Go ahead," he said, "start the conversation." He was full of plans — for the election of a pope! He wanted us to work on a profile and on a programme; he felt that at the conclave, we should have one already in hand!

Dear Helder is definitely a poet and a dreamer. He even told me one of his dreams. Fortunately, he has a great sense of humour, and he is a very holy man.

He also informed me that he had recently received an anonymous phone call. The caller told him to leave his house immediately, claiming that a bomb had been set in the house, and that it was timed to explode within the hour. He had replied: "Well, how kind of you to let me know! So few people are lucky enough to know an hour in advance that they are about to have the joy of dying. Can you imagine...the ultimate joy of being, at last, with the Lord!" At the other end of the line, the anonymous caller had cried "You're quite mad!" and hung up. And Helder stayed in the house.

I forgot to ask him what exactly he did, during the hour that followed the phone call. This could provide us with a new version of the classical tale of Saint Aloysius Gonzaga who said that if he were told, in the middle of a game, that he was to die before the game was over, he would continue to play.

Munich — the academic opening of the Olympics
I was quite surpised to find myself in Munich on the opening day of the Olympics, delivering a solemn speech at the introductory academic session. When Cardinal Doepfner first asked me, I refused, but he insisted; he finally managed to convince me that I had to accept, in order to offset, as he put it, the presence of a Russian Communist speaker.

The choice of subject for such a lecture baffled me at first. Finally, I settled on "Humanising Factors in Sports"; this allowed me to discuss team-spirit as an element of co-responsibility (a favorite theme during the Council), and fair play in games, a quality that needs to be developed in everyday life as well.

Joy in illness
One of our priests, Fr G. Demol, had a serious heart attack, and was taken to the hospital in the Rue des Cendres. On the eve of my visit, he seemed to be dying; his warm and friendly welcome when I arrived in the morning was therefore a delightful surprise.

He had asked to be in a room with other patients, because he wanted "to be able to witness to the very end".

Memories and Hopes

He took both my hands in his and told me, "Your visit is the greatest joy I have had in a very long time. I am telling you this because I doubt that you have very many consolations. I look upon death with faith and with joy. I know the One in whom I have believed. Now let me introduce you to my friends here." And he introduced his two room-mates with great gentleness and kindness.

This was one of the most beautiful visits I have ever shared with someone seriously ill. It was very obvious that every person in the room was in great harmony with this priest — this faithful witness, to the very end, to the paschal meaning of death. Death was eclipsed by life, and we parted in joy.

An intense audience with the Pope

On Thursday October 19, 1972, my audience with the Holy Father lasted close to an hour. He greeted me with the words "You're looking wonderful!" He himself appeared to be in excellent form, although he had aged somewhat; as our conversation progressed, it was clear that he was not always fully attentive. At any rate, he welcomed me very warmly.

He suggested that I should some day go to Jerusalem, to stress the fact that it is sacred to us as well. Then he asked for my advice concerning the Holy Year he was planning to announce, and the central theme for it. At that point, I gathered up all of my courage to speak to him of the conclave and of the procedure governing all future succession.

I introduced the problem by mentioning a recent article by Cardinal Garrone, who claimed that this subject was one that the Pope alone should deal with. Mgr Benelli had just said to me, "The Pope is very happy with Cardinal Garrone's article; it might be useful to let him know that it does not reflect the general opinion." I said to the Pope, "Holy Father, this matter concerns the entire Church, and the credibility of the next conclave is at stake."

The Pope replied "This is not an easy matter to decide; at the moment, journalists are weaving imaginative tales on the subject." He did not indicate what direction the new rules for the conclave would take. My own impression was that nothing would change in this area. From an ecumenical standpoint, the underlying issue — and the crucial one — would be to determine the fundamental criterion for a pontifical election. What is the basic assumption? Are we choosing a bishop of Rome, who then becomes pope, or a pope who then is bishop of Rome? But this was not the time for theological discussions.

I told the Holy Father that in my opinion, the most important issues were at the level of the cardinal-electors, where it is essential to have an equitable representation of the various parts of the world; this would put an end to the many centuries of Italian preponderance. I added that, in my view, the regulations should in any case include a clause stipulating that no candidate could be elected pope if he was over the age of sixty. The Pope asked me why, and I replied: "Because beyond this age, it is almost impossible for a man to shoulder the heavy burden of the pontifical responsibilities of this day and age."

We then went on to speak of Europe, and of the role of Brussels. He gave me a brief lecture on the history of the relationship between the Latin peoples and the Germanic peoples, going back to Aix-la-Chapelle. Finally, he gave me a luxuriously bound book about St Peter's See in Rome.

1973

The audience of February 19, 1973
This audience lasted one hour and fifteen minutes. I first spoke to the Pope about the next Marian Congress. I explained why I hoped that it could take place in Rome, in 1975, at the very heart

of the Marian Year, rather than in Spain or in Brazil. My wish was very much in line with what the Pope himself wanted, and he said he would be happy if this idea were adopted. He was a little concerned about the possibility of offending the Spanish, who were making grandiose preparations for 1976 in Saragossa; but at any rate, he seemed very grateful for my suggestion.

Next I mentioned the upcoming synod, and told him how much better it would be if he were to speak personally at the synod, expressing his opinions and giving us a chance to contradict him, as the most natural thing in the world. He replied: "I choose not to speak, precisely to give freedom to the Fathers."

We then discussed the theme of the next synod. Finally, I asked him: "Do you know the charismatic movement?" He told me he didn't, so I gave him a half-hour talk on the subject.

In conclusion, I said to the Holy Father: "Could you perhaps invite the charismatic prayer group which already exists in Rome, with the professors of the Gregorian University, to pray in your chapel, in your presence? You would not need to do anything except listen as they pray. It would be a very enlightening experience."

Encouraged by the friendly atmosphere of our talk, I went a step further: "Would you perhaps invite a priest of the Renewal to preach the Lenten retreat to the Roman Curia?" The Holy Father did not pursue any of these points, and we moved on to other matters.

Among other things, we discussed Bulgakov's rather heavy book on the Holy Spirit, which the Pope was then reading. I recommended Heribert Mühlen, a first-class theologian on this particular subject.

Charismatic renewal in the United States
The publication of a book I was writing, *The Holy Spirit — Source of all our Hopes,* had already been announced in *The Tablet;* then Veronica O'Brien called my attention to a prayer

group in New York, which described itself as a "Catholic pentecostal" group. The group met at Fordham University, a Jesuit
institution, and Veronica O'Brien had been with Margie Grace to
one of their meetings. Her reaction was: "I believe it is a 'Pentecostal' grace, but it must be separated from any kind of Pentecostalism."

I gave up writing the book; I thought it was a matter of the
most basic courtesy to pay attention to the possible action of the
Holy Spirit, however surprising it might be. I was especially interested in the talk of the awakening of charisms; at the Council, I
had pleaded the cause of such an awakening.

I established contacts with the larger Renewal groups. A first
meeting took place at a charismatic weekend at Convent Station;
this was directed by Jim Ferry, a priest of outstanding piety. He
had been the spiritual director of a Legion of Mary group, and
was now assisting a very dynamic group of "charismatic" women
religious. As I write these words, in 1989, Jim Ferry has just died,
leaving memories of a priest who was deeply rooted in the
Church and who believed strongly in the living presence of the
Holy Spirit in the present time*.

What I found at Convent Station was very convincing. This is
what I wrote in my notes at the time:

> Suddenly, St Paul and The Acts of the Apostles seem to
> come alive and become part of the present; what was
> authentically true in the past seems to be happening once
> again before our very eyes. It is a discovery of the true
> action of the Holy Spirit, who is always at work, as Jesus
> himself promised. He kept and keeps his "word". It is once
> more an explosion of the Spirit of Pentecost, a jubilation
> that had become foreign to the Church, for the sky is dark
> over the Church today. "Happy are those who know joy",
> says the Psalm.

---

*A biography of this priest, to be published by the University of Steubenville, is in prepara-
tion.

Memories and Hopes

I now decided to make contact with the principal initiators, starting in the university town of Ann Arbor, Michigan. I went at a time when a Presbyterian charismatic meeting, for which about three hundred members had come together, was taking place. They had been informed of my presence in town, and had invited me to come to the meeting. I was impressed by their faith and their evident piety, but I felt alien to their exuberant pentecostal style.

I spent more time with Catholic leaders — Ralph Martin, Steve Clark, and others. I discussed my impressions in an interview I gave at the time to Ralph Martin, founder and editor of a magazine called *New Covenant*.

I met male and female members of life communities who were living out the realities of their renewed Christianity with tremendous courage.

The Grottaferrata Congress

It had become a matter of urgency for Rome to give the Renewal movement the go-ahead, in order to avoid the possibility that it might develop in isolation, rather than at the heart of the Church. It was decided to convene a meeting of the leaders of this movement, which had already spread to every continent. The term "leaders" did not refer to duly elected and qualified representatives, but rather to those people who had in fact initiated and organised Renewal groups in their respective countries.

At the suggestion of Veronica O'Brien, it was decided to hold this Congress not in Puerto Rico (as had been originally planned, in view of the central location of the island), but rather in Grottaferrata, in the foothills of Rome, in the mother house of the Franciscan Sisters of Mary. The place had been chosen because, while it was very close to Rome, it would not directly involve the Holy See nor oblige it to take an official position — something the Holy Father might have considered premature.

I wrote to the Pope to inform him of these plans. In my letter I mentioned, as inconspicuously as possible, that I was planning to be there — without, however, formally requesting his authorisation; I thus gave him the option of not reacting. In Rome, the presence of a cardinal at a ceremony implies at least the implicit approval of the Holy See. As was to be expected, I received a letter from Mgr Benelli, requesting, on behalf of the Holy Father, that I should not attend the Congress.

Having received this negative response, I wrote to the Pope once again; this is the letter I sent him.

July 24, 1973

Most Holy Father:

I have received a letter from Mgr Benelli, in which he informs me that Your Holiness has requested that I should not attend private meetings arranged by the international leaders of the Charismatic Renewal in Grottaferrata next October.

Should you decide to confirm these orders, I shall of course abide by them — that is not in question. Before you do so, however, I would like to explain some aspects of this matter; in so doing, I hope to avoid the shock that your decision would cause, on an international level, to the leaders of the movement. They had hoped that I would be present among them to help them translate, on the spot, their desire for a profound communion with the Holy Father and with the Church. They chose to meet in Rome — rather than in Puerto Rico, as they had originally planned — partly at my insistence, and precisely with a view to promoting and strengthening this hierarchical communion.

The situation is precisely the following: here are men and women of absolute good will and total loyalty to the "institutional" Church — a rare thing these days! — humbly submitting to anything the hierarchy might ask of them, even to the point of being willing to disappear at the slightest sign – as is stated in a declaration made and acclaimed before twenty-five thousand people, a few days ago, in South Bend. I understand that Your Holiness may wish to avoid taking any position, at this early stage, with respect to this new movement; and that each local hierarchy should be free to take its own position as the movement grows, which it is doing at an extraordinary rate.

The American hierarchy, the first to be involved, has taken a cautious stand, but an open one; a bishop has been appointed to serve as liaison agent. However, even a "benevolent" attitude "from outside" cannot replace the need for a hierarchical or theological presence at the local level, "from within". Only by being among them can a priest guide them and help them in that discernment of spirits which is both delicate and essential.

Instead of remaining on the outskirts as an observer or a critical judge, the bishop must make sure that the flock is not left without a shepherd. Should the sheep stray for lack of a shepherd, we – and not the sheep – would be to blame. A policy of presence is vital – I would even say urgent – from the very outset, while it is still easy to provide those guidelines which the laity are anxious to receive. There is a temptation for local priests to remain uninvolved and simply to observe, with more or less benevolence, on the pretext that their bishops are also merely observing as they await instructions from Rome. This "wait-and-see" policy cannot last, and could in itself bring about errors due to faulty communication.

The central concern of the laity, at the moment, is to obtain basic orientations and solid rules, so as to avoid the possibility that this movement, which has started so well, should veer off course as it becomes universal. They are knocking at Rome's door in a spirit of filial obedience and of respect. They ask for no favours, except to be allowed to breathe freely and to help the Church in its spiritual renewal, which is the very purpose of the Holy Year. It is my opinion that they represent one of the most powerful graces of renewal in today's Church.

Having said this, I return to the matter of my presence in Rome in October. I had intended in any case to go to Rome in October, as I believe I wrote to you some time ago, in hopes of obtaining an audience to report on certain pastoral problems.

I can understand full well that if a cardinal were to preside over a public convention in Rome, this might raise problems, and might indeed be inappropriate. In the event, it is rather a matter of private meetings of a working nature, with no publicity and no official presidency – in my opinion, quite a different situation. At any rate, my specific request is the following: in order to avoid the possibility that the leaders should interpret my absence as a sign of distrust and of indirect condemnation, would Your Holiness object to my being in Rome – without attending the meetings in Grottaferrata, but privately meeting with some of the leaders in Rome itself, at the Christian Brothers', where I intend to stay?

> L.J. Cardinal Suenens,
> Archbishop of Malines-Brussels

The Pope's reaction was favourable. Mgr Benelli wrote to me, privately, that my letter concerning the charismatic movement had been very well received by the Holy Father, who had said to him:

> The Cardinal is very good to us; we must trust him. If he so wishes, let him invite his friends to the Brothers'; if he thinks it is appropriate, let him visit them in Grottaferrata, perhaps to celebrate the Eucharist.

Mgr Benelli added: "I shall write you an official letter on the subject." He specified, however:

> The "number two" [that is to say Cardinal Villot] had serious reservations on this matter. The Pope was also pleased with your letter concerning Edel [Quinn] [and her beatifi-

cation]. The request was greatly appreciated; there is, however, one obstacle: the rule according to which a procedure of this kind can only be initiated fifty years after the death of the person concerned. He instructed me to ask the relevant department whether it might not be possible to make an exception in this case.

With respect to the Renewal, a first bridge had been sucessfully crossed.

The first fruit of the meeting in Grottaferrata was a private audience with the Pope, granted – at my request – to about fifteen of the participants, including Fr de Monléon, OP, now Bishop of Pamiers. I had carefully avoided taking an active part as cardinal, in order not to implicate Rome in an approval that had not yet been granted.

On the morning of the audience, the Pope's entourage managed to have the audience cancelled, to make sure that the Pope would not commit himself. *In extremis*, I had to turn for help to my friend, Mgr Benelli.

The Pope welcomed the group very benevolently. The text he read was already, in itself, an encouragement; the improvised words that followed, and which I quoted in *A New Pentecost?*, were even more cordial.

A further fruit of the Congress was an initiative due to Veronica O'Brien, who proposed the establishment of a theological and pastoral commission to study necessary clarifications from a Catholic standpoint. The idea was adopted and implemented in May of the following year, by a team that met in the Archbishop's House in Malines to prepare the first orientation document.

South Bend

The Charismatic Renewal continued to grow throughout the world. A large national convention was held in Montreal in June 1973, and at the same time, an international congress took place

This was preceded by a day of theological reflection for priests + bishops of which the Cardinal was present + I gave a paper.

Active Service (1965-1980)

at South Bend, Indiana, in the United States. I attended both.

I would like to underline that, for me, the importance of the Congress in South Bend lay in the stand I felt compelled to take in order to situate the role of Mary in the Renewal. This was a sort of ecumenical crossroads, and I believe it marked an important turning-point in the history of the Renewal. I was accused of betraying ecumenism because I had spoken of Mary to a crowd of thirty thousand Catholics; the presence of a few non-Catholic guests should have been sufficient reason, some felt, to silence me on the subject of the Virgin Mary. This incident has countless implications; it invites us to reflect on the true meaning of an authentic ecumenism, which respects the identity of each faith.

* * *

I attended the first charismatic congress in the United States, invited by Fr H. Cohen, SJ, who to this day continues to play an important role in the Catholic orientation of Renewal.

I travelled to the US via London. I celebrated the Eucharist at the airport, and exchanged greetings with the Belgian Ambassador. I was offered a first class seat on my next plane by the flight captain, but I declined his offer because I did not want to be separated from my travelling companion, Canon Servotte.

When I arrived, I was completely exhausted, weakened by a bad cold, practically sleep-walking, and voiceless. Physically, the hours that followed were an excruciatingly painful experience; spiritually, they were a feast.

More than thirty thousand people had gathered at the stadium. The sight of so much harmony and spontaneity was spiritually exhilarating. When Fr Harold Cohen begged the absent bishops not to delay, to join their flocks and guide them, and when he proclaimed the loyalty of the participants to the Pope, the crowd rose for a long ovation.

"Lord, help us to hasten the reunification between the "institutional" Church and the "charismatic" Church" – this was my prayer. My presence there had no other purpose than to assist in hastening that hour.

I was the only cardinal at the Congress, but there were also about ten bishops present, as well as six hundred priests. It was a poignant moment when the procession of priests, in white albs, crossed the stadium, greeted by a long acclamation from the crowd — who in this way expressed their gratitude to their pastors for remaining faithful to the priestly vocation, which some had rediscovered through the Renewal. After the Gospel reading, I gave the homily, although I was not sure, when I started out, if I would be able to say more than two words, since I had practically lost my voice.

After a few hesitant words, aided by a microphone, I found that I was able to continue. I started out by saying that it seemed to me that the Lord was saying to me; "Tell them why you are there, why you love them, and what the Church and the world expect of them." I spoke for twenty minutes — "twenty minutes and a lifetime". Each word reached them, each sentence brought a reaction and a vibrant response. These were evidently words spoken "in the power of the Spirit", so great was the disproportion between the words I spoke and the response of the crowd. The talk was interrupted by laughter and applause at least ten times, maybe as many as fifteen times.

In conclusion, I said to them, "And now, if you like, I will tell you a secret which will help you to welcome the Holy Spirit: it has a name; it is union with Mary." At these words, the crowd stood up and gave Mary a long and fervent ovation.

A visit from Archbishop Ramsey

While I was deeply involved in the evolution of the Renewal Movement in the United States, my ecumenical meetings with Archbishop Ramsey, head of the Anglican Church, continued.

Our first meeting was in 1963, in Malines. I remember it well. On that occasion, I had suggested to him that before starting our discussion, we should open the Bible to ask the Lord for a word to guide us. I happened upon a passage about the apostles, when Jesus appeared among them after the Resurrection. Together, we read the following lines: "Suddenly, while the doors were still locked, the Lord stood among them and said to them: 'Peace be with you'" (John 20:26). Archbishop Ramsey saw in this, as did I, an invitation to continue the dialogue that had begun under my predecessor, Cardinal Mercier. The doors were still locked, but a window was beginning to open.

I remember asking Ramsey the following question: "Do you feel closer to Rome than to the Orthodox Church?" He replied: "Ten years ago, I would have answered that I felt closer to the Orthodox. Today, I feel closer to Rome. I say this with some surprise, and somewhat regretfully," he added, laughing. "Since Vatican II, Rome is closer to me; the Orthodox world is too conservative. In the past, I felt very close to the Orthodox because of their concern for spirituality; their development, however, is far too slow."

Clearly, the wind of Pentecost had been blowing beyond our own walls as well. The visit was brief, but very friendly.

Ecumenical meetings in Bristol and in Exeter

I was invited to an ecumenical conference in Bristol. On the programme was an early morning ecumenical prayer meeting, in a small church that had traditionally been a Baptist church. The event was to be broadcast on national television in the UK, and every detail of the ceremony had been rigorously timed. It was agreed that my homily would last no more than fifteen minutes – not one second longer. To be on the safe side, I had asked someone at the back of the church to signal to me when my time was up. Due to a misunderstanding, the person in question was not at the appointed place in the church, and I ended up speaking for twenty minutes! As a result, the end of the ceremony could not be broadcast, for lack of time.

The Anglican newspaper, *Church Times*, described my homily as "superbly simple"; I found this very encouraging.

Archbishop Ramsey and I were both scheduled to speak that afternoon. Our messages, each in its own style, converged; the dialogue between us was relaxed and friendly. In the evening, we continued the same dialogue on national television.

The next day, I attended a meeting of Catholic priests in Exeter. I had been invited by the presbyterial council, from which the initiative for the meeting had originated. Having made an absolute rule for myself never to accept an invitation without prior agreement from the local bishop, I checked with the secretary of the council, who assured me that the bishop had agreed, but had expressed some reservations concerning my orthodoxy! Luckily, he watched my exchange with Ramsey on television; this reassured him, and he gave me a very warm welcome.

Later, one of the priests at the Exeter meeting wrote me a letter, saying: "Our bishop is enthusiastic... which is really quite out of character." If the kind bishop is still alive and reads these lines, I thank him once more for his fraternal welcome!

1974

The First Malines Document: **Charismatic Renewal***

In response to a request made in Grottaferrata, I set up an international group, whose task it was to give theological credibility to the Charismatic Renewal Movement, and to clarify certain points in order to avoid confusion and misunderstanding. This was necessary because the Movement was meeting with serious opposition, both in the United States and within the Roman Curia and its entourage.

---

*Published in French by *Lumen Vitae*, Brussels, and in English by Ann Arbor Press, Michigan.

This theological and pastoral commission met in my residence in Malines from May 21 to 26, 1974. The commission included the following:

- from the US – Fr Kilian McDonnell, OSB, and Kevin Ranaghan;
- from Chili – Fr Aldunate, SJ;
- from France – Fr de Monléon, OP (today, Bishop of Paniers);
- from Ireland – Veronica O'Brien;
- from Germany – Professor Heribert Mühlen of Paderborn;
- from Mexico – Fr Carrillo.

The document they prepared was sent to a few theologians, who were asked to give their comments; these included Congar, Ratzinger, Rahner and Küng.

Fr Lebeau, SJ, was the secretary of the working group.

Fr Kilian McDonnell, director of the Collegeville Ecumenical Institute in the United States, did the actual drafting of the document. He later published three large volumes, *Presence, Power,*and *Praise!,** containing all the official statements of various Christian Churches concerning the Renewal.

My role involved chairing the meetings, and assuming the consequences of acceptance or rejection from Rome.

Pope Paul welcomed the document. Some time later, he showed it to me, lying on his desk, and commented, "This is precisely the sort of study that is needed. Please continue to provide us with similar reports, which serve the Renewal."

The second Malines Document: Ecumenism and Charismatic Renewal

Document No. 2 was intended for members of the Renewal; its purpose was to clarify the meaning of ecumenism, which must be lived, in Catholic groups, from a position of respect for their own

---

*Published by The Liturgical Press, Collegeville, Minnesota. This includes Malines Documents Nos. 1 to 4.

identity. They must avoid the sort of ecumenism that belittles them; and on a positive level, they must propose a strengthening, together, of the celebration of Pentecost. This was published in French by *Le Centurion, 1978.*

The third Malines Document: **Charismatic Renewal and Social Action**

This document was a response to some of the criticism which Christians involved in social service had voiced against the Renewal. They feared that the Renewal might turn Christians away from their responsibilities with regard to human problems. I wrote this document together with my friend Dom Helder Câmara, whose credentials as a social activist are impeccable! (published by *Lumen Vitae, 1979*).

The fourth Malines Document: **Renewal and the Powers of Darkness**

This was a reminder that, alas, the powers of evil are no myth; this does not mean, however, that we must freely engage in wild exorcisms, with direct challenges to demons. The preface was written by Cardinal Ratzinger (published by *Cahiers du Renouveau,* 1982).

The fifth Malines Document: **Nature and Grace in Vital Unity**

The title of the English edition had broader connotations than did the French: *Le culte du moi et foi chrétienne.* It was written as a reaction against an overdose of introspection, which can be very harmful to full supernatural development, and which is often flawed with naturalism (published by *Les Editions Desclée,* 1985).

The sixth Malines Document: **Resting in the Spirit**

A Controversial Phenomenon — *Resting in the Spirit* called upon the reader not to look upon this phenomenon as a new charism for our day, and counselled caution. I stressed the ambiguity of all corporeal manifestations in general, and emphasised the discreet action of the Holy Spirit; I called attention to natural forces which have yet to be explored, or are only now being explored (Les Editions Desclée, 1986; Veritas Publications, 1987).

As a whole, these documents were meant to support the Renewal in its vital renovating thrust, while at the same time winnowing the inevitable chaff. For me, this was one way of living out concretely what is asked of every bishop at the time of his consecration:*"Ut evellat et destruat ut aedificet et plantet"* ("That he may discard and destroy in order better to build and plant").

It is painful for me to realise that there continue to be ambiguities in all of these areas. It gives me joy to know that I am not everywhere "a voice crying in the desert", and to have received from Pope Paul, shortly before his death, a moving and friendly letter expressing gratitude for my efforts.

Meanwhile, I kept the Pope informed about all that was happening in the United States.

A New Pentecost?

My next task was to write a book introducing the Renewal to a wider public. My commitment to this project was similar, in many ways, to the commitment I had felt earlier, in writing the *Theology of the Legion of Mary*. It was a duty to which I felt conscience-bound — to make known the powerful action of the Holy Spirit, at work before our very eyes.

René Laurentin reviewed the book for *Le Figaro*, and summarised its central idea as follows: "The author wants to show us that the breath of the Holy Spirit is active today in very broadly-based groups, creating and offering a 'democracy of holiness'." This is exactly my point. What I actually said was that the Council had not proposed the democratisation of the Church, but rather the democratisation of that holiness which is inherent in baptism.

The question mark in the title was important to me. I felt that the Renewal ran the risk of not being recognised for what it was: an act of the Holy Spirit, available to all movements, and capable of renewing many aspects of the Church. It was an anguished call to those in power within the Church to accept this challenge, rather than reducing the Renewal to one movement among many others. The book was, in my eyes, something like a message in a bottle, tossed out to sea.

It is not a book I can summarise here; instead, I will reproduce a review which I found particularly perceptive. It was written by Fr Lebeau, SJ, who, on a number of occasions, was my private theologian at ecumenical meetings in America, England and Switzerland. He understood both my words and the thinking behind them very well. Here is the full text of his review:

> Cardinal Suenens' new book — his thirteenth — is not easy to label. Doctrinal teaching; pastoral suggestions; reflections on the state of the Church; discernment of the signs of the times; personal witness; guidelines for prayer — they are all there, in the lively style of the Archbishop of Malines-Brussels, punctuated by the striking phrases and poetic touches which by now are familar to those who have read his books or heard him speak.
>
> Yet, in the end, what makes the strongest impact on our hearts and on our souls is the live witness. It is true that in this witnessing, what is personal and what is ecclesial are closely interwoven. Here we see a man who has been marked to his very core by the charism of his ministry, opening himself to the reader with a new abandon. In other words, here is a bishop "sharing in solicitude for all the churches" (Vatican II, *Christus Dominus*, 1), and intent on not avoiding this collegial responsibility. After being one of the main craftsmen of the great work of Vatican II, L.J. Suenens, like many of his brothers, found himself at the heart of the turmoil and confusion of the post-Council period — that "dark night of hope", which, for a pastor and

guardian of communion, was "a long and painful Calvary". Today, however, he sees the early signs of what he believes could be (for a question mark tempers the boldness of his statements) "a new Pentecost" such as John XXIII had prayed for for the Church.

Cardinal Suenens discerns these signs as an attentive witness − indeed, a contemplative witness − of the life of the Church, both in its enduring tradition and in its living actuality. As in earlier renewals, these signs originate in the rediscovery of the charismatic nature of the Church, about which the author once made a crucial statement to the Council. Since then, Paul VI has many times underlined, in his teachings, the fundamental significance of this aspect of the nature of the Church (chapter 1). These charisms produce and determine all that allows the Church to be what she is and to become more fully herself. The author defines them, in the light of Scripture and of Tradition, in these terms: "gifts of the Spirit recognisable by their visible presence, and by their common goal within the community − to build anew the Kingdom of God". He reminds us of their fruitfulness and of their power for renewal throughout history, from the earliest days of the Church (chapter 2). The liturgical renewal inaugurated at the Council witnesses and attests in many ways to this permanent presence and this tangibility of the Holy Spirit (chapter 3). This leads to the experience that is essential to Christianity − that of "the immediacy of God at the heart of man and of history".

The author points out that, as Jean Mouroux also noted, this lived experience corresponds to one of the most typical aspirations of contemporary consciousness, which, in this respect, echoes that of biblical believers: "For the children of Israel, to know God was to experience God." "The Hebrew does not occupy himself much with what is, but with what happens, and with what he concretely experiences." (quoted from W. Kasper). In the Christian economy, the objectification of the salvific experience into a dogmatic "argumentation", signifying the ecclesial communion of faith, has meaning only through constant reference to this experience.

"The doctrinal teaching which enunciates truths regarding Christ is first of all rooted in the experience of meeting him. The same applies to truths regarding the Holy Spirit." The abusive emphasis on the experiential, in the context of illuminisms of various sorts, does not authorise us to minimise "the role of religious experience at the heart of authentic Christianity". The decisive hours in the history of the Church, and in the history of every Christian, are determined by the experience of a God who lets himself be known, touched, and tasted, even in his silence, by the communion of his Spirit (chapter 4).

"The fact, however, that we recognise this universal presence of the Spirit, should not prevent us from discerning, analysing, and reflecting upon a special and privileged presence where he manifests himself in a particular way." The author recognises, today, such a privileged presence, in the "Charismatic Renewal", which has manifested itself within most branches of the Christian faith – and, since 1967, within the Catholic Church itself – as a rich and promising spiritual event. After presenting its signs, and the words of witnesses, in chapter 5, the author goes on to analyse the significance and the scope of the Renewal in chapter 6.

"Presence and discernment" – in these words Cardinal Suenens summarises the attitude which he adopted, from the very beginning, in the face of this event. A Council document defines the episcopal charism as "the charism of discerning charisms". This is not really an adequate definition; according to the Archbishop of Malines-Brussels, it is rather "a call to assume our responsibilities in the service of the Church, and not shirk them". As other pastors (beginning with Pope Paul VI himself, whose words – from a speech made in 1973 to a group of leaders who had come to Rome from various continents – the author quotes here) have done and are still doing, he gives us a theological and pastoral evaluation of the symptoms of

Christian vitality and spiritual renewal which have characterised the Charismatic Renewal, and which in many cases
he has verified personally: Christocentricity; a deepening of
prayer life, both on a personal and on a communal level (of
particular interest are the pages concerning an anthropo-
logical and theological interpretation of glossolalia, or
"praying and speaking in tongues"); an increased love of
the Scriptures; a sense of the Church.

Perhaps by temperament — but no doubt also by virtue
of a healthy theology — the author, like St Irenaeus, is
mainly sensitive, in this evaluation, to the continuity and
the coherence of divine action in the history of salvation.
He warns the reader against the temptation to believe that
"God is doing something absolutely new, unheard of
before, and reserved for our times". He stresses also that
this is in no way "an exclusive manifestation that replaces
everything else". Chapter 8, entitled "The Holy Spirit and
New Communities", goes well beyond the description and
analysis of those Christian life communities born from the
Charismatic Renewal. There is, in particular, a positive and
careful analysis of the communal experience of the "Foco-
larini" and of "Marriage Encounter". None the less, the
Charismatic Renewal holds for the author a privileged
ecclesial significance; in his view, this is not "just a movement to set alongside other movements", but rather "a
breath of grace that passes, and carries to a higher level of
conscious tension, the charismatic dimension inherent in
the Church". The dynamic of the Renewal is by nature one
that leads it to fade away as a distinct movement, "like the
waters of a river which loses its name as it reaches the
ocean".

The Holy Spirit, in bringing about, at the heart of the
Church, this renewal of hope, of freedom and of fraternal
communion, leads Christians today to find their true place
in the world, in relation both to its affinities with the Kingdom and to its incompatibilities (chapter 9). "Known or
unknown, he is at work in every effort that tends toward
more light, more sincerity, greater closeness among men."

He is the power of communion and of reconciliation; he leads us to "integrate prayer and politics, prayer and social behaviour, prayer and justice, prayer and peace". Like Jesus, whom Luke shows us "going towards men, moved by the Spirit" (Luke 4:1), we are called by the Spirit to be "fully present to human distress and to the building up of the world".

Those who have met Cardinal Suenens, even briefly, know of his passionate interest for all that concerns ecumenism, as well as his sense of the Marian mystery. Two further chapters clearly describe the impact of Charismatic Renewal on these two areas, which are central to the life of the Church.

In the final chapter, "The Holy Spirit, my Hope", his witness takes on a personal character. With a sobriety that increases its value, we are given an invitation to enter the inner world of the bishop, of the Christian, of the man; to learn about his questionings and his discoveries. And we give thanks for this invitation, for this availability, for this fraternal abandon.

Fr Lebeau, SJ

A surprise from Pope Paul

During the Bishops' Synod, Pope Paul would regularly leave us, on Wednesday mornings, for his usual public audience with pilgrims. On one of these occasions, he spoke to the pilgrims of signs of hope in the Church, and mentioned the importance of charisms today. Suddenly, setting aside his prepared text, he showed them a copy of my book and said, "I am alluding to a book recently written by Cardinal Suenens — *A New Pentecost?* — in which the Cardinal describes and justifies expectations of a Renewal. The abundant outpouring of those supernatural graces which we call charisms can indeed be the sign of a providential hour in the history of the Church."

The following morning, before resuming the presidency of the Bishops' Synod, he called me and said "I must apologise for being so brief yesterday at the public audience; I should have said much more." I replied, with heartfelt gratitude for his friendly gesture, that "to have one's book personally and publicly endorsed by the Pope is indeed a rare event, and a great surprise!"

"Fervent and unanimous prayer" around the Synod

Inspired by the primitive Church, by the early Christians "in communion of prayer with the apostles", Veronica O'Brien proposed that members of the Charismatic Renewal might assume a similar task. She suggested to the leaders that they should send a few members of the movement to Rome, to live the Synod with the Bishops, in communion of prayer with them and for them.

On her own initiative, and with financial support from Margie Grace, she invited a few Renewal members from each continent to Rome. Their programme included daily Mass together, prayer meetings — spontaneous and liturgical — frequent contacts with various bishops outside the assembly hall, and, in the evenings, a prayer meeting and a briefing with cardinals, bishops and visiting personalities. During each of the Synods, about twenty members of the movement came to Rome for this purpose; they were divided into two language groups (French and English), which alternated at two-week intervals.

I gave a few talks to these groups. Among the more assiduous participants was the humble and dynamic Padre Arrupe, Superior General of the Jesuits, in whose generalate, in Borgo Santo Spirito, the meetings were held.

Pope Paul was aware of this initiative, and asked me to thank the members of the Renewal; at each Synod, he sent them a gift as a memento of the occasion. The tradition still continues; and today, John Paul II invites these international groups to his private Mass, which gives him the opportunity for some direct contact with them.

Donald Coggan is installed as 101st Archbishop of Canterbury
Those invited to the Archbishop's installation were to meet at Victoria Station, in London, where an entire train had been reserved for their journey. I travelled with Cardinal Marty and with the Archbishop of Utrecht, of the Old Catholic Church.

When we arrived in Canterbury, we were met by coaches, which took us to the Cathedral. Here we were all meticulously searched by the police; even our suitcases, which contained liturgical vestments, were opened, and their contents examined.

In some ways, the ceremony resembled a royal wedding; it was broadcast in colour on television. As I walked past one of the cameras, an English cameraman whispered in my ear: "Thank you for providing the colours."

It was a flawless procession; everyone was very stiff and dignified. A few wigs were scattered here and there. You could tell that all the participants were very conscious of their rank, of the quasi-feudal privilege that assured them a particular place in the procession. An Anglican bishop — Allin, a friend, President of the Episcopal Conference of the United States — greeted me with a big smile.

I shared a stall in the choir with Cardinals Willebrands and Marty. The music was magnificent. The sermon's leitmotif was realism and confidence. A curious allusion was made to Pope John XXIII, in relation to General Booth of the Salvation Army.

The ceremony culminated with the installation of the new Archbishop to the See of St Augustine of Canterbury.

Later, Archbishop Coggan sent someone to find me in the crowd of guests. With great cordiality, he invited me to give a speech at the Nicean Club, in London, in honour of his fiftieth birthday.

Finally, there was time for conversation with the guests — people from every corner of the world.

In the coach, on the first leg of the return journey to London, I sat with the Secretary of the British Council of Churches, a Methodist and a man of extraordinary depth and spirituality. In my notebook, I wrote "A man worth watching". On the train, my travelling companion was Satterthwaite, the Anglican Bishop for Europe.

We arrived in London at 7:15 p.m. I barely had time to catch my breath at the Belgian Embassy; at 8 p.m., I joined the Nicean Club and their other foreign guests at a hotel, for a reception in honour of the Archbishop. I happened to be seated with Archbishop Runcie, Bishop of St Alban's; Philip Potter, Secretary of the World Council of Churches; and the Archbishop of the Orthodox Church of Ethiopia, who was distinctly anti-papal, and quite certain that he was in full possession of the truth. As for Dr Runcie, I was struck by his openness; it was a great contrast to the simplistic attitudes of the Ethiopian Archbishop.

When the time came for toasts, a Finnish bishop said a few words, as icy as the snows of his land. Others spoke as well, but there was little fire in what they said. All were exhausted and in a hurry to get home; for me, "home" was the Belgian Embassy, where I was welcomed warmly by Ambassador Rothschild. At dinner, I met the British Minister for Prices and Consumer Protection, who is a Catholic. I felt very much at home.

Ecumenical meetings in Texas
My friendship with Doctor Outler, Dean of the South Methodist University in Dallas, dated back to the Council, and continued beyond it. He was particularly open to ecumenical dialogue. I had the opportunity to meet him on his own home ground, in Dallas.

As a result of my brief visit to Texas, I was made an honorary citizen by official decree. In the course of a ceremony, this parchment was handed to me by the civil authorities. The ceremony was followed by a luncheon; I remember the occasion with some amusement because of a minor incident which occurred during the meal. I suddenly noticed that someone had surreptitiously made off with my hat. I mentioned this to the person sitting next to me, in the hope that he would stop the thief and salvage my hat — but I could elicit no answer, no reaction whatsoever. I repeated my request, but his indifference was so total that, rather than provoke a scandal, I simply gave up all hope of ever seeing my hat again.

The key to this mystery was provided at the end of the banquet. One of the organisers had borrowed my hat and taken it to the local hatter; he wanted to buy me a Texan hat, and he needed my own hat to be sure of the size. Thus I got my old hat back along with a Texan hat, of the kind made famous throughout the world by cowboy movies, and to which I, as an honorary citizen of Texas, was fully entitled.

I have excellent memories of the ecumenical aspects of my visit. Albert Outler had invited me to deliver the Perkins Lectures at the First United Methodist Church in Wichita Falls. We had chosen the theme for the lectures together: "Can I experience God?" Outler had personally written the introductory leaflet, which mentioned Vatican II. The paragraph that served to introduce me ended on a very Methodist note: it announced that I had come "to preach what John Wesley called 'a religion of the heart'".

The meeting with the Methodist audience took place in a delightful atmosphere. There was definitely some concern, at the outset, about this encounter with a Catholic bishop — and a cardinal to boot. This was the first time they had ever invited a non-Protestant speaker.

Their fear melted like snow in the sun. At the end of each talk, many members of the audience came to shake hands with me and to say a few kind and charming words; someone asked me: "May I kiss you and receive your blessing?" One Episcopalian minister even asked me, there and then, "How can I become a Catholic?"

Question-and-answer sessions took place on two different evenings. I believe that they dispelled a great many doubts concerning the Charismatic Renewal and the Catholic Church. The local Catholic parish priest later wrote me a letter that filled me with joy.

The eve of Pentecost

As 1975 had been proclaimed a Holy Year, Rome was chosen as the venue for the Marian Congress. On the eve of Pentecost, I had to — simultaneously — preside over the Marian Congress; welcome ten thousand pilgrims of the Charismatic Renewal, who were arriving in Rome to celebrate the Holy Year; and be at the airport with the Vatican authorities to welcome King Baudouin and Queen Fabiola, who were coming to Rome as Holy Year pilgrims. For once in my life, I would very much have liked to have the gift of trilocation!

The Pope came to the Marian Congress in person. A public letter — which he addressed to me, in my capacity as President of the Congress — was published in the *Osservatore Romano*; it is an important document concerning the role of Mary in the mystery of salvation.

At the Congress, I met Cardinal Ottaviani and a few other Roman theologians, from whom I had somewhat distanced myself during the Council; the climate, among all of us, was now extremely cordial.

Rome — Pentecost 1975

Pentecost of 1975, which the pilgrims of the Charismatic Renewal celebrated in Rome, marked a historic turning-point for the Movement; for it was on this occasion that the Renewal was fully received into the Church.

The leaders of the Movement deliberately decided to gather in Rome so as to indicate their explicit desire to be vitally inserted into the Church, and to proclaim that there are not two Churches — the one institutional and the other charismatic — but only one

289

Church of God, whose various aspects are inseparable and complementary. During one of the sessions, Cardinal Willebrands spoke on the theme "The Holy Spirit and the Church"; captivated increasingly by the atmosphere of piety, equilibrium and joy, he was able to find the right words, giving encouragement while stressing the need for discernment.

The strongest moments of the charismatic pilgrimage included the Pontifical Mass of Pentecost, which was celebrated by the Pope, in St Peter's, in the presence of a crowd of about twenty-five thousand, of whom ten thousand were pilgrims of the Charismatic Renewal. We lived unforgettable moments of fraternal communion with all those present. I shall never forget what one newspaper referred to as the "musical joust" between the Sistine Chapel choir and the spontaneous chants of the pilgrims of the Charismatic Renewal. In the silence that followed the consecration, they raised their voices in a song of great and delicate beauty; in a moment, it filled the Basilica and then softly ebbed away, like a wave which dies gently on the beach.

On the following day, the Monday after Pentecost, I had the joy of celebrating the Eucharist at the papal altar, in front of the confessio of St Peter, surrounded by about eight hundred priests in white albs and a dozen bishops. Another five thousand passing pilgrims had joined the original group. The procession of priests and bishops, arms raised in prayer, made its way towards the altar along the central nave, as the crowd chanted a seemingly endless flow of Alleluias. The eucharistic celebration proceeded in a climate of extraordinary symbiosis between traditional liturgy and spontaneous prayer.

We all felt that nothing could have been more natural than for the people of God to sing their jubilation. The prayerful and radiant crowd translated into action the words of the pontifical exhortation on "Joy in the Holy Spirit", which had just been proclaimed to the world. The Pope was to receive us in special audience — something we were all looking forward to particularly. In preparation for the arrival of the Holy Father, the crowd continued to alternate prayers and chants.

When the Pope appeared, he was greeted by wave upon wave of Alleluias. He gave a very important speech – in French, in English, and in Spanish – and then, very relaxed, improvised in Italian. He told us that the Church welcomes the Charismatic Renewal; he called it "an opportunity that the Church must ✓ seize". To help the Movement in its future development, he gave his own guidelines for discernment, alluding to the ones St Paul gave to the Corinthians. This statement was to become the basic charter of the Charismatic Renewal.

I felt that we were living a privileged moment of grace for the Church as a whole and for each one of us individually. Only the future can tell what its scope will be, but even then its richness could be felt; the Lord was there, very near to his own.

It is up to us to grasp this passing grace by making ourselves open to the breath of the Spirit with humility and faithfulness. God is still alive today! Alleluia!

At the foot of the altar, the Pope embraced me with profound emotion, and made a gesture, pointing to me as if to designate me his representative to the pilgrims of the Charismatic Renewal. He thanked me, quietly, in these words: "I thank you – not in my own name, but in the name of the Lord – for all that you have done ,and all that you will still do, to bring the Charismatic Renewal into the heart of the Church."

Pentecost of 1975 is also an important date in the history of the Charismatic Renewal because of the seeds of ecumenical hope which it contained. This was clearly brought out in an article written by Sr Jeanne d'Arc, which was published in *Vie spirituelle* in July 1975:

> The embrace which Pope Paul gave Léon Joseph Suenens had as much significance as the one he gave Athénagoras some years ago – perhaps even more. The embrace to Jerusalem was the first fruit of an ardently desired union; yet, this union of the Churches can only come about if the

Church is wholly open to the Spirit. Communion cannot take place simply by means of an agreement between hierarchies, in the manner of a diplomatic treaty. It can only happen through the action of the Spirit.

Obviously, this group of "charismatics" does not have a monopoly on the Spirit — who, like the wind, blows wherever he pleases. If this group had not been welcomed and recognised, however, the consequences for the Catholic Church, and for ecumenism, would have been very serious indeed. What happened in Rome on Pentecost is a sign and a promise. It is also a message, a call to spiritual combat: armed with the Spirit, we are called to stand up against the forces of disintegration.

On the official level, the Monday after Pentecost 1975 will be remembered as the date on which the Church fully welcomed the Renewal. On a more private level, an important meeting took place, the following day, at a side altar in St Peter's; I and a few of my closest collaborators met with two American leaders, Ralph Martin and Steve Clark, whom I had invited to come and pray with us for the future. I now asked them to move to Brussels, where we would have the opportunity to study at ease the full integration of the Renewal into the heart of the Church. They accepted my suggestion; as a result, they came to live in Brussels for several years.

A letter of thanks to Paul VI

Malines, June 4, 1975

Most Holy Father,
In order better to express my profound gratitude for the days of Pentecost which we recently shared in Rome, I

chose to wait for a moment of calm and clarity before writing to you.

I now turn to you, with profound emotion, to thank you from the depths of my heart — both for the personal welcome which you gave me, and for the words of encouragement which Your Holiness had the kindness to speak to me "on behalf of Our Lord". Later, I found an echo and a continuation of these words in what your Holiness said to me, at the foot of the altar in St Peter's Basilica, at the end of your moving speech to the ten thousand participants in the meeting of the Charismatic Renewal — a speech that has reached deep into the hearts of those present.

Your Holiness must know that I take to heart the mission with which you have entrusted me: to integrate further the Charismatic Renewal into the Church, into the very heart of the Church. I believe that everyone has felt and understood the importance and the significance, for the Charismatic Renewal, of the paternal welcome of the successor of Peter to this renewing breath of the Spirit — a breath that can only renew if it comes from within the Church and is carried and sustained by her.

The "opportunity offered by the Charismatic Renewal", which Your Holiness spoke of, is for everyone a call to greater responsibility, so that the Spirit may find us receptive to his inspirations in fidelity to his Church.

The six lay leaders whom I introduced to you, and who represent various continents, were very moved and grateful for your words. I truly believe in their total desire for full adhesion to the Church, to the Head of the Church, and to the bishops. The presence of Veronica O'Brien — who was the inspiration and the soul of this charismatic pilgrimage *"ad limina Petri et Pauli"* — among these leaders is a further guarantee that the Marian aspect will receive an ever-growing attention, to the extent that this will depend on us. The union of the Holy Spirit with Mary is so completely at the heart of the Incarnation that it is impossible to divide "what God has united".

Thank you also, once again from the depths of my heart,

for the magisterial letter which Your Holiness addressed to me as President of the Marian Congress; it too, I hope, will be a charter for the Charismatic Renewal, and for all Christians, who must "receive Mary without fear". With respect to the immediate future, I can see the need for doctrinal and spiritual clarification along the lines of the Malines Document on Charismatic Renewal and of the "pastoral suggestions" which I sent to you last April. In particular, it will be important to situate the Charismatic Renewal, with respect to ecumenism, so as to remain faithful both to the call for visible unity among Christians and to the demands of our own Catholic authenticity. We shall continue our efforts in this direction, in Malines, with a team of theologians who belong to the Charismatic Renewal, and who, for this reason, ally theological science with the kind of lived spiritual experience which is essential to verify the theology itself and to understand the workings of the Spirit. I will take the liberty of keeping Your Holiness informed of the progress of our work, and of the contacts we establish; your trust reinforces my awareness of the responsibility which I carry as a result of the spiritual mission that has been entrusted to me within the worldwide Charismatic Renewal.

On the evening of the Monday of Pentecost, at a reception at the Hotel Columbus, I was surrounded by a dozen Protestant charismatic leaders; they were on their way to Venice, to continue their ecumenical dialogue with members of the Secretariat for Christian Unity. One of them said, speaking for all: "Pope John opened a window; Pope Paul has just opened a door". They were overwhelmed by the way in which the Catholic Church welcomed the Spirit; they looked back, with nostalgia, to the days of the Reformation and of the breakaway. We prayed together for a while in the garden of the hotel, and they prayed spontaneously and at length – I am almost tempted to say with filial piety – for Your Holiness.

It is my hope that these days of Pentecost have been days of spiritual fulness and joy for Your Holiness, as they have been for us. Thank you also for the magnificent apostolic exhortation on the joy of the Holy Spirit; its words are still echoing in our hearts.

With affectionate respect, Most Holy Father, in the union of our hope,

L.J. Cardinal Suenens,
Archbishop of Malines-Brussels

More ecumenical meetings in the United States
On my travel schedule for that summer, I find Philadelphia, Minneapolis, Ann Arbor, Collegeville and Steubenville.

At the World Eucharistic Congress in Philadelphia, I met Bishop Allin, President of the Episcopalian Church; he is a good friend of mine and has visited me in Malines. At the Congress, I presided over the Day for Priests and Religious, where I spoke on the theme "The Eucharist and the Epiclesis of the Holy Spirit".

On the evening of August 5, an unforgettable "charismatic" Mass was celebrated in the stadium, in the presence of four cardinals, fifty bishops, five hundred priests and about forty thousand faithful. Here, the Renewal was truly at the very heart of the liturgy and of the Church.

One evening, in the context of the Congress, a panel discussion, on American television, brought together Mother Teresa of Calcutta, Cardinal Pignedoli, and Dom Helder Câmara, with a journalist. I heard the story from Dom Helder. He told me that the journalist began by praising Mother Teresa; then, by way of contrast, he embarked on a diatribe against the Pope, the bishops, the Catholic Church, and the riches of the Vatican. Mother Teresa interrupted him to say quietly, "You seem very tense; you need more calm, more inner peace."

His aggressive outburst cut short, the journalist retorted: "Inner peace? Where do you expect me to find that?"

"Inner peace is a grace of God," she replied; "you must ask him for it, and pray for it."

"I don't know how to pray."

"Then we shall pray for you, and we shall ask God for this grace."

She then took Cardinal Pignedoli's hand in one of hers, and Helder Câmara's in the other, and began to pray for the bewildered journalist.

* * *

From Philadelphia I went to Ann Arbor, where I met with the Bishop to discuss charismatic renewal and some of the questions it raises. In the evening, there was a huge meeting at the high school — a send-off for Ralph Martin and his wife and children, who were moving to Brussels so that we could study together and in detail the full insertion of the Renewal into the Church. The assembled people prayed over them. Among the foreign visitors whom I met there was Pierre Goursat, who later founded the Emmanuel Community.

In Collegeville, I visited the Benedictine community; I was greatly impressed by the large number of monks, and by their activities. Small lateral chapels, with more than thirty altars, had just been completed. Meanwhile, in Rome, the Council had voted to allow concelebration. What a change of perspective!

My last stop was in Steubenville. Here, there was a congress of about seven hundred women religious who were meeting with Michael Scanlan. I celebrated the eucharistic liturgy beneath an immense canopy, in a relaxed, prayerful and charismatic atmosphere. In my homily, I told them that if I were to rewrite *The Nun in the World*, I would be more precise; to avoid all misunderstandings, I would specify "The Holy Spirit in the nun, and the nun in the world".

My friend and travelling companion, university professor Jan Van der Veken, gave a charming little speech; he commented on a text by Saint Paul on widows, which he transposed and applied to women religious, to the great amusement of all present.

An oversight and a luncheon

During one of my visits to the United States, I opened the paper one morning only to discover that I was expected to give a lecture, on the following day, in a Jesuit college not far from New York, on the occasion of some event or other. Since no one had mentioned this to me, I asked someone to telephone the college, ask for information, and express the presumed lecturer's puzzlement and concern.

The mystery was soon solved: Cardinal Cushing (the Archbishop of Boston, who, at the Council, had offered to pay all the expenses involved in setting up simultaneous interpretation), had promised that I would give this lecture, and had arranged the day and the time; he told the organisers that he would ask me personally, and that they could count on me. He forgot one minor detail, however − he neglected to tell me about it!

I immediately rang him up, and he exclaimed "Oh, I had forgotten all about it! But please don't let me down; I'm depending on you!" And so the lecture took place at the appointed time − 11 a.m. the following morning.

This, however, raised another problem: at 1 p.m. I was to have lunch, in New York, with the editors of *Life*. Once again, I was able fully to appreciate American efficiency. At the end of my talk, I was met by two police officers on motorcycles; in their wake, my car crossed New York City at high speed, preceded by their screaming sirens, and ignoring traffic lights. I arrived at my destination in time for my appointment.

There, about fifteen journalists bombarded me with questions on Vatican II and the Church of yesterday and of tomorrow. I have seldom met reporters who were so professional and so well-prepared. As I was leaving, I gave the director a copy of one of my books, in which I wrote the following words: "In memory of a meal during which we solved all of the world's problems". A few days later I received a note from him, in which he said: "Thank you for the meeting during which we solved all of the world's problems. Problems have a way of not staying solved, unfortunately; and so we hope to see you again."

Cardinal Cushing was famous for the kindness of his heart, his generosity, and his honesty. Speaking of him reminds me of a lecture he once asked me to give to his clergy. He was presiding over the meeting, and was expected to say a few words to introduce me. He had been forewarned that I had to catch a plane as soon as the meeting was over; but his introduction was so lengthy that several notes had to be slipped to him, reminding him that my plane would not wait for me. At last, I was able to give a lightning-quick speech, and I just managed to catch my flight.

My memories of him bring a smile to my lips and a warm feeling to my heart. I look forward to meeting him in Heaven.

Italy

In response to an invitation from Mgr Delmonte, I travelled by plane to Milan, then by car to Novara; Delmonte, who was Bishop of Novara, had asked me to speak about the Charismatic Renewal — first to the people, and then, at a more intimate dinner, to a few of his collaborators. The atmosphere was such that our meal ended with a spontaneous prayer, in which every one of the twelve guests took an active part — such stuff as dreams are made of!

On the following day, the Bishop took me to Arona, near Lake Maggiore. There I spoke about the Renewal to all the clergy of the diocese. As usual, there was time for questions afterwards, but I could sense that this was all very new to them. The Bishop supported and reinforced all that I said. At lunch, I met the then nuncio to Thailand, Mgr Moretti, who has just recently been appointed nuncio to my own country.

Then I returned to Milan. My schedule included a lecture on Charismatic Renewal at the Ambrosianum. I had been told I could speak in French, because of the cultural background of "the sort of people who come to the Ambrosianum". One look at my audience, however, was enough to convince me that I should speak in Italian. I was glad I had when, at the end of my lecture, my audience spontaneously burst into Alleluias of a distinctly charismatic style. Apparently the charismatic groups of Milan had arrived early, and had taken all the good seats in the front of the hall, leaving so little room for the upper-crust intellectuals that most of these had to make do with a basement room, where they watched the lecture on closed-circuit television!

1976

New York – Washington

On this trip, I travelled in Peter Grace's private plane. The journey took twelve hours, because we refuelled in Iceland in order to be sure that we would have enough fuel to circle over New York for as long as necessary. A strange procedure; but nevertheless, what tremendous progress!

I was to give three lectures: "Theological Reflections for Today", "New Christians for New Times", and "Charismatic Renewal – what it can give and what it must receive".

My first stop was in Gracefield-Manhasset, where I had a meeting and an intense discussion with Ralph Martin and Steve Clark, the two leaders of the Renewal. We needed to find a common wavelength, to build bridges which, in human terms, were sometimes as long as those spanning the Hudson River in New York.

From New York we went to Washington, where we had been invited to pray at the Capitol with a group of about one hundred senators, representatives, and Supreme Court judges. We gathered in one of the Capitol lounges, and Douglas E. Coe, organiser of these spiritual sessions, opened the meeting with an improvised prayer.

Later, we all had lunch together. I sat next to a Supreme Court judge on one side, and a lady from the Treasury on the other side. They asked me to tell them "what I had in my heart". I improvised, and felt that all were listening very attentively, in an ideal climate of religious receptivity.

I later had excellent meetings with Jesuit Fathers D'Orsy, Dulles, Haughey and McCormick.

In the evening, I gave a lecture at the National Shrine, in the middle of a snowstorm; the door to the sacristy was locked, and we were left out in the cold. My mind drifted off to Christmas night in Bethlehem, where no welcome had been planned.

Next, I gave a lecture at Howard University. The audience comprised a mixture of various sects, and it was difficult to speak of the Church, which was so foreign to most of them. I therefore tried to explain every word before using it. At the end, a group of black Pentecostals offered to pray with me. It was a very moving prayer; we held hands, in an atmosphere of extraordinary fraternity, and ended with a warm embrace — much more meaningful than any lengthy discussion. We were all deeply affected by the experience.

Finally, I gave a lecture at the Episcopalian Union Theological Seminary in Virginia. This began with a two-hour ecumenical discussion with a group of about twenty faculty members. At the end, I was bombarded with questions. I was astonished to discover how many of those who argued with me had not read certain basic Catholic books, and were not familiar with some of the authors who could have cleared up, or at least partially dispelled, many of their apprehensions. I had to explain the meaning of papal infallibility, and a few other points concerning which all misunderstandings should long ago have been clarified. I fear that this kind of discussion will never lead to ecumenical unity. May the Lord lead us to a few short-cuts! Perhaps Renewal in the Holy Spirit will prove to be just such a short-cut.

In the evening, I gave a talk at the Seminary, in an excellent atmosphere. Finally, I travelled back to Gracefield for a meeting with Catholic theologians Montague, Lauge and Maloney.

A MAN SENT FROM GOD

*The text of a speech by
Leon-Joseph Cardinal Suenens
in memory of Pope John XXIII, delivered at the opening of
the second session of Vatican Council II*

VERITAS

Published 1992 by
Veritas Publications
7-8 Lower Abbey Street
Dublin 1

ISBN 1 85390 225 X

British Library Cataloguing
in Publication Data.
A catalogue record for
this book is available
from the British Library.

Cover design by creative a.d. Dublin
Printed in the Republic of Ireland by
Criterion Press Ltd

Preface

On 2 April 1992 the English language edition of **Memories and Hopes,** the autobiography of Leon-Joseph Cardinal Suenens, was published. **A Man sent from God** is the complete text of the address delivered by Cardinal Suenens at the Solemn Assembly in memory of Pope John XXIII, referred to by the Cardinal on p. 123 of his autobiography.

Most Holy Father,
Venerable Fathers of the Council,
Brethren

> *Fuit homo missus a Deo cui nomen erat*
> *Iohannes.*

> There was a man sent from God, whose name
> was John (Jn 1:6).

I

THERE WAS A MAN SENT FROM GOD

John the Baptist and John XXIII

It is true that, in their literal sense, these words refer to John the Baptist, the precursor of the Lord. Yet they come irresistibly to the mind of anyone who thinks of the Pope who has just left us: John XXIII of holy and venerated memory.

He came, like John the Baptist, to bear witness to the light; to make the rough ways plain, to prepare a path, to show Christ to the world; like him too, his mission was short, cut off by death.

When he was elected, John XXIII might have seemed to be a "transitional pope". He was indeed transitional, but not in the way expected nor in the ordinary sense of the word. History will surely judge that he opened a new era for the Church and that he laid the foundations for the transition from the twentieth to the twenty-first century.

But it is not our purpose to assess the full significance of the pontificate that has just ended; that would be rash and premature. What we should like to do in this solemn gathering, called at the wish of Pope Paul VI now gloriously reigning, is simply to try to represent before us for a few moments the figure of John XXIII, in a collective act of filial piety and deeply-felt gratitude.

The farewell

Each one of the Council Fathers keeps in his heart the vivid remem-

3

brance of our last meeting with him, here in this very place, close to the tomb of Peter. Each one, as he listened, asked himself: "Is this a final goodbye? Will the father, talking to us now, ever see his children again?" We realised that we were listening to a kind of Discourse at the Last Supper.

Returning for the second session of the Council, we have looked in vain for his kindly face, his cheerful smile, his gesture of welcome. John XXIII is no longer in our midst. God has recalled to himself his good and faithful servant.

The death

The television, the radio and the press brought his death so close to us that it was like a death in the family. Never has the whole world taken part at such close quarters in the poignant stages of a mortal sickness. Never has it shown such unanimity of feeling. "The death of the saints", says Holy Scripture "is precious in the sight of God". The death of John XXIII was precious also in the sight of the world. The Pope transformed it into a final proclamation of faith and hope; he made it something like the celebration of an Easter liturgy.

A few weeks before his great leavetaking, the Supreme Pontiff had said in the course of an audience: "Every day is a good day to be born, and every day is a good day to die. I know in whom I have believed". He went to meet his end with the serenity of a child going home, knowing that its father is waiting there with open arms. What could be simpler?

When he heard the members of his household sobbing round his bed, he protested: "Don't cry, this is a time of joy". When the end drew near, he asked to be "left alone with the Lord" to recollect himself. But some echoes of his prayer could be heard when he recovered consciousness. He could be heard repeating the words of the Master: "I am the Resurrection and the Life", words which in such a moment took on their fullest meaning. And then his lips formed this last, barely audible, heartfelt cry, full of filial love for the Blessed Virgin, "My Mother, my hope". And it was the end.

John XXIII breathed his last on the day after Pentecost just as the priest in Saint Peter's Square had spoken the words: "Ite missa est", "Go, the Mass is ended". For him too the mission was at an end, his offering completed in a spirit of supreme fidelity to the Holy Spirit.

A twofold presence
John XXIII has left us.

Yet we dare to believe that he is more than ever present in our midst. The dead do not cease to live, but live more fully. In the mystic reality of the Communion of Saints they act more penetratingly and intimately and with greater power. It is right and fitting that we should ask him to intercede for us now with God, so that our conciliar labours, which he inspires, should evolve and come to perfection in entire docility to the thought and desires of God for his Church.

John XXIII is present in our midst in a twofold way.

In his successor
First of all, he is present in his well-beloved successor, Pope Paul VI, the august continuer of his work, who gave expression on the morrow of the Pope's death to the unanimous hope of the Church and the world: "The tomb of John XXIII", he proclaimed, "will not be able to confine his heritage". And in the first days of his pontificate he affirmed his profound continuity with his predecessor in these words: 'We are deeply grateful to God who gave to us the precious gift of a supreme pastor of the Church so deserving of our love. In the candour of his simplicity, in the splendour of his virtues, in his tenacious effort to promote peace, he has not only filled the whole world with love and admiration for himself, but has also, by his calling of the Ecumenical Council, opened new avenues to the saving activity of the Catholic Church. God grant that the great work which he began may be brought to a happy conclusion and that the glorious day, which he foresaw in calling the Council, may soon dawn upon the Church and the world" (letter of Pope Paul VI to Cardinal Tisserant, September 12, 1963).

And more recently still, have we not ourselves heard the solemn witness to this continuity, expressed in the never-to-be-forgotten discourse which opened the second session of the Council? On each line and between the lines, the same breath of Pentecost was perceptible. We heard the same invitation to openness and dialogue, to doctrinal and pastoral charity, the same insistence on constructive, positive work, the same solicitude to translate the Gospel's eternal message into a language modern people understand. It is clear that Providence has given Pope Paul VI to the Church to give form and substance to the prophetic intuitions of his predecessor.

5

By his sacrifice

John XXIII is present in our midst in another way, mysterious and profound. He is with us by reason of the sacrifice of his life, which he offered up for the happy outcome of the Council's labours.

On this point there comes to mind an incident at Castel Gandolfo in July of last year. John XXIII had spent the day, pen in hand, studying the preparatory schemata. In the course of an audience he read aloud some of the notes he had written in the margin. Then, suddenly, he stopped and said: "Oh, I know what my personal part in the preparation of the Council will be..." And after a pause, he concluded: "It will be suffering".

He did not specify what the suffering would be, but it was easy to see that he was thinking of his coming death. Not in vain had he read in the Gospel that the grain of wheat must die in the earth for the sake of the harvest. With all his heart he believed in the spiritual value of total sacrifice fully accepted. He knew that, once again, death would be the source of life. In accepting it with his truly noble spirit, he has given to God and to all of us the supreme gift: he has loved us unto the end, as his Master did.

In finem dilexit eos.

II

HIS NAME WAS JOHN

We must now try to describe the figure of the Pope, whose memory is forever fixed in the heart of every one of us. His winning personality was too rich to be reduced to a few characteristics: all we can do is to sketch some dominant traits which brought him so close to us and to the men of our time.

If one had to express it all in one word, it seems to me that one could say that John XXIII was a man surprisingly natural and at the same time supernatural. Nature and grace produced in him a living unity filled with charm and surprises.

6

Everything about him sprang from a single source, In a completely natural way he was supernatural. He was natural with such a supernatural spirit that no one detected a distinction between the two.

Filling his lungs, as it were, he breathed the faith just as he breathed physical and moral health.

"He lived in the presence of God," one wrote, "with the simplicity of one who takes a walk through the streets of his native town."

He lived with both feet on the ground, and with vibrant sympathy he was interested in the everyday concerns of people. He knew how to stop at the side of a road to talk with ordinary people, to listen to a child, to console an invalid. He was concerned with the construction of an airport and he prayed for the astronauts.

But he also lived completely in the world of the supernatural, in the familiar company of the angels and saints. He loved to share his preferences with others, and here also he showed the courage that characterised his friendships. He surprised St Joseph by introducing him into the Canon of the Mass, and some saints from the region of Venice and Lombardy by raising them to the altars: we recall the names of St Gregory Barbarigo and of Blessed Innocent of Berzo and Luigi Palazzolo.

Teaching and life
This successful alliance between grace and nature explains another harmony, so striking in John XXIII, that existed between his life and his teaching. In him there was no dualism. After the example of the Lord, of who St John said that "His life was light", the deceased Pope enlightened men by the very course of his existence.

In him light and warmth were inseparable, like the sun which simultaneously illumines and warms the world.

John's spontaneous, forthright, ever-alert goodness was like a ray of sunshine which dispels the fog, which melts the ice which filters its way through, as of right, without even being noticed. Such a ray of sunshine creates optimism along its path, spreads happiness with its unexpected appearance, and makes light of all obstacles.

It is thus that John XXIII appeared to the world, not as the sun of the tropics, which blinds one with the intensity of its brilliance, but rather as the humble, familiar, everyday sun which is simply there in its place, always true to itself even though it may be momentarily veiled by a cloud, a sun which one hardly notices, so certain is its presence.

John XXIII was not so naive as to believe that goodness would solve all problems, but he knew that it would open hearts to dialogue, to understanding and to mutual respect. He had confidence in the power of the charity of Christ burning in a human heart.

He knew also that truth penetrates more easily into the hearts of men when it appears to them as a revelation of love. Did not the master say: "My words are spirit and life"? And does not Scripture teach that "he who does not love does not know God, for God is love"? And, in the unspeakable oneness of his nature, is not God himself love and truth, truth and love?

John XXIII could reveal God to men, perhaps better than others more brilliant or more scholarly, because for so many years he was the faithful witness of the living God, of the God who loves men.

On the day after his entrance into the Church, a certain convert justified his choice by these words: "I believe that the greatest truth exists where there is the greatest love. "

John XXIII had made these words his own. They were strikingly illustrated in his life, the memory of which will endure through the course of centuries

Forgetfulness of self

But there is a secret to loving others to this extent: a man must forget himself. Charity, it has been said, is "pure concentration on the existence of others" (Lavelle).

To be completely dedicated to others, one must banish all self-interest. Forgetfulness of oneself conditions the gift of oneself.

John XXIII leaves us the memory of someone who, in his own eyes, did not exist. He put himself beyond all earthly vanity: self-denial was a constant value for his soul. This fundamental humility allowed him to speak of himself with detachment and with humour, as if he were speaking of somebody else.

Let us listen to him as he introduces himself to his newly acquired subjects, the faithful of the Patriarchate of Venice:

"I wish", he told them, "to speak to you with the utmost frankness. You have waited impatiently for me; people have told you about me and written you accounts that far surpass my merits. I introduce myself as I really am. Like every other person who lives here on earth I come from a definite family and place. Thank God, I enjoy bodily health and a little

8

good sense which allows me to see matters quickly and clearly. Ever ready to love people, I stand by the law of the Gospel, a respecter of my own rights and of those of others, a fact that prevents me from doing harm to anybody and which encourages me to do good to all.

"I come of humble stock. I was raised in the kind of poverty which is confining but beneficial, which demands little, but which guarantees the development of the noblest and greatest virtues and which prepares one for the steep ascent of the mountain of life. Providence drew me out of my native village and made me traverse the roads of the world in the East and in the West. The same Providence made me embrace men who were different both by religion and by ideology. God made me face acute and threatening social problems, in the presence of which I kept a calm and balanced judgement and imagination in order to evaluate matters accurately, ever preoccupied, out of my respect for Catholic doctrinal and moral principles, not with what separates people and provokes conflicts, but rather with what unites men."

The same authentic accents are heard again a few weeks before his death on the occasion of the bestowal of the Balzan Peace Prize: "The humble Pope who speaks to you", he said, "is fully conscious of being personally a very small thing in the sight of God. He can only humble himself....

"In all simplicity We speak to you just as We think: no circumstance, no event, no matter what honour it may bestow on our poor person, can puff Us up or do harm to the tranquillity of Our soul."

No one was surprised to read in his personal diary reflections such as the following:

"This year's celebrations for my priestly jubilee have come to an end. I have allowed them to be held here at Sofia and at Sotto il Monte. What an embarrassment for me! Countless priests already dead or still living after twenty-five years of priesthood have accomplished wonders in the apostolate and in the sanctification of souls. And I, what have I done? My Jesus mercy! But while I humble myself for the little or nothing that I have achieved up to now, I raise my eyes toward the future. There still remains light in front of me; there still remains the hope of doing some good. Therefore, I take up again my staff, which from now on will be the staff of old age, and I go forward to meet whatever the Lord wishes for me" (Sofia, October 30, 1929).

"My recollections are delighted with all the graces received from the

Lord, but at the same time I feel humiliated for having been so niggardly in the use of my talents, for having rendered a return without any proportion to the gifts I have received. I find here a mystery which makes me shudder and at the same time stirs me to action" (August 10, 1961).

"The Vicar of Christ? Ah! I am not worthy of this title, I, the poor son of Baptist and Mary Ann Roncalli, two good Christians, to be sure, but so modest and so humble" (August 15, 1961).

III

HE CAME TO GIVE TESTIMONY OF THE LIGHT

If we shift our gaze from the man to the work he accomplished, his life appears as a threefold grace: a grace for the faithful of the Catholic Church; a grace for all Christians; a grace for all men of good will.

A grace for the faithful

His life was a grace for the faithful, above all because of the Council he convoked; this was the culmination of his pastoral activity.

John XXIII wanted this Council: he rightly saw this desire as an answer to an inspiration of the Holy Spirit, inviting him to assemble in Rome all the bishops of the world.

He obeyed this inspiration with the same simplicity he showed in all matters: "Obedientia et pax" was his motto.

At the opening of the Council he made a calm declaration of "his complete disagreement with those prophets of doom who are always forecasting disaster". "We have no reason to be afraid", he added; "fear comes only from a lack of faith."

He obeyed God's call, peacefully and without knowing exactly how all of this was to be worked out. "When it comes to a Council," he once said smilingly, "we are all novices. The Holy Spirit will be present when the bishops assemble; we'll see."

Indeed, for him, the Council was not first of all a meeting of the bishops with the Pope, a horizontal coming together. It was first and above all a collective gathering of the whole episcopal college with the Holy Spirit, a vertical coming together, an entire openness to an immense outpouring of the Holy Spirit, a kind of new Pentecost.

10

This is why, on the eve of the Council, he invited us to reread in the Acts of the Apostles, the description of the Cenacle of Jerusalem, where the Apostles, with one mind continuing steadfastly in prayer with Mary, the Mother of Jesus, awaited the fulfilment of the Master's promise.

Thanks to John XXIII, God has once again visited his people: Christ the Saviour sends his Spirit to his own, to teach them, in his name, all truth, and to explain to them what before they could not bear nor fully grasp.

The Council is the light of the Holy Spirit which will penetrate deeper into the Church, and through the Church, into the world; it is a gift of God's magnanimity to our age.

The Pope followed the various phases of the Council with that superior wisdom which was his and which appeared in these lines which date from his mission to Paris:

"By the grace of God, my affairs are going well. I go about them calmly and watch over them all. And I see them fall into their proper place one after the other. I bless the Lord for the help he gives me, thus preventing me from complicating simple matters, and assisting me rather to simplify the more complicated. "

May John XXIII receive, from the heights of heaven, the expression of the Council Fathers' deepest gratitude for the singular grace of the Council, for his confidence in the Episcopate which is more than ever unshakeably united to the successor of Peter, to Peter who yesterday was called John and who today is named Paul, and to whom we pledge the same love and the same indefectible loyalty.

A grace for all Christians

His life was a grace for all Christians. For to him we owe a new atmosphere, a new climate, which enables us together, as brothers, to meet the obstacles which remain to be overcome on the path to a full and visible unity. This climate we owe to his charity and to his sincerity.

To his charity, which opened the hearts of men to dialogue, to a predisposition to judge favourably, to understanding. Better than anyone else, John XXIII knew that the search for Christian unity does not proceed along the path of diplomatic negotiations, but looks rather to the very depths of men's spiritual lives.

We grow in closeness, one with another, in his judgement, according to the very measure each one allows himself to be taken over by the life and charity of Christ. As we become more and more one with him, we cannot but grow in closeness to our brothers. Every effort for union, by the very fact that it is an act of charity, has in itself unitive value.

This climate of *rapprochement* we owe also to his sincerity which was so manifest. No one, contemplating his life, could charge him with authoritarianism or ambition.

One day, as he was showing a visitor his private library, he stopped before the edition of writings and speeches dating back to his years as Patriarch of Venice. He took down one of the volumes and said: "Do you know what I feel when I look at these volumes?" He hesitated a moment and then said, "I feel sincere."

This confession gives us the secret of his influence. Is it not this moving sincerity which struck the Observers during the audience he had with them the day after the Council opened?

"As for you," he told them, "read my heart: you will perhaps learn more there than from my words. How will I forget the ten years spent in Sofia and the other ten in Istanbul and Athens?... I often met Christians belonging to various denominations.... We did not debate; we spoke; and though we did not discuss, we loved each other. Your presence here, which we cherish, the emotion which fills my priestly heart ... urge me to confide to you how my heart burns with a desire to work and to suffer for the coming of that hour when Jesus' prayer at the Last Supper will be realised for all men."

A grace for the world
His life was a grace for the world.

John XXIII was the pope of dialogue, and this has special reference to the men of our times.

It is not easy to make the world of today hear the voice of the Church. It is drowned by too much noise; there is too much static and interference in the air for the message to get through.

In spite of these obstacles, John XXIII managed to make himself heard: he broke through the sound-barrier.

The words of John awakened a response.

Men recognised his voice, a voice speaking to them of God, but also of human brotherhood, of the re-establishment of social justice, of a peace to be established throughout the whole world.

They heard a challenge addressed to their better selves, and they raised their eyes towards this man whose goodness made them think of

God. For men, whether they know or not, are always in search of God, and it is the reflection of God that they sought in the countenance of this old man who loved them with the very love of Christ.

And this is why they wept for him as children for their father, pressing around him to receive his blessing.

And the poor wept for him; they knew he was one of them and that he was dying poor like them, thanking God for the poverty that for him had been such a grace.

And the prisoners wept for him: he had visited them and encouraged them with his presence. Who does not remember that visit to the prison of Rome? Among the prisoners were two murderers. After having heard the Holy Father one of them approached and said: "These words of hope that you have just spoken, do they also apply to me, such a great sinner?" The Pope's only answer was to open his arms and clasp him to his heart. This prisoner is surely a sort of symbol of the whole of mankind, so close to the heart of John XXIII.

Now that his pontificate has come to an end, how can we without deep emotion reread the words he spoke in 1934 as he was leaving Bulgaria? We recognise John XXIII in this farewell message, a message that has prophetic value.

"Oh my brothers," he said, "do not forget me, who, come what may, will remain always the fervent friend of Bulgaria.

"According to an old tradition of Catholic Ireland, on Christmas Eve each home puts a lighted candle in the window to show St Joseph and the Blessed Mother, searching for a place to stay, that inside there is a family waiting to receive them. Wherever I may be, even at the ends of the earth, any Bulgarian away from his native land passing by my house will find in the window the lighted candle. If he knocks, the door will be opened, whether he be Catholic or Orthodox. A Brother from Bulgaria, this will be title enough. He will be welcome and will find in my house the warmest and the most affectionate hospitality."

This invitation has gone far beyond the borders of Bulgaria; John XXIII addressed it to all men of good will, irrespective of national frontiers.

He will be for history the Pope of Welcome and of Hope. This is the reason his gentle and holy memory will remain in benediction in the centuries to come.

At his departure, he left men closer to God, and the world a better place for men to live.

Tampa

On Sunday March 14, I left for Florida. I was in Tampa from the 14th to the 17th, to participate in a meeting on healing directed by Fr Francis McNutt (this was before his break from the Church). Despite the very valuable help we received from Professor Jan Van der Veken, of the University of Louvain — who had come with me, and who tried in vain to shed some light on all of these issues — we were unable to find a common theological ground on miracles, exorcisms, or the charism of healing.

The Templeton Prize

I received this award in April of 1976, at Buckingham Palace, from the Duke of Edinburgh. Mrs Thatcher gave the official address at the public ceremony in the Guildhall in London.

The award came as a complete surprise; few Catholics had ever received it (Mother Teresa of Calcutta had been one recipient, and Chiara Lubich was to be another). This prize is unusual in that it is not awarded exclusively to members of any particular religion, and in that its jury includes Jews, Muslims and Christians of various denominations. In my case, one result of this event was a friendship with Mr Templeton, the generous American Presbyterian donor. His purpose in instituting this award was to give recognition to efforts, all over the world, which are aimed at promoting religion.

Later that year, we both took part in a panel discussion for American television, on the *Today* show; we took the opportunity to stress the importance of the religious dimension at the heart of all human beings.

Meetings in England

In July, I was invited to York by the Anglican Archbishop, Mgr Blanch, in the context of a projected "twinning" (which has since taken place) between the chapter of canons of Malines and that of York. I received a very friendly welcome in Bishopsthorpe. We

301

were surrounded by a magnificent park; it was bordered by a river, and we could see rowing and sailing boats passing by. As we took a leisurely walk, we covered a wide range of subjects; we did not, however, discuss ecumenical problems.

I still remember how intrigued I was by the Archbishop's humorous explanations of the mystery of that British logic which is so alien to us. He told me that during the recent Synod, someone spoke up against the absurdity of the fact that landlords, even non-Christian ones, have the right to appoint parish priests in the parishes on their land – a prerogative which the Queen enjoys as well. In my own country, we certainly do not have such a deep-rooted sense of tradition!

The Archbishop had asked me to give a talk, at his residence, to an audience of eighty seminarians. The following morning, I gave a homily at the Cathedral; this was followed by an official lunch hosted by the Lord Mayor of York.

On the way back to London by car, we stopped briefly to pray at the tomb of Lord Halifax; we also made a brief stop at Cardinal Hume's residence. Finally, we reached my Anglican friend Tom Smail's country house, where two days of ecumenical meetings had been scheduled; both sides had requested this opportunity for an exchange of views. I received a warm welcome; the atmosphere, during both the prayers and the discussions, was excellent. With me were two Catholic theologians: Fr Lebeau, SJ, and Professor Jan Van der Veken of the University of Louvain. On the non-Catholic side were Tom Smail; J. Dunn, a professor at Nottingham University; Watson, Vicar of St Mary's in York; the Evangelist Richard Hare; and the Irish Presbyterian Cecil Kerr. Our discussions centred on "Baptism in the Spirit" according to Scripture, its relation to the sacrament of confirmation, and the Christian spirituality which stems from it.

J. Dunn is an extremely learned exegete, and his studies on the Holy Spirit are very thorough. His presentation, however, left many questions unanswered; each of the texts he used could easily have been interpreted in several different ways. It seemed to me that Paul Lebeau dominated the discussion, through the clarity of his presentation on Charismatic Renewal. At the end, we touched on the role of "Mary in the Christian life"; despite our feelings of friendship, which were never for a moment in doubt, we were at an impasse. Alas, the Marian Ecumenical Society still has a long way to travel if there is to be a *rapprochement* at this level!

An evening with young people in Brussels

I spent an evening with a dozen young people between the ages of twenty and thirty, who had come from various countries; they belonged to the Charismatic Renewal. During the meal they each, in turn, told me their stories. All had left the Church around the age of sixteen or seventeen; some had turned to various forms of oriental wisdom; others had opted for atheism, sexual promiscuity, or drugs, or had sought refuge in some sect. The end of each story was the same: "And then I found Jesus Christ." One of them added: "Actually, to be more precise, Jesus Christ found me; and that changed my whole life."

From this starting point of an encounter with the living Christ, each of them had oriented his or her life in the direction of a Christianity that is lived, active, and apostolic.

I asked them: "Tell me, where and how did you meet the living Christ?" In substance, the answers they gave me were identical: "I came back to the Lord because I met him in the Christians who live in him and through him."

This, indeed, is the path of every conversion: we are ourselves the proof of Christianity. What a magnificent and awesome responsibility!

1977

Neuchâtel

I went to Switzerland from April 26 to 28, with Fr Lebeau, SJ. Pastor Molinghen was there to meet us at the airport. He is Belgian, married to a Swiss woman, and is at present pastor at La Chaux-de-Fonds. I had once dined at his home in Mons, and had found him to be very close to us – and, moreover, a charming man. He drove us to Neuchâtel; along the way, we discussed theology, and stopped briefly at the Sisters of Grandchamp, an order associated with Taizé.

In Neuchâtel, we had dinner at the home of Professor von Allmen, of the Reformed Church. He is a very open-minded man, delightful in his humility. He said to me once, "Catholics have made a caricature of our Protestant ancestors, and somewhere around the seventeenth century we identified with this caricature. Our early reformers were not what they have been made out to be." He was trying to rediscover the original common roots, lost somewhere beneath the jumble of centuries and polemics. He promised to send me a copy of his book on the Eucharist, and one of a second one, soon to be completed, on the Pope; this is an unusual subject for a Protestant writer, and he was expecting some difficulties as a result.*

After dinner, I gave a talk on "Renewal in the Church"; I had been asked to do so by the dean of the Protestant faculty at the University of Neuchâtel. Von Allmen had told me that he had read the dean's welcoming speech and had found it excellent. Indeed, it was humorous and friendly. He reminded the audience that more than five hundred years had gone by since the last cardinal had set foot in Neuchâtel; so I began my own talk with the words: "I felt the time had come for this visit!"

The lecture was followed by a big dinner at the Hotel du Lac. I had already eaten dinner at Von Allmen's, since I had been told that there would be only "a small reception". I know of no worse ordeal than to be obliged to eat two full meals in one evening. But I was assured that the fish from the lake of Neuchâtel is unique; in none of the other great lakes is the water so pure. It seemed I had no choice but to sit down to my second dinner, which lasted till one in the morning.

---

*This book has since been published under the title *La Primauté de l'Eglise de Pierre et de Paul (The Primacy of the Church of Peter and Paul)*, Paris, 1977.

Geneva

On the following day, Pastor Molinghen drove us to Geneva. Along the way, Fr Lebeau provided us with a wide range of theological exposés on such matters as ministry and intercommunion. These were beautifully explained and very well received, even when we explored the role of Mary in the Church.

Our first appointment in Geneva was at the Cenacle. After a brief rest, I went to the studios of Radio Romande for an hour-long interview. The speaker had a reputation of always managing to unsettle the guests on his programme. He did, in fact, attempt a few insidious questions; very soon, however, he gave me free rein, and thus provided me with the opportunity to give a full-length presentation on the Charismatic Renewal.

That evening's lecture had originally been scheduled to take place in the Protestant Cathedral of St Peter. Some local authorities, however, considered this to be something of a provocation; earlier, they had also denied access to the cathedral to the Prior of Taizé. At the last moment, therefore, we had to fall back on a Catholic church.

In the church, I was met by a mixture of Catholics and Protestants. Some of the audience sat on the floor, others on the steps of the pulpit. A few hymns were sung, and then I spoke for a little over an hour. I believe this was one of the best lectures I ever gave.

My Swiss programme was now drawing to an end, but my schedule still included a visit to the offices of the World Council of Churches. On a personal level, Philip Potter and his staff gave me a warm welcome, but they did not express much interest in the Charismatic Renewal; they did not seem to be aware of the ecumenical opportunity that this movement could provide, if it were to be allowed to take its proper place. Father Lebeau made a few excellent comments, but we both felt that the atmosphere was far too administrative for the message to be understood.

Back at the Cenacle, we had dinner with Mgr Mamie and his episcopal council. Toasts were made, and the Bishop spoke of St

Francis de Sales, of Mercier, and of Cardinal Journet. This gave me the opportunity to mention Journet's prophetic words concerning the renewal of charisms. I had been advised, "If you want to win Mamie's heart, quote Journet."

Finally, to conclude my stay in Switzerland, I had a two-hour meeting, the following afternoon, with the pastors of Geneva and some theologians — a few Catholics, but mostly Protestants. There were in all about 160 people present, including Visser't Hooft. Seldom have I taken part in a more lively and interesting exchange (which included a discussion of Mary). In conclusion, we prayed together in the chapel, in a cenacle atmosphere and with a merging of hearts which was very moving.

Mission to Oxford

This mission, which was amply and sympathetically described in *The Tablet*, was a unique ecumenical experience. *The Tablet's* report is quoted in full further on; but first, a few personal comments.

I had received a touching and unexpected invitation to preach the University mission for Oxford students — a mission which Archbishop Ramsey had also once preached. This mission went back to the days of William Temple, a great historical figure of the Anglican Church. In 1968, it had been abolished for fear of disruptions; now it was felt that the time had come to re-establish the tradition. For the first time since the Reformation — and in response to a request from the students themselves — a Catholic bishop was invited to preach.

I was welcomed by Dean Chadwick, of Christ Church, whose kind and charming hospitality I enjoyed during my stay; he was a particularly thoughtful and attentive host. In his home, I was at the very heart of Oxford, a sanctuary of the Anglican tradition; on the walls was an impressive array of portraits of Deans of bygone days. The mission began with a service celebrated by the Bishop of Oxford.

Every evening, I gave a lecture, in the Sheldonian Theatre, to an audience of about fifteen hundred students and faculty members. The silence that greeted me, as I entered the crowded hall, was astonishing. The hall itself was extraordinary: a vast rotunda crowned by a cupola, with people sitting in rows of seats that rose well above the speaker's head. And what a magnificent pulpit! In some ways it resembled St Peter's throne at the very back of the Basilica in Rome, poised on high, between the four Doctors of the Church. On the first evening I felt about as comfortable, sitting there, as if I had usurped the papal throne! As for the thick red cushions along the balustrade — they were not designed to hold lecture notes. Altogether, it was quite an ordeal! Luckily, on the following day there was a change of scenery, and I was able to speak from another, less majestic lectern.

The audience was extremely attentive and responsive — smiles and laughter were always on cue. I prayed as hard as I could that the words I spoke would come from the Lord, rather than from me, and that they should be something other than "words of human wisdom".

I believe that what I said was clear, simple, and warm — "convincing", as I was later told, with no cumbersome theological jargon. The lectures, on the theme "Your God?", have since been published as a book.

The public was faithful to the very end. I remember a curious detail: every evening, but also during the day, whenever I had to go somewhere in the town, a group of four or five young people would come to fetch me and to escort me. One of the young men attracted my attention. He always carried an umbrella, even in sunny weather; to me he seemed very English — always elegant, and never caught off guard.

In the intervals, I was busy with the press, the radio, and question-and-answer sessions — sometimes with the seniors, and at other times with the younger students. The latter had chosen to meet at Saint Mary's Church, which had been Newman's church; they had heard me preach there two years earlier, and this had apparently been their reason for inviting me back.

I did not look forward to the question-and-answer session at the church; it is always much easier to ask a question than to answer it, especially in a very few words. Moreover, the chaplain who had organised this encounter had insisted that students, who were to ask their questions in writing, should then be allowed to follow them up orally. Providence had mercy on me, for after about two or three exchanges with someone at the back of the church, we were forced to give up – the microphones had broken down. This gave me the opportunity to speak at length in response to each written question, with no interruptions. Questions were primarily directed at the issue of the relationship between science and faith. I was thus able, in all intellectual integrity, to speak of the path I had personally travelled, and to explain how it is possible to "seek light with light".

A further item on my programme was a press conference at the Newman College, during which photographs were taken of me in front of Newman's bust. Newman's presence can still be felt at Oxford, where he appears to be loved by one and all, Catholics and Anglicans alike. I was very moved when a professor at Keble College said to me, by way of thanks, that, during my stay in Oxford, we had remained very much in the tradition of *"cor ad cor loquitur"* ("the heart speaks to the heart") – which was Newman's motto.

On the last evening, I spent an hour with some Anglican students in a charismatic prayer group. Professor Jan Van der Veken, who was in Oxford with me, was at the same time answering questions from a group of theology students; this was a joy to him, and a feast for them.

While in Oxford, I went to the famous Blackwell's bookshop to autograph some of my books. It is a fortress of the printed word, an unfathomable construction of shelves and floors! It reminded me, more than anything, of an airport car-park.

This mission was one of the most important moments of my life. The preparation it required of me was, in itself, a grace; but what made it even more special was the ecumenical communion in which I lived during those days. At no point did I step out of that area in which we were able to commune "in the unity of the Father, of the Son, and of the Holy Spirit", and to be united at the deepest levels of the Gospel. "I did not believe that a Catholic could ever be so 'evangelical'", one student confided to an Anglican chaplain.

Here is the text of the article, by Ronald Jenkinson, which appeared in *The Tablet* on February 26, 1977, "Cardinal Suenens Preaches the Mission at Oxford University":

The chandeliers were ablaze. The splendid building was filled with light and with sonorous music from the organ. Seat after seat was taken as the audience streamed in, first the chairs set out across the floor, then the benches in the circles and galleries, the rows of spectators arising ever higher and higher, until the topmost of them almost reached the allegorical figures of Streater's ceiling and the house was full. The setting was the Sheldonian Theatre at Oxford, but the 1500 or so present, students for the most part, were not awaiting an overture from a symphony orchestra or the pomp and circumstance of the Encaenia, but the arrival of one man, the Belgian Cardinal Suenens.

This must have been an occasion altogether without precedent, and therefore likely in itself to be impressive. But in the event the impression made was deeper than and different from what might have been forecast. The cardinal duly appeared, neatly attired in black suit and clerical collar, and walked, with erect carriage, to the rostrum. He began by praying that God would speak to us rather than he, and then simply and meditatively addressed us for half an hour and, after a pause for silent prayer, for a further half hour. And that was all. The audience was held in silence throughout, except for an occasional ripple of laughter when the cardinal – spontaneously, it seemed – tempered his talk with humour.

How did all this come about? A plan for a University Mission was afoot, and it was undergraduates who heard Cardinal Suenens preach a University Sermon some two years ago who first suggested that he should be invited to lead the mission. The history of Oxford University missions goes back at least to Bishop Gore's mission in 1914, and perhaps the most memorable in the series was that conducted by William Temple in 1931. This year, for the first time, the missioner was a Roman Catholic who, moreover, came from abroad.

It is a sign of the times that the choice of the cardinal has not met with any substantial opposition from any body of Christians in Oxford. By coincidence the mission came fast on the heels of the Agreed Statement on Authority, and I find it touching, even humbling (and I think Cardinal Suenens would approve of these adjectives) that Christians outside the Roman Catholic Church should be looking to us increasingly for leadership, sensing a new vision and a new openness in our attitude to our fellow Christians. The cardinal stated in one of his addresses that he regarded it as no accident that he was a protegé of, and a successor to Cardinal Mercier, who conducted the 1920 Malines Conversations from the Catholic side.

The Mission Committee was headed by Dr Geoffrey Rowell, chaplain-fellow of Keble College, and included representatives of the Roman Catholic, Anglican and Methodist Churches, and from the student Christian societies. The mission had the support of the Orthodox, of Evangelical Anglicans, of Baptists and of the United Reformed Church. Dr Rowell has stated the aim of the mission as "the presentation of the Christian faith to present members of the university, not just as a theory to be considered, but as a way of life which may be wholeheartedly and intelligently followed".

The occasion to which I alluded in my opening paragraphs was the first of four appearances of the cardinal in the Sheldonian. On each of the nights the theatre was filled to capacity. It would be impossible in this article to give even a summary of all that the cardinal said, but I will try, by a process of selection, to convey an impression of the way in which he communicated his message. The titles of the talks were (1) How and where to find God;(2) God as my father; (3) God as my brother; (4) God as my breath of life. Behind all the cardinal said was the Christian doctrine of God, of the Incarnation and of the Trinity, but it was not with any brilliant theological exposition that he captured his audience. Rather he told us, simply and firmly, that love is the key to understanding – to love is to see; if we are to know God, we must love him; theology, in the last resort, is prayer. We must empty ourselves so that "the Lord may take over"; we must each of us become, in St Paul's words, a "new creature", with new eyes through which God may look, with new ears listening always for his voice and a new heart loving with the love of God. He spoke of "baptised non-Christians" – we have received the sacrament indeed, but to what extent, in fact, has the Lord taken over? He suggested that perhaps some formal act of commitment should be introduced, later on than baptism and confirmation, particularly as in our time – when a traditional Christian upbringing will so often be lacking – allegiance to Christ will tend to be a matter of choice, a personal decision. The cardinal reminded us that many young people are rejecting materialistic standards, but this leaves a vacuum which is crying out to be filled.

The cardinal dwelt intensely on God the Father's incredible love for each one of us, setting out how this mystery was made vivid in the parable of the Prodigal Son. God, he said, would wish to invent along with each of us our special vocation. God our brother is shown to us in Christ, who puts to all of us a personal question: "Whom do you say that I am?" The divinity of Christ brings us a "first hand" knowledge of God; his humanity identifies us closely with him as our brother. Through the ages man asks "What am I?" and must reply that the reason for his existence is Jesus Christ. The operation of the Holy Spirit makes Jesus universally, eternally present. By the Spirit the face of the earth is indeed to be renewed, but first there must be a personal renewal, alone and then – inevitably – in community with others. There can hardly be too many Christian communities, and the Church, which embraces them all, with the Spirit is alive, without the Spirit dead.

The cardinal's line of thought is known to those who read his books – for example *A New Pentecost?* – but the spoken word was fresh and compelling, and one had the feeling that the Holy Spirit, through the speaker and the listeners, was breathing new life into our university's ancient motto, *Dominus Illuminatio Mea*.

At a separate session the cardinal answered questions on such topics as the problem of suffering, the relationship of Christianity to other religions, the *raison d'être* of the Church, the function of theology and how best to make the Christian religion relevant to non-believers. But neither here nor at the press conference (at Trinity College, which gave the cardinal the opportunity of expressing his great admiration for Newman) nor at any point during the mission was I aware of any controversy concerning the particular doctrines of the different Christian communions. The essence of Christianity and its relevance was the subject.

Unavoidably the presence of Cardinal Suenens was the central feature of the mission, but a tribute should be paid to the ancillary missionary work carried out by many from within and from outside the university, including the Bishop of Truro. I would like to say something of two preliminary events. By way of a prelude, about 100 Catholics and Evangelical Anglicans met together for an hour of prayer in the chapel at the Catholic chaplaincy. Prayer was largely spontaneous, and young men and girls asked for God's blessing on the cardinal and his visit. Then, in the evening at the University Church a Eucharist of Rededication was celebrated by the Bishop of Oxford in glittering mitre and chasuble against a background of Catholic, Anglican and Non-Conformist clergy – the latter clad soberly in black. Our Catholic chaplain conducted the Renewal of Baptismal Vows. In darkness we held our candles, lit from the Mission

Candle, as the Gospel was read. After the Consecration 400 went forward to receive communion dispensed by Anglican, United Reformed and Baptist ministers. Another page was turned in the history – both glorious and tragic – of that great perpendicular church.

Thus the mission was launched – it ended with a variety of discourses, meditations and discussions, including an open retreat at the Catholic Chaplaincy, where the cardinal had celebrated Mass each morning. As to the effects of the mission, there seems to be general agreement that it will have been of direct benefit to those who already have some belief rather than to unbelievers. And yet I cannot but feel that the cardinal's obvious sincerity and conviction will have impressed some of the latter. Then there are those who would have liked rather more "matter", more food for discussion. Nonetheless night after night the theatre was packed. As one wandered down St Aldate's under the stars and looked up at Christ Church with its floodlit tower, where the cardinal resided as the guest of the dean – within a college originally the project of how different a cardinal – one could not but reflect on the historic nature of this mission, and at the same time one felt assured that a measure of fruitful outcome would not be lacking.

The Holy Land

To celebrate the fiftieth anniversary of my ordination to the priesthood, I had expressed a wish to go to the very place where Jesus instituted the Eucharist, and where the Church was born on the morning of Pentecost – the Cenacle in Jerusalem. This was for me a symbolic and evocative gesture, rich in meaning and in hope. At the same time, it provided an opportunity I had often dreamed of – the chance to make a pilgrimage to the Holy Land, where I had never before set foot.

I had planned to travel incognito, with a few of my friends, on Pentecost 1977. Ralph Martin heard of my plan and asked if he, with a few leaders of the American Free Churches, could join us.

313

In the end, there were nearly fifty of us, counting children; about three-quarters of the group were Protestants. They asked if they could meet me in Malines and travel with me to Rome and to Assisi, then by plane to Jerusalem, where we would gather at the Cenacle.

The Pope, who had been told about this trip, welcomed them at his weekly public audience. From Rome, we left for Assisi, and then flew to Tel Aviv. At last, we arrived in Jerusalem.

I celebrated the Eucharist for my jubilee in the chapel closest to the Cenacle. The Latin Patriarch of Jerusalem, Mgr J.B. Beltritti, had insisted on joining me in my jubilee celebration. Together — mindful of the suffering caused by the separations among Christians, and each assuming his part of co-responsibility — we all expressed at length an "ecumenical Confiteor", in the literal sense.

Our small private group then headed off for Nazareth, while the ecumenical group went for a retreat in the Sinai. Before leaving us, the American group presented me with a gift — a silver goblet, and a letter that expressed our joint hopes:

Dear Cardinal Suenens,

The pilgrimage to Jerusalem on Pentecost 1977 will live forever in our hearts as a special gift from Our Father in Heaven. The privilege of celebrating with you the fiftieth anniversary of your priesthood was a great honour and blessing.

This small gift — a water goblet — is a modest expression of our affection for you. You have dedicated your life to others. Through you, the Lord has spread his Holy Spirit on many, and he shall continue to do so for multitudes to come.

May those who see this goblet remember the Water of Life that has united us in a deeply appreciated friendship.

Your brothers,
Don Basham
Ralph Martin
Ern Baxter
Bob Mumford
Paul De Celles
Derck Prince
Larry Christenson
Kevin Ranaghan
Steve Clark
Charles Simpson

and their families

On my return from Jerusalem, I was more than ever imbued with the image of the Cenacle, the place of birth of the Eucharist and of the Church. In my heart, Eliot's unforgettable words acquired a meaning that became increasingly compelling and precise in the context of the growth in ecumenism:

> We shall not cease from exploration
> and the end of all our exploring
> will be to arrive where we started
> and know the place for the first time.

1978

The International Charismatic Congress in Dublin
One of the most important events of 1978 was the International Charismatic Congress, which took place in Dublin from June 12 to 19.

We decided to hold the meeting in the capital of Ireland in hopes that the Renewal would take root in that country, and thus grow and bloom in a truly Catholic climate; this would give it greater credibility within the Church itself, and thus promote its spread throughout the world. The fears concerning the Renewal which Frank Duff shared with our other friends within the Legion of Mary were based on a few local experiences of a pentecostal sort.

The programme of this World Ecumenical Congress included a day with Tom Smail, theologian and pastor, and Presbyterian minister in Northern Ireland; and a day with me. Questioned by the press, we both spoke openly and with loyalty about our friendship, but also about the issues which divided us. This Congress was a very new experience for Ireland – a moving call to unity in a communion lived together in the Holy Spirit.

The final solemn Mass, celebrated by the Archbishop of Dublin surrounded by a crown of concelebrating priests, was an invitation to an alliance between traditional liturgy and the spontaneity of the Holy Spirit. It was broadcast on television, and its impact throughout the land was considerable. I have since heard many echoes of it.

These were days rich in hope. In the Dublin convent where I stayed, I noticed a poster on a wall; the words, and their message, are still with me to remind me of those days: "We cannot control the wind, but we can adjust our sails."

The wind was blowing in Dublin, during the Congress.

* * *

On the international level, 1978 was most significantly the year of Pope Paul's death, and the year of the unexpected election of two popes – John Paul I and John Paul II – in close succession.

Here are a few personal memories of these three popes.

Paul VI

A brief sketch
It is no easy task to capture Pope Paul's personality in a few

words. Poor health prevented him from attending the regular seminary; as a result, he was somewhat isolated in his youth. He was also marked by the political upheavals in Italy, in which his father took a courageous anti-fascist stand. Finally, he was influenced by the many years which he spent, in various capacities, at the Vatican. In the last of these positions, he was in daily contact with Pius XII, whose concept of the papacy was not open to the ideas of co-responsibility or collegiality of the bishops – he was his own Secretary of State. Against this backdrop, Montini became a self-educated man, an assiduous reader of French authors – Maritain, Journet and Guitton were among his favourites. This distinguished him from his immediate entourage: Mgr Felici was overheard once, after an audience, complaining about the "dangerous French books" the Pope was reading.

It may also be significant that in his diplomatic posts, where compromise played an important role, he very naturally learned to seek to maintain a balance between opposing trends. He later applied this to the Council, attempting to keep a balance between, on the one hand, the majority, and on the other a very strong minority whose strength lay in the local power of its members, and who did not hesitate to put pressure on the Pope. At our weekly audiences, he often spent most of the time explaining that he was attempting to reconcile opposites, and that the majority had to take this into account.

He was also very anxious that pontifical prerogatives should remain intact; he took care to redefine them clearly (see the *Nota praevia*) in traditional legal terms, and to develop statutes, for future synods, which would turn these into consultative assemblies rather than instruments of co-responsibility.

Paul VI was called to guide Peter's barque over troubled waters, perturbed by opposing currents. In Rome itself, some felt that he was far too receptive to the majority tendencies, and his local reforms met with much local opposition; outside Rome, however, what was noted most was a certain deliberateness and hesitancy.

Memories and Hopes

Our personal relationship

Pope Paul was a shy man; the gesture with which he greeted the crowds, as he entered St Peter's on the *Sedia*, always stopped halfway, remained somehow unfinished.

I have many times experienced with him what I termed the "thawing phenomenon". Whenever the audience was brief, Pope Paul's manner was reserved, conventional; if I stayed about an hour, however, the atmosphere became more relaxed, and it was possible to speak freely, without oratorial precautions. Whenever I stayed longer than an hour, in private, a different man surfaced: well-read, artistic, fond of classical music, often surprising in his reactions and in his comments.

Early in his pontificate, I boldly asked him to cancel the decree *Veterum Sapientia*, issued by John XXIII, which required the use of Latin for instruction in seminaries (John XXIII had privately apologised for this!). Pope Paul replied: "Perhaps you are familiar with an Italian saying that teaches how to deal with a decree that is too restrictive or simply impossible to apply:

> *Prima si fa quello che si deve;*
> *Poi si fa quello che si può,*
> *Poi si fa quello che si vuole.*

> At first, you do what you have to do;
> Then, you do what you can;
> In the end, you do what you please."

This was a hidden side of the Pope, full of humour and subtlety. But please do not misuse this quote!

Once, at the end of an audience, Pope Paul said to me: "Pray for me, because my task is a difficult one." I replied: "I pray for you faithfully every day, not because your task is difficult – but because it is simply impossible!" He had already opened the door to let me out; now he closed it again, and asked "Why?" I answered candidly, "Holy Father, take a look at the Pontifical

Directory. On the first page, you will see the list of your functions: Bishop of Rome, Metropolitan of Latium, Primate of Italy, Patriarch of the West." I compared this to a President of the United States who would add to all of his present charges those of Mayor of New York City, Governor of the State of New York, and so on... He interrupted me: "So what is the solution?" Briefly, I once more summarised my arguments for some measure of decentralisation, and our conversation ended there.

Some time later, I had to defend myself because, in an interview, I had criticised the mechanics of the Roman Curia — not the actual people involved. I told a journalist: "Surely criticism of a car engine implies no criticism of the driver!" Shortly after this interview, as I introduced my private secretary, Canon Brieven, to the Pope, I said: "Holy Father, here is my very devoted secretary; not only does he take care of my mail, he is also my driver through the chaotic streets of Rome, which is not an easy job!" The Pope, who had obviously read the article, smiled and said, "I can assure you that being the driver of God's Church is no easy task either!"

These were the last words we exchanged on the subject of co-responsibility — an issue on which we have at times disagreed, although I never questioned the priceless grace of pontifical authority, supreme guarantor of the communion of the Churches, in itself.

Pope Paul's reign was also marked by the fact that he was a deeply spiritual man. It is this side of him which was so open to the Charismatic Renewal, despite the opposition of his immediate entourage (with the exception of Benelli). An important book, containing his major writings on the Holy Spirit, has been published;* I was asked to write the preface.

What emerges from all of this is an unusual personality. His pontificate was a painful *via crucis* for him, and a grace for the Church. Only time will allow us adequately to evaluate his role.

Pope Paul and the Holy Spirit, by Edward O'Connor, CSC, Ave Maria Press, Notre Dame, Indiana.

319

Memories and Hopes

I have kept preciously the last letter he wrote to me, a few weeks before his death, on May 27, 1978:

> We have read with great care your letter of April 15, concerning the Charismatic Renewal Movement. We were unable to respond as promptly as we would have liked, to express our satisfaction with the caring attention with which you are attempting to ensure the full integration of this movement into the life of the Catholic Church; we are happy to do so now, and to tell you how very much we appreciate these efforts. We ask the Lord to fill you with his grace in this ecclesial service, and we renew from the depths of our heart our affectionate apostolic benediction.
>
> Paulus P.P. VI

His farewell to the world

Shortly before he left this world, which for him was so full of tribulations, Pope Paul wrote in his testament these touching words:

> Now that the daylight is dimming — now that all is dissolving and fading on this astonishing and dramatic temporal and earthly scene — how can I thank you again, Lord, for giving me not only the gift of natural life, but also the far greater gift of faith and grace, in which, in the end, what is left of me takes refuge? I close my eyes on this sorrowful, dramatic and magnificent world, calling yet again for your divine goodness to descend upon it.

A poignant goodbye from a man who consumed his life in the service of the Church so that that she might be more than ever at the service of humanity. He had to face countless challenges. From the outset, he had to bear a twofold burden: coming as he did after John XXIII, he was constantly compared to that legend;

moreover, he had to assume leadership of the Council in mid-course, and then implement its work.

His personality was very different from that of Pope John: his shyness and his personal style made it impossible for him to be at ease and on equal footing with the people.

He bravely undertook an immense task: first, to bring to conclusion the Council's work; secondly, to translate its documents concretely into the life of the Church and into its newly developed structures. His pontificate was for the most part a ministry of suffering; as Peter, the first Pope, experienced in Nero's circus, the Cross is never far from those who wish to follow the Master.

During the Council years, I was frequently asked to inform Pope Paul of the true feelings of the bishops on one subject or another. This was obviously not an easy thing to do. I often thought of what the Patriarch Athénagoras once said: "The Pope needs brothers who have the courage to speak to him with total honesty." This, of course, requires great mutual trust. From time to time, Pope Paul and I had differences of opinion, but these never in any way affected my loyalty to him.

Pope Paul was profoundly aware of his responsibility, and this awareness often seemed to overwhelm him. He wrote his speeches with great care. I sometimes said to him: "Holy Father, why not improvise?" — but he found this extremely difficult, because he felt that the Pope's words must be carefully weighed in order to avoid any cause for criticism.

He loved the Lord passionately, and served him to the extreme limits of his strength — often in particularly difficult circumstances, in a troubled and torn world. He never missed an opportunity to speak out and to proclaim the Gospel. At the United Nations, he begged his audience to put an end, for evermore, to fratricidal wars. In Italy, he called insistently on terrorists to put an end to the suffering of his friend Aldo Moro. He offered his own life in exchange for the freedom of hostages held in Mogadishu.

He fulfilled his duty towards humanity in heart and in conscience. He loved the human race with a strong and tender compassion. The question most frequently on his lips was "What can I do to help?"

> Lord,
> May Pope Paul VI,
> Who wrote an admirable encyclical on joy;
> Who, on the morning of Easter,
> Began his homily with a resounding Alleluia,
> Vibrant with his faith in the Risen Christ;
> Who suffered so profoundly,
> In the last years of his life,
> both in soul and in body,
> Enter, not only into restful peace,
> But into the Joy of God —
> Life and Rejoicing,
> For all time.

John Paul I

His election

In my notes, I find a few details concerning the election. In revealing them, I will not betray any conclave secrets, but perhaps I can give the reader a sense of the atmosphere.

We arrived at 4:30 p.m. to enter into conclave. My room was No.88; it forms a suite with No.86, which had been assigned to Cardinal Duval. This meant that I had to cross his room to go in or out of mine. Fortunately, it is one of the rooms where Benelli has had running water installed. Cardinal Luciani, like many others, had to make do with a pitcher of water. Our suite even had a shower — the ultimate luxury! Cardinals Silva and Landazuri very humbly requested the immense favour of using it, which I was happy to grant!

My room was a sort of sauna. It is difficult to describe what it's like to sleep in an oven — it is enough to make one feel quite sick.

The only window was hermetically sealed. On the second day, by sheer force, I broke the seals. Oxygen, at last! Fresh air! What a wonderful gift from God!

The first night, and the first morning – and it was the big day.

We concelebrated Mass in the Sistine Chapel at 9:30. On the previous evening, a Latin American cardinal had whispered in my ear the name of the candidate he favoured; now another stepped into my room, exchanged a few pleasantries, and suggested the same name, pointing to the man who happened to be walking down the gallery, praying the Rosary.

A first vote produced a wide range of names. On the second vote, the list was somewhat reduced. On the third, we could begin to glimpse the light of dawn; and a fourth vote brought the full light of daybreak. John Paul I was elected. Immediately, we all went to embrace the new Pope, as he exclaimed to us all, "May the Lord forgive you for what you have just done!" This quip reached the press, which, incorrectly, took it to be a reproach.

Next we followed the Pope as he stepped out on the *loggia* to give his first blessing. He then came back to have dinner with us, and took time to chat with each one. When we reached dessert, an American Cardinal asked the new Pope for permission to smoke – something definitely contrary to protocol. The Pope looked very solemn; he kept everyone waiting while he gave the matter some thought; finally he said: "Yes, Eminence, you may smoke, but on one condition: the smoke must be white!"

There was another amusing moment, when all the cardinals were preparing to process to the Sistine Chapel for a concelebrated Mass. By custom, the master of pontifical ceremonies calls out the name of each cardinal, as we line up according to rank. He absent-mindedly called out the name of Cardinal Luciani at the place he would have occupied on the previous day. Naturally, there was much laughter!

I trust I have betrayed no conclave secrets!

* * *

323

On Wednesday, August 30, those Cardinals who were still in Rome were unexpectedly called for a first audience with the Pope. Smiling, the Pope listened to a speech by the dean of the cardinals. For a moment he played with the papers in his hand; he reflected, aloud, "Shall I read this prepared speech, or shall I improvise?" This was a foretaste of a mood we were to see quite often in later audiences. He decided to improvise; I attempted at that point to provoke some applause for his decision, but my venerable colleagues remained unmoved. In the course of his improvised speech, the Pope told us that Cardinal Felici had handed him a small gift at the conclave, saying, *"con voce soave"* ("in a gentle voice"), "A message for the Pope." It was a metal reproduction of the stations of the Cross. Pope John Paul resisted the temptation to give a grim commentary, and remarked instead that one of the stations represented the meeting of Jesus with Simon of Cyrene; he would count on us to play the role of Simon.

Then he continued: "I am new to the Vatican; I know nothing of its inner workings, of its machinery. The first thing I did was to open the Pontifical Directory to find out 'who's who' and how the whole thing works."

Finally, he picked up the paper with the speech prepared for him by the Secretariat of State, which concluded with the traditional apostolic blessing. Halfway through, he stopped reading: "I find it a little embarassing to bless you; all of us here are the Lord's Apostles, and the wording is quite pompous." Nevertheless, he gave us a quick blessing. After that, one by one, we kissed his ring.

He had a few personal words for each cardinal. Ahead of me was the Franciscan Cardinal Landazuri of Peru, to whom he said *"Ecco San Francesco!"* ("Here is St Francis!") He greeted me with these words: "Here is the Cardinal of the Holy Spirit, who writes so magnificently about him." I whispered in his ear: "Would it be at all possible – as a kindness to the Protestants, and for television, where lengthy things are not appreciated – for you to omit the long Latin formula announcing indulgences at the end of next week's pontifical benediction, after the ceremony in St Peter's Square?" The Pope answered: "Speak to the master of ceremonies." To this I responded, "No, Holy Father, you must tell him: my role is merely to make suggestions to you, nothing more." However, nothing came of this.

One last memory: one morning, as I arrived at the Vatican, I met a group of five cardinals in the elevator; like me, they were on their way to an audience with the Pope. Among them was Cardinal Parente, former assessor at the Holy Office; for many years, he had been second-in-command in that Congregation, and Ottaviani's right-hand man. He had not taken part in the conclave due to his advanced age. Like the rest of us, however, he had been invited to the first plenary audience with the new Pope. I felt I should somehow make amends to him for the age limit which had excluded him from the conclave. As the elevator, in which we were very tightly packed, rapidly ascended, I put out my hand across various shoulders and said to him, in a very loud voice: "Cardinal Parente, I salute in you a very brave defender of collegiality at the Council. Your statement will always be remembered, and we all know the price you have paid for it!" I was alluding to a speech he had made at the Council pleading in favour of collegiality — a speech which caused great consternation at the Holy Office, and which was greatly appreciated by the majority of Council members.

We stepped out of the elevator, and continued the conversation privately. He said to me: "During the first millennium, the Church experienced true collegiality; in the second millennium, all of that was 'officialised'. Now we must revert to the genuine conception, and no *Nota praevia* will stand in our way!" Coming from him, this remark was so unexpected that I wrote it down; the future will tell whether he had the gift of prophecy.

* * *

What used to be known as the Pope's "coronation" took place on September 3, 1978. John Paul I transformed this into a pastoral inaugural ceremony of great simplicity, officially described as a "solemn Mass marking the beginning of his ministry as Supreme Pastor". In line with tradition, this involved a procession during which each cardinal made an act of obedience. As he embraced me, the Pope joked: *"Ecco, l'incontro con lo Spirito Santo; mi raccomando."* ("An encounter with the Holy Spirit – don't forget to pray for me.")

That day, I went to Ciampino Airport to greet the King and Queen of the Belgians, who had come for the inaugural ceremony. In the airport lounge, I met Mgr Caprio, a Vatican prelate representing the Holy See, who was also there to welcome them. As we waited, he told me about his first working session with Pope John Paul, which had taken place earlier that same day. "When we had finished our business," he told me, "the Pope stood up to see me to the door. I said to him: 'Holy Father, it is not the custom for the Pope to walk to the door with one of his collaborators.' He replied, *'Nessuno può impedire al Papa di fare due passi'* ('No one can keep the Pope from walking a few steps.')." He definitely belonged to the same school as John XXIII – a Pope full of surprises, with a style all his own.

John Paul's anguish, and his spontaneity

John Paul I came and went like a meteor in the Church's sky. His election was a surprise to one and all, but above all to him. When my turn came to embrace him during the ceremony of obedience in the Sistine Chapel, a few moments after his election, I said to him: "Thank you, Holy Father, for accepting such a heavy burden!" He quickly replied, with a smile that softened his words: "Perhaps I would have done better to refuse!" These words were not spoken casually.

On the following morning – he had spent the night in his conclave cell – I ran into him in the hallway and walked with him to the Sistine Chapel, where the concelebrated Mass was to take place. I asked him, quite naturally, "Well, did you sleep well, after yesterday's events?" and he replied to me: "No, I had only doubts." These words confirmed those he had spoken on the previous day; but this time they definitely suggested a pessimistic interpretation.

We were not aware at the time that he had undergone several operations because of circulatory problems, and that this was a hereditary condition in his family. He revealed it himself, several days later, at an audience for sick people. I mention this because it sheds some light on the sudden death of the dearly-beloved Pope John Paul I, and may serve to discredit the wild speculations that surrounded his death.

A memory
This is a story that goes back to the days before John Paul I was elected Pope; it gives us a glimpse of that special spontaneity that gave him so much charm, and shows how unexpected and amusing his reactions could be. Most readers are probably familiar with the fictional letters he wrote to famous writers of the past — Dickens, Mark Twain, Briand, Poincaré, Clemenceau, Chesterton, Goethe, Manzoni, Péguy and Teresa of Avila. Here is a letter he wrote to me, at the time when he was still Patriarch of Venice.

Between two session of a synod, we once discussed the Charismatic Renewal, and I told him of my book, *A New Pentecost?* I promised to send him a copy, provided he in turn promised not to write me the sort of letter which, all too often, I find myself writing, and which says: "Dear Sir, thank you for your book. I will read it very soon. I am quite sure that I shall greatly benefit from reading it, etc. etc." We laughed together, and he promised that he would truly read the book before writing to me, and would not send me the kind of form letter I had described. When his letter came, this is what it said, with the thoughtfulness and freshness that characterised him:

Venice, December 10, 1974

Your Eminence,

On page 260 of your book *A New Pentecost?*, you claim that your words are somehow "inadequate", that "all of this is not well said". I beg to disagree: you have said it all very well indeed. You have a gift for writing in a way that captures the reader, interests him and captivates him.

So much for the form. As to the substance, I must admit that as I went along, I often felt the need to go back, with new eyes, to certain passages in St Paul and in the Acts of the Apostles — passages which I thought I knew well (p.128). For me, your book has been, and will continue to be, a precious guide to the Acts.

Thanking you for the good you have done to my soul, and for the service you have given in motivating the Church, I wish you all the best for Christmas and a very happy New Year.

Respectfully yours,

A. Luciani, Patriarch

In the sudden death of this beloved and spontaneous Pope, we see that the richness of a life cannot be measured by its length.

John Paul II
Here are my unedited notes on the election of John Paul II, as I wrote them on October 25, 1978.

I have just returned from Rome. This second conclave started on October 14 and ended on October 22, culminating in a "coronation" with no crown.

Now we are back home, after those long busy days, so heavily involved with the future.

In contrast to the previous conclave, at which I had made no effort to establish contacts before the opening, this time I saw a great many people: Hume, Lorscheider, Jubany, Arns, Silva, Marty, Gouyon, and others, with whom I exchanged ideas.

We set out on an adventure with the Lord. Thinking that we were off on a trip to the South Pole, we ended up at the North Pole. Once again, the Lord has worked wonders. There is indeed a conclave secret — it is the Holy Spirit. All the rest is human games and very trivial secrets. It has been said that God speaks through the signs of the times; among these signs we must include mathematical signs. At the conclave, God uses this language of numbers, and it is important to know how to read it. The convergence of votes on a given name is the sign of that communion, which the Lord expects and brings about.

And now, here we are, standing before John Paul II, the new Pastor of the Universal Church. I have met him two or three times, at various synods; he was in my *circulus minor* — the French language working group. At the last Synod, in 1977, his name was not on our list. I ran into him in a corridor, and asked him why he had not chosen the French group. He replied: "This time I decided to join the Italian group; I thought that perhaps our experience with communism in Poland might be useful to them." An open letter from Bishop Bettazzi to the head of the Italian Communist Party had recently brought this issue to the forefront of public attention. Later, in the Synod assembly, I requested that, for the sake of realism, the working-groups should be organised on the basis of issues, rather than languages; to support my argument, I mentioned this conversation, without revealing the name of the bishop with whom I had been speaking.

I heard several of the statements he made, as Cardinal, within our working group; but I have never had a full conversation with him.

I am convinced that the new Pope will find the appropriate "dimension of the Church" within which to situate himself, as the third millennium draws near. Normally, he should be the one to guide Peter's boat to those shores. It will not be our dear Luciani's Venetian gondola – more likely, it will be a vigorous steamer that will give confidence by its solid construction and the power of its motors. In what direction will he set our course?

My feeling is that he will resolutely break away from the curial style and from that certain Italian "decorum" – which is all for the best. All too often, "yes" meant "perhaps" and "perhaps" meant "no". It is likely that in future, "yes" will mean "yes" and "no" will mean "no". The real question is, to what will he say "yes", to what "no"? I have a feeling that the *"idem velle"* will be much broader.

After the election, during the obedience ceremony in the Sistine Chapel, where he stood to embrace us – a very good touch, that – the Pope said to me: "Thank you for all that I owe to Belgium, and in particular for the years I spent at the Belgian College. And thank you, Eminence, for all that we owe to you." I have no idea what he was alluding to; I suppose it was to the Council, since later, during the Cardinals' audience, he said to me: "It will now be possible to bring about what you had hoped for." Once more, I'm not sure what he meant by this; perhaps he was thinking of collegiality, since it is of this that he spoke to me after the concelebrated Mass in the Sistine Chapel, saying, "And now, let us have some affective and effective collegiality."

The day of the inauguration was a great day indeed. The Pope exudes an air of faith and of power. I feel that God himself has chosen him for us, for no one has more spirit than the Holy Spirit. He will be a man for new times; a man of bold decisions, not routine ones; one who will go beyond muffled diplomacy, facing into the wind, and even into the storm. He will need to be strong at the helm and very weak in prayer before God. One of his fellow students in Rome, Paul de Haes, used to say that the intensity of his prayer "is enough to make you jealous". He prays with his whole body – he is an incarnation of prayer – and at those moments he looks years older. He bows deeply, bending close to the ground; in the Sistine Chapel, during his prayer of thanksgiving, he looked as though he had collapsed, and I feared that he had been taken ill. But as soon as he stands up straight and smiles, he looks amazingly young.

During the public obedience ceremony, *in piazza*, I suddenly had the very unconventional impulse to tell him something that would go straight to his heart: I suggested that he should have a swimming-pool built in the Vatican, immediately, to protect himself from the Roman heat. He burst out laughing. This intrigued those of my friends who were watching the scene on television; I promised them that I would reveal the secret if the Pope took up my suggestion. He did, and I kept my promise.

A first trip to Poland

A few weeks before the conclave, the future John Paul II had invited me to go to Poland, on the occasion of the sixth centenary of Our Lady of Czestochowa. His election gave a different slant to this invitation. I had already accepted it; now I was looking forward to the added joy of being present when the first Polish Pope in the history of the Church returned for the first time to his homeland.

I left Brussels on June 8, accompanied by my secretary, Canon W. Brieven, and by Mr Galawski, the leader of the Polish community in Brussels, who was to be our very valuable interpreter.

As I got off the plane in Warsaw, I could see from a distance a group of people, waving bunches of flowers, in the airport waiting-room. I had no idea who was being welcomed in this festive manner; only gradually, as I made my way into the lounge, did I understand that this was all in my honour. These were members of a charismatic renewal group, and some executives from a publishing house; they had come to present me with two icons and a chalice, to thank me because I had not asked them for royalties from the translations of my books.

The Belgian Ambassador was there to meet me; he made sure I was spared the lengthy customs formalities, and was very thoughtful and kind. That evening, as we were having dinner at the Embassy, I asked his wife if the government authorities had hidden microphones in the house. She replied with serene humour: "Oh, I suppose they must have, but that does not bother us in the least; everyone already knows what we think!"

We left Warsaw on the following day, heading for Cracow, where the Holy Father had already arrived. As soon as we met, at the Archbishop's House, he asked me for news of his friend at the Belgian College, Mgr Marcel Uylenbroeck, who was gravely ill and who died soon afterwards.

The Pope was definitely at home here, on his own territory; one sensed that the people, who never stopped cheering and applauding in the street outside the building, were truly his flock. They continuously chanted the Polish words of greeting *"Sto-lat!"* which mean "May you live a hundred years!"

The Pope left us and went back to the window, and I listened to the following family conversation. The Pope called out a question: "Do you really want me to live a hundred years?" "Yes! Yes! Yes!" they shouted back. "And do you really want me to have good health?" "Yes! Yes! Yes!" came the answer. "Well, then, I beg you, go home and let me sleep!" he concluded, with a smile and a blessing.

The main public events were scheduled for the following day, Sunday, June 10. A crowd of two million people gathered for the Eucharist, in a huge public park, to welcome their former archbishop. I have never seen such a crowd – there were enough people there to fill St Peter's Square in Rome ten times over. I was listening to a translation of the Pope's homily, and I gathered that the Pope was appealing urgently to his people, calling every Polish man and woman to become rooted more strongly than ever in the grace of baptism, in order to overcome the trials to which they were being subjected.

In the afternoon, I was present for the Pope's departure from his homeland, back to Rome. As the plane left the ground, the crowd took up a popular local song: "Mountaineer, come back, do not forget your native mountains...". It was a moment of great emotional intensity; I felt sure that the Pope would indeed return, for he is in every fibre of his being a child of his native land.

On the day after his departure, we went to visit the Cathedral in Cracow — a place of marvellous beauty, with great historical significance. Then we drove to the sanctuary of Our Lady of Czestochowa.

When we arrived at the Convent of Jasna Gora, I met a Czech woman who had illegally crossed the border to see the Pope. She recognised me, and told me that a story she had read in one of my books — *Christian Life Day by Day* — had forever changed her life. The story was about a child who survived a fire because he jumped out of the second-storey window, even though he was blinded by the smoke, simply because he could hear his father's voice calling: "Jump into my arms: I can see you, and that is enough." "My creed", she told me, "lies entirely in the similar invitation which God addresses to his children."

In the evening, I celebrated Mass at the sanctuary, with Mgr Mamie, Bishop of Fribourg, and another Swiss bishop. Mgr Mamie told me that when he was a close collaborator of the future Cardinal Journet, the latter had said to him: "Make sure you always read whatever Cardinal Suenens writes about the Holy Virgin." This filled me with joy. In a way, it was a quid pro quo, because during the Council, whenever I and the other moderators discussed collegiality with Paul VI, we always quoted Journet; his words, more than those of any other, seemed to convince the Pope of the validity of our arguments. I must add that in his very important book on the Church, Journet has written a few pages on the subject of charisms which are quite extraordinary, particularly in the context of his day and age.

Our travels resumed; together we went on a pilgrimage to Auschwitz, that Golgotha of human suffering. The sight is staggering, almost unbearable in its horror. We went to pray in Father Kolbe's cell; here we were face to face with the opposite extreme, a luminous peak of evangelic charity. Never have I experienced so intensely the reality of the powers of evil. What happenend there goes far beyond human perversion.

I returned to Poland in 1982, invited by the Primate of Poland and by the Charismatic Renewal Movement, which was holding its first National Congress in Czestochowa. These groups were only beginning to come out of hiding, and it was impossible to predict how many people would show up. It was quite a surprise to see six thousand pilgrims. The police were visibly anxious about such a large gathering, and helicopters hovered vigilantly over the crowd.

We, who are Christians living in free countries, do not appreciate sufficiently the price of freedom, and we are too afraid to affirm our faith. The Church of silence is not where we think it is. This should be an invitation to each one of us to examine our consciences. I can understand how it came to be that Poland gave us a Pope who challenges our inertia and the timidity with which we proclaim the Gospel. What I find most striking in his lifestyle is his obedience, a literal obedience, to the Master's command: "Go take the Gospel to the very ends of the earth." He incarnates brilliantly the Church in mission.

1979

A few last commitments

As I waited for my successor to be appointed, I fulfilled a few last commitments I had made in London, at Princeton, USA, and in Biella, in Italy.

London: I went to London with Fr Lebeau, who came along to provide theological support. I had been invited to meet with twenty-four Anglican bishops at Windsor Castle; I was to be the only Catholic bishop there.

As it turned out, we discussed no major doctrinal issues. We had the opportunity, however, to learn a great deal about the English mentality, which is so much more pragmatic than ours; and we had a chance to admire the famous chapel where the standards of the Order of the Garter are kept. In other words, it was above all a friendly get-together, very intense and busy.

Later that summer, I returned to London to speak at the ecumenical conference of the Fountain Trust, on the theme "Charismatic Renewal, Evangelisation and Social Action". Most of the participants appeared to be Protestants. I prayed very specially to the Holy Spirit to inspire my words as I tried to find a common ground; I literally plunged in, trusting in God's grace.

The reactions were overwhelming, and I mention them here in a spirit of thanksgiving to the Lord. Non-Catholics came to see me later, to tell me, "We were deeply moved by your every word." "Forgive us for not applauding — we were too moved." "My heart was burning as I listened, as at Emmaus; and let me assure you that when a Presbyterian Minister, and one who comes from Northern Ireland, says this, these are not empty words."

Thank you, Lord.

Princeton: In the United States, a variegated itinerary took me to Pittsburgh, Little Rock, Palm Beach and Princeton.

At Princeton University, I met with Mgr G. Danneels, who was also visiting the United States, and who was then Bishop of Anvers; in 1980, he was to become my successor. Together, we listened to the witness of a professor of psychiatry who had been converted by the Charismatic Renewal; he described, in amazing technical detail, the ways in which the action of grace had transformed even his medical approach to his patients. This was followed by a colloquium with faculty members of the Department of Theology.

Memories and Hopes

The Head of this Department, Professor McCord, invited me to come to Princeton as a visiting professor, to give courses in pastoral ministry in the perspectives opened up by Vatican II; I did not accept his offer, as it would have required too much travel.

Biella: The Bishop of Biella had invited me to speak to his clergy about the Charismatic Renewal, and so I went there for a brief visit. I was greeted very cordially by the Bishop; the audience, however, was very reserved, and only thawed gradually. A famous reporter, Vittorio Messori, author of the best-selling book *Ipotesi su Gesù,* came to talk to me there. I have seldom met a journalist so knowledgeable about religious matters. He asked me a great many questions; I particularly remember a very complicated one concerning the hellenisation of the theology of the Holy Spirit by the Greek Fathers. I was struck by the contrast with an hour-long television interview, on the charisms of the Holy Spirit, which I had once given to a Baptist journalist in Philadelphia. These kinds of interviews can be risky; all too often, the reporter knows absolutely nothing about the subject, and is only looking for something sensational. There are times, however, when such dialogues are a real joy. This was the case that day in Biella.

On the same trip, I visited the sanctuary of the Madonna of Oropa. Both in size and in style, this is an impressive centre for pilgrimages; two thousand pilgrims can be housed there at one time. I slept in the royal apartments of the Kings of Piedmont, in a canopied bed with steps leading up to it; on the walls were portraits of the Princes of Savoy, looking proud and conceited, with curled moustaches, rows and rows of decorations, their chests puffed out — the stuff of nightmares! It all belongs to such a distant foggy past.

My goodbyes to the diocese

I was approaching the age of seventy-five; the time had come to retire. I therefore requested the *"nunc dimittis"* from Pope John Paul. This I did, first to remain consistent with myself, since I had been the instigator of this pastoral innovation; it also meant that I would no longer have to carry the burden of service to my country's Church in addition to all of the work which had sprung from the Council – in particular in the service of ecumenism in English-speaking countries.

My resignation, offered on July 14, 1979, became effective on January 4, 1980.

The diocese had been divided into three pastoral sectors, which meant that there were three sets of goodbyes and many touching memories. In the Cathedral of Brussels, in the presence of King Baudouin, I called one last time on Christians to be consistent in their faith and to witness more fully to Christ, at all times and in all places.

A solemn goodbye ceremony was held in the Palais des Beaux Arts in Brussels. I remember it vividly for a number of reasons.

Cardinal Etchegaray, who was at the time President of the French Episcopal Conference, came to the ceremony to bring the fraternal greetings of the Church of France. I had known him during the Council, when, full of vitality and initiative, he had been Secretary to the same Bishops' Conference.

Cardinal Benelli came from Florence, in a gesture of friendship, and to guarantee my Roman orthodoxy by his mere presence. I was overcome when I saw him, for he was physically almost unrecognisable: the day before, he had been in a serious motor accident on the road between Rome and Florence, and he should have been resting in bed and seeing a doctor. He brushed aside all such sensible advice, and gave a warm and friendly speech in honour of our shared past. He then returned to Florence and was immediately admitted into hospital.

The last speaker at the ceremony was Léo Moulin, a great scholar, a social scientist and a non-believer, and a specialist in a wide variety of fields, including St Benedict's Rule and the Rule of the Chartreux – and an old friend of mine. He opened his speech with these words, which made everyone laugh: "I wonder what I'm doing here; I suppose I'm here because, not being a

Catholic, I'm used to obeying bishops' orders!"

A further cause for joy, as I said goodbye, was the appointment of my successor, Cardinal Danneels: I knew that the diocese would be in good hands. During one of the farewell gatherings, Cardinal Danneels made public the words that the Holy Father had said to him about me: "Cardinal Suenens played a crucial role during Vatican II, and the Universal Church owes much to him."

Ultima verba

Here is a brief text that was distributed to members of the diocese, as my goodbye — my last message to them:

> As Christians, we are a people of hope.
> We know where we come from
> and where we are going.
> We know that we come from God
> and shall return to him,
> to enter for all time
> into the fullness of life —
> which is the Father, the Son and the Holy Spirit,
> in communion with the angels and the saints
> and Mary, their Queen.
>
> We know that we are invited to enter
> into a new world,
> "that no eye has seen
> and no ear has heard
> that is beyond the heart of man,
> that God has prepared
> for those who love Him" (1 Co 2:9) —
> a world that is greater than all hope.
> May every one of us,
> at the end of this life on earth,
> sing in joy and thanksgiving
> the moving antiphon
> that the liturgy for Advent

has so often placed on our lips:
"O Wisdom, who imbues all life
from beginning to end,
who guides its every detail,
who brings it to its appointed end
with a powerful hand
and with tender gentleness."

L.J. Cardinal Suenens

7

Active Retirement (1980-1990)

Three memorable events have marked this decade of active retirement: the celebration, in Washington, of the anniversary of a branch of the Ecumenical Marian Society; the prayer-lunch with President Carter in Washington; and the Pastoral Days in Chattanooga with about one hundred Episcopalian bishops.

1980

The Ecumenical Marian Society in Washington
The American branch of the Ecumenical Marian Society was celebrating an anniversary Mass at the National Marian Shrine in Washington, and I was invited to preside and to give a homily. At the offertory, two charming Protestant professors, Donald Dawe and Ross Mackenzie (both of whom taught at Union Theological Seminary in Richmond), walked through the church towards me, cruets in hand, like well-trained altar boys — a most unusual sight, and one which greatly surprised me.

I spent the following day with them. Donald Dawe invited us to a small private dinner at La Petite France, where the refined gourmet style was definitely that of *la Grande France*. He was delightful in his spontaneity and his wild erudition. He speaks a wide range of Indian and other dialects; he has written a book called *How to Introduce Saint Paul in India*; he has taught in India and in Japan; he speaks with equal ease of the courses he taught in these countries and of a vast array of strange and exotic sects he has studied. Keeping the conversation going is not a problem; he never stops talking! And everything he says is fascinating. His sentences are punctuated by bursts of laughter as

340

funny memories spring to his mind. He defends the Pope against
Küng; he once wrote an article on this subject. In other words,
he is the ideal preacher for Catholics enamoured of the anti-
Roman syndrome!

His friend Ross Mackenzie is very different; he has an almost
Benedictine placidity, but he is just as ecumenical and Marian. He
had just written a book about Mary, and asked me to write a preface for it; it is called *Mary, Teacher of Praise.* I have not yet seen
it on sale.

Then I spent a day with other members of the Theology faculty
in Richmond. The climate was excellent, and we had a friendly
discussion concerning Peter's ministry in the Church of tomorrow.

In the *Commonweal* issue of February 15, 1980, I found an
article by Donald Dawe, entitled "Protestants and the Pope";
every line of this article deserves to be read with great attention.
I sent a copy to the Pope, because it contains valuable guidelines
on which words to use and which to avoid using. The author
would like Rome to stop using expressions that imply an exclusive ownership of the Pope by Catholics – a rather original
request!

A prayer-lunch with President Carter

My central purpose on this particular trip was to participate
actively in a prayer-meeting with the American President.

In the huge ballroom of the Washington Hilton, some two
thousand guests – every one of them a very important person –
had assembled. At eight in the morning, we had a quick breakfast
at small tables. The religious event began with a few prayers and
exhortations, and readings from the Old and New Testament.

At about 10:00 a.m. President Carter took the floor and spoke
about "human growth". He took the opportunity to stress the
need for spiritual growth as well. He spoke like a Baptist preacher. He looked kind and generous; he is more likeable in person

than in his photographs, where he often has a constrained smile. His wife looked very unaffected; she inspired confidence. When he had finished his "homily", the President retired, and the guests broke up into "seminars" in the adjoining lounges. I was to speak to them on "The Role of the Christian in the World of Today".

After my talk, I answered a few questions. The most unusual one was the following: "Would the Cardinal tell us where he has learned to speak about Jesus Christ like a Southern Baptist Preacher?" It was said humorously and gently, as a way of thanking me.

This morning session, presided over by Senator Douglas E. Coe, lasted two hours: various people bore witness in a touching, direct way. It is difficult to imagine our own senators and representatives talking about their personal religious experiences aloud – or even in a whisper, for that matter!

Next, we all made our way back to the Ballroom, where we were served lunch. I had to finish mine rather quickly. I was sitting with the organising committee on the stage, from where I was about to give a talk to the assembled crowd. I found that giving a speech to a group of people who are eating lunch is far from exhilarating; worse yet, half-way through, I was handed a note asking me to make the speech as long as possible, since the speaker who was supposed to follow me had been taken ill. I told myself that I should chalk this up to experience, and avoid similar situations in future! I remember this prayer-meeting particularly well because it did much to help me understand a people who have few inhibitions, for whom God is still, always and openly, the God who created humanity and the world – even though the image they have of Him is often somewhat Americanised!

Chattanooga

My last trip to the United States was in October 1980. The bishops of the Episcopalian Church of the United States and of Canada were holding their annual assembly. I had been asked to lead them in prayer for an hour each day, before their working sessions. There were about 120 participants, and the meetings went on for ten days. Every year they choose a new venue; that year they had decided to meet in Chattanooga.

I left from Rome, where I had taken part in the Special Synod, which met from September 25 to October 20. That very morning, the Pope had celebrated the Eucharist in his private chapel for our small charismatic group, which had come specially to pray for the bishops at the Synod. I had suggested to the participants that they should chant in tongues after communion, as a prayer of thanksgiving. When the mass was over, I asked the Pope whether the spontaneous chanting in tongues had disturbed him during his prayer of thanksgiving. He replied: "On the contrary; it helped me to pray more deeply."

I left Rome with Fr John Catoir – the successor to Fr Keller, founder of *Christopher News-Notes* – whom I had introduced to the Pope. The plane flew to Atlanta, via Boston; from there, we proceeded by car to our destination. We arrived absolutely exhausted.

I stayed in Chattanooga from October 3 to 8, leading the Episcopalian bishops in prayer every morning from 9:00 to 10:00; this morning prayer was supported by a lay "charismatic" choir. We all stayed at the same hotel; this made conversation easier, and was convenient for the informal prayer meeting which we held in my room after each meal. About twenty Episcopalian bishops came to pray with me, many of them sitting on the floor. It is difficult to imagine this kind of spontaneity in our own lifestyle!

This was to be my last contact with the Episcopalians. The time was not right for ecumenical *rapprochement*: sixty-three Episcopalian ministers had opted for the Catholic Church, and one of the Episcopalian bishops had publicly put an end to ecumenical dialogue with his Catholic colleague in the diocese (Mgr Gerety). This, however, did not affect my own relationship with the Episcopalian bishops; Bishop Allin, the President, was still very much my friend, and had even invited me to come to the working sessions of the commission – which invitation, through discretion, I declined. When my "occasional" secretary, Fr John Catoir, had to leave, Dean Collins, of Atlanta, came to serve at Mass – without receiving communion – in my hotel room.

On the way back, I flew from Atlanta to Brussels. I could see from afar the fairy-tale outlines of a restaurant whose brightly-lit elevators were suspended on the outside of the building, as if to defy every convention.

This will remain, for me, the last memory of a country to which I felt very close – which I have loved for the warmth and the kindness of its people, and for the friendships I made, which are still very precious to me today.

Scotland

A "charismatic" invitation from Scotland took me to Glasgow, Dundee and Edinburgh, where I stayed with Cardinal Gray – I had been told that I had to win him over to the cause of Charismatic Renewal.

In Glasgow I had a rather strange experience. I had been warned that a group of Scottish Protestants were planning a demonstration against my presence in Glasgow; this was scheduled to take place during the charismatic service that was to be celebrated in a Catholic church in the city. And indeed, there were demonstrators waving posters and banners at the main entrance to the church, but I did not see them, because I entered through the sacristy. There were no disruptions during the ceremony itself. However, there were more protests on the radio that evening, when one of the Protestant leaders was vehemently attacked for his benevolent attitude towards Catholics. I heard harsh explosive words, full of hatred: "You are betraying Knox! You forget the Spanish Armada!" The entire history of the sixteenth and seventeenth centuries was brought in. It was all unbelievably anachronistic, but it was a clear indication that ecumenism is a delicate problem at the grass-roots level, and that the

344

burden of the past is still very heavy indeed.

My day in Edinburgh with Cardinal Gray was, by contrast, a source of great joy, both for him and for me. About fifteen hundred young people of the Charismatic Renewal greeted their bishop and the day's speaker with such warmth and enthusiasm that the Cardinal was deeply touched and filled with new hope.

In the Tyrol

Two American Methodist bishops, retired from active ministry, have specialised in accompanying American tourists to the Holy Land during Easter vacations, and around Europe in the summer. The bishops organise cultural and religious events which give a spiritual dimension to these tours.

They came to Brussels to ask me if, during the month of August, I would give four religious talks to their group in Ellman, a small Austrian village in the Tyrol, which they used as a base for trips to Switzerland and Bavaria.

I, too, was retired by then, and so I was able to accept their invitation. This was the reason for an unexpected stay in a colourful little Tyrolean hotel whose balconies were decorated with brilliant geraniums. Quite late every evening, when the exhausted tourists returned from their excursions and museum tours, I would give my talks. All of this was organised with a very American efficiency: they were accompanied by a university professor from Chicago, who was an expert in the literature and theatre of the sixteenth and seventeenth centuries. I was impressed by such details, and by the thoroughness with which this tourist organisation was run.

Every morning, I celebrated the Eucharist privately in the little village church in Ellman, whose curate was away on vacation. I had not hidden this fact from my tourists, nor had I advertised it. When the kindly Methodist bishops heard about this, they asked me, with much embarrassment, whether I expected their flock to be present and to receive communion. I answered that I did not.

345

Deeply relieved, they thanked me profusely: for a moment, they had feared that the group's absence from the celebration would offend me. As it turned out, their little flock decided on their own to come to Mass; both bishops were at the door of the church to inform each new arrival that "the Cardinal does not expect you to receive communion". I gave a homily in English for them, and at the end of the celebration I invited the Methodist tourists to sing a hymn of their choice. They sang beautifully and wholeheartedly. At the end, many photographs were taken in the little cemetery beside the church.

At the end of my stay in Ellman, the professor from the University of Chicago, who turned out to be a Mormon, drove me to Zurich airport.

The kindly Methodist bishops taught me that we must love God and our neighbours actively, even when we have reached the age for retirement, and that we must use creative imagination and a touch of humour to deal with unexpected situations.

Dublin

The university chaplain had invited me to speak to the students at University College Dublin. This time, in contrast to other lectures I had given at universities, I was to meet groups of students by department. This new approach, which allowed for more individual contact, was of course much more demanding, but also more direct.

I arrived in Dublin eight days after Frank Duff's death. All the Irish bishops had been present at his funeral. I went to pray at his tomb with the leaders of the Dublin "concilium" of the Legion of Mary.

Frank Duff's name is known everywhere in the world. He was the founder of the Legion of Mary, and was its main organiser for almost sixty years. The apostolic organisation he developed has spread to five continents and is active in more than two thousand dioceses. I know of no other evangelical effort of such scope.

Today, the Legion counts among its past members an impressive number of martyrs – primarily in China and in Africa – and two of its envoys are on the list for future beatifications: Edel Quinn, for former British Equatorial Africa, and Alfie Lambe for South America.

During the Council, I asked Pope Paul to invite Frank Duff to be one of the lay observers. When he arrived in the Council hall, the 2,300 Council Fathers gave him a touching and enthusiastic ovation – a vote of thanks from the Universal Church to this pioneer of the lay apostolate.

Frank Duff founded the Legion of Mary in 1921, on the Feast of the Nativity of Mary. He did not like to be refered to as its founder. In 1971, when the Legion celebrated its fiftieth anniversary in Dublin, in the presence of all the Irish bishops, the organisers had trouble finding Frank Duff, who was lost in the crowd and had to be extricated from it.

When I speak of him as a pioneer of the lay apostolate, I am merely underlining his prophetic mission. When I describe him as a genius, I wish to give recognition to the unequalled merit of having instituted a concrete and practical method of apostolate, available to every baptised person, and of having given it a soul: lived consecration to the Holy Spirit in filial union with Mary.

To end this section, I cannot resist the pleasure of telling, to the glory of Irish humour, the story of a misadventure which occurred at the end of a long night's drive from Limerick to Dublin. My friend and driver, Fr Martin Tierney, who was at the time Secretary of the Irish Bishops' Conference, was taking me to the seminary in Dublin where I was supposed to spend the night. It was almost midnight when we arrived. We knocked at the door, but there was no answer. Finally, he climbed over a wall and up to the second floor of the building, found the President's room, and announced: "The Cardinal is here." "What cardinal?" asked the President. "We are not expecting anyone."

My friend had made a mistake; he had taken me to the wrong seminary. Up to this point, the story has nothing very extraordinary about it, but it did not end there. The President of the seminary came to the door, in his pyjamas, explained the mistake to me, gave us the correct address, and asked me if I would autograph his visitors' book! Which of course I did!

When I returned home from Ireland, I found a piece of paper on which I had written a few lines by way of thanksgiving for this country, to which I owe so much, on a spiritual level and also on an evangelical level:

"The Lord is my shepherd; I shall not want.
He maketh me to lie down in green pastures."
In my mind, I see the Irish shepherd,
his face hewn from rock,
his smile a web of wrinkles;
by his side a faithful dog
who does his work unassumingly,
taking it for granted,
vigilant and discreet,
gathering the sheep together
by his mere presence.
And I think of the fields and the meadows —
Lord, how green they are
on Erin's Green Isle!
And how fresh the grass,
fresh as nowhere else in the world,
in this paradise of colours —
lavender, yellow, red —
but above all green,
a tender, newborn green;
a green that God has reserved for "His" land,
the land of the shamrock,
which is also green,
and symbol of the Trinity.
Thank you, Lord, for creating Ireland
at the dawn of Creation,
one spring morning
in the freshness of daybreak;

348

for offering us these landscapes,
these shores, these islands —
these three hundred and sixty-five islands
in one distant corner —
these rocks, these pebbles, these promontories.
Thank you for opening up new horizons
on the beauty of God,
on the freshness of His love,
on the loving vigilance
of the ever-attentive Shepherd.
Thank you for the fresh grass of your pastures,
and for having linked us
to the springtime of your Church,
so hesitant still, and yet so necessary
if your Church is to find again its first vitality —
the smooth face with which it was born,
in the early morning,
as on the day of Pentecost.
Amen.

1981

On the threshold of the future
What does getting old mean?

Old age is a strange experience; it is living all ages at once —
the past, the present, and the future.

As I approached my eightieth birthday, a magazine asked me
for my thoughts on this turning-point. I replied that I had a
strange feeling with respect to the past — a past which is less and
less familiar to those around me, and which I must increasingly
explain in detail if I want to be understood. The War of 1914-
1918, Cardinal Mercier, Eisenhower, and even Vatican II — all of
this was my life, and now, for the new generations, it is lost in the
distant fog. The past vanishes as gradually as a ship that slowly
sinks into the sea, far off on the horizon.

The present is also strange; for me, it is the past taking shape, becoming real and realising all of its substance and its richness. I can well understand the answer Corot gave when he was asked "How long did it take you to paint this picture?" He replied, "Five minutes and a lifetime."

Finally, I have a very new feeling about the future; the communion of saints; Heaven, which is there to be discovered; and – at the very heart of the future – the immense tenderness of God reaching out to me. It is an invitation to make haste, to look up at the stars that make the night so bright, and to give thanks to the Lord for that world which is yet to come.

Impressions of a retired bishop

For me, the last stage actually began in 1981, when I made the decision to accept no more invitations to the United States and to concentrate on the "global village" which we call Europe. I continued to accept invitations to meetings in Italy, Switzerland, Denmark and other countries, for ecumenical and charismatic events; the two quite often coincided.

Providence provided me with a travelling companion, Fr Albert Van de Ven, who is also retired, and whom we have privately renamed "Timothée". Once he was the spiritual director of the Flemish "senatus" of the Legion of Mary; his devotion had been unflagging, as had been his practical efficiency.

Before sharing a few last memories of my active life, I will try to respond to a question which journalists are always asking me: what is it like to be a retired cardinal? At first, I used to tell them that they should give me time to find out what "retirement" means. Today, I still have not discovered the meaning of "rest" and "retirement", because I have continued to be intensely active. The only difference is that the scope of my activities is more simple, and that I set its boundaries myself. Given all of this, here is what I felt at the beginning of that decade: I rediscovered the right to dream; the right not to know; and the right to transcend time.

Let me explain.

The right to dream

By this I mean the right to start afresh, not from what is, but from what "ought to be" — to go back to the first, the original, the "normal" meaning of Christianity — and from that starting point, to dream about what a "normal" Christian ought to be like, a "normal" priest, a "normal" bishop, a "normal" seminary, a "normal" synod, "normal" ecumenism, the "normal" logic of Vatican II.

It is the right to dream of a pastoral approach which would go straight to the heart of issues, rather than having to deal with immediate problems; all too often, these are insoluble — attempts to fit square pegs into round holes — at the level of persons and situations.

The right to dream is one that the Scriptures give to the old, while reserving "visions" for the young. It is the right to say what should be; the right to point to the horizon beyond the roofs; the right to proclaim a Gospel with no glosses; the right to speak out clearly, to speak true; the right to stop balancing sentences — "on the one hand... on the other hand"; the right to say, clearly and simply, with no false precautions, that two and two are four.

In *La Croix* of October 18, 1990, Noel Copain made a remark which I liked very much: "Is it unrealistic to dream that the dreamers of today might be the realists of tomorrow?"

The right not to know

I remember an evening I spent with about one hundred theology students in Innsbruck. I gave a talk, which was followed by a great many questions. In answer to one particular question, I told them I hadn't a clue. Apparently this answer — which created quite a sensation — endeared me to the audience, who were very surprised that a cardinal would dare to admit to his ignorance.

I have spent my life searching for answers to innumerable questions — trying to understand how grace and freedom could be reconciled, and how God could know the *"futurabilia"* (and what a relief it was to discover that the entire hypothesis had to be rejected!). I have spent thousands of hours reading philosophy books, theology books and literary works, in search of answers. The poet's familiar words come to mind: "Alas! the flesh is weary, and I have read all the books."

I now have the right to set them all aside in a corner of my library and lock them up. They were my friends, once, but those days are gone. What matters more today is the sense of mystery — apophatic theology, that which goes beyond rational thought. Mary asked only one question: "How can that be?" She received only one answer: "The Holy Spirit will come upon you and the power of the Most High will cover you with his Shadow." That was enough for her. Today, what matters to me is the luminous shadow of the Spirit.

Nocturna lux viantibus. It is the hour of silent adoration of the ineffable God, of the Revelation which surpasses all understanding, of the God who is beyond "our" God, of the transcendence of the One who is completely Other and yet so near. The words "Father of immense Majesty" include also the majesty of what we cannot understand.

The right to transcend time

By this I mean the right to see past, present and future merge into the eternity of God, who is "present" in all his fullness. I experience intensely the actuality of the past which I carry in myself — the actuality of the wonders God has done for me — and the actuality of each one of yesterday's stages. I feel that my present is nourished by all of this, that it receives life from all of God's great tenderness at work.

I also feel that the future is already here, that eternity began in the waters of baptism. And I feel that the real transition is not death, but baptism; through Jesus Christ, and in him, we are already on the other shore. We cannot see him, and yet it is here that my faith finds once again the whole mystery of Easter and the unchanging nature of God who is beyond time and beyond space.

Thus, for me, growing old is a new birth, a gradual entering into another world. And it is a call to shout, through the skies and over the roofs, that the real life is that of tomorrow. I tried to say some of this in a booklet which I called *Spiritual Journey* * Copies of this booklet were distributed to the six thousand priests who came to Rome for a retreat in September 1990, to replace the final lecture which I was supposed to deliver but which my doctors prevented me from giving because of a problem with my health.

1982

A letter from Pope John Paul II
The approach of a New Year is always an opportunity for bishops to express to the Holy Father the feelings of fraternal communion that bind us to him.

The year 1981 had been one of great turmoil for Pope John Paul II and for his country. In response to my good wishes, I received the following letter:

To His Eminence Cardinal Léon Joseph Suenens, former Archbishop of Malines-Brussels

I was deeply moved and comforted by your thoughtful wishes for my daily ministry and for my future apostolic travels, and by the fervent witness of your communion with the suffering and the invincible hope of my beloved countrymen. I thank you from the depths of my heart. It is also a joy for me to wish you a New Year of fruitful service to the Church, with the powerful help of Our Lord and of your long experience of the discernment of spirits. I entrust your person and your evangelical endeavours to

*Published by FIAT, 9 Gravenplein, 9940 Ertvelde, Belgium.

353

the maternal protection of the very holy Mother of Christ, and I bless you with the affection you know.

From the Vatican, January 11, 1982

Johannes Paulus II

Looking back at Vatican II after twenty years
Since I was the only surviving member of the team of four moderators of the Council — Cardinals Agagianian, Lercaro and Doepfner having already gone back to the Father — the editors of the *Osservatore Romano* asked me to write about my thoughts on Vatican II, as I looked back with the benefit of time. My comments were published in full on November 16, 1982. Here are a few excerpts from the article:

I. LOOKING BACK AT VATICAN II

1. The Context of the Council
To understand the impact of the Council, it would be useful to situate it in the ecclesial and international context of that decade of 1960-1970. Such a vital contextualisation — *Sitz in Leben* — would enable the reader to understand both its significance and its limitations. However, such a task is too vast and too complex; we will merely recall a few of the major problems which produced turmoil and anxiety during the Council years, outside its halls, and which were not part of its agenda.

After a few hesitations, the Council had accepted to concentrate on the Church as such — *ad intra* and *ad extra*. This was to be the central theme of its work. However, it only touched incidentally on the issues which were dividing and troubling people's minds and hearts in the theological controversies of the day.

I believe it is important to remember this, if we are to avoid blaming the Council for problems that originated elsewhere.

2. The Mystery of the Church

The very title of the first chapter of *Lumen Gentium* – "The Mystery of the Church" – was a statement of faith which immediately situated the Church in its true dimension. The Council had to answer the question "What does the Church say about herself?" From the outset, the answer went to the heart of the matter by linking the Church to the mystery of the Trinity. It is regrettable that the public – and even the Christian public – hardly noticed this title, or what followed; for this is where we stand – at a crossroads: what do we mean when we speak of the "Church"?

Almost invariably, we remain on a superficial level; we think of the Church as an institution – an establishment like many others – with its rigid juridical machinery and its history of turbulent events, of which we remember the more sensational ones. Nowadays every institution, whatever its nature, is a target for criticism. It was therefore particularly important, from the outset, to make clear the nature of the Church.

An immense catechetical effort is still needed, at every level, if Christians are to discover the true face of the Church, which is Christ alive in his Mystical Body. Christians must know – must live and experience in faith – that which they profess in the Creed, when they say that they believe "in one, holy, catholic and apostolic Church". Christians must be fully aware that there are not two Churches – the one "institutional" and the other "charismatic" – but only one with a twofold dimension, visible and invisible.

3. The powers of evil

If indeed the Church is "Jesus Christ communicated in the Holy Spirit" (Bossuet), it is likely, *a priori*, that till the end of time she will be struggling against the attacks of the one whom the Scriptures call the Enemy. It is impossible to read the Gospels without being struck by the presence of evil in conflict with Jesus. From the very first hour, there is constant confrontation.

I recall a conversation I had, during the Council, with Dom Helder Câmara. We were concerned about the fate of one of the Council documents, and we both regretted the conflicts around this issue, as well as the resulting echoes in the international press. The time was a crucial one for the future of the Council's work. As we parted, Dom Helder exclaimed: "The Devil would be a real idiot if he were not hanging around the Council!" I have never forgotten these words.

In the aftermath of the Council, we entered not the dark night of faith, but the dark night of hope, both in the world and in the Church. We need only look around to discover a world which is making great progress on some levels, but which on others is still tragically dark, suicidal and apocalyptic.

Even the most "optimistic" of the constitutions, *Gaudium et Spes,* contains the following words: "A monumental struggle against the powers of darkness pervades the whole history of man. The battle was joined from the very origins of the world and will continue until the last day, as the Lord has attested."

We must go against the currents to affirm once again that this spiritual struggle is a real one, and that it alone gives its true dimension to our history, even in our own time.

This subject is so unpopular, and so difficult to talk about, that there is in our teachings a sort of vacuum in this respect. For a variety of reasons, I personally believe that we must break out of this "conspiracy of silence" which is itself a demonic ploy. The devil has succeeded in his most devious ruse: he has made us believe that he is an anachronism.

4. The People of God

Continuing our reflection on *Lumen Gentium,* let us move on to chapter 2. This time, far from going unnoticed, the title has been bandied around indiscriminately. The substance of the chapter, on the other hand, has given rise to ambiguities and misinterpretations. All too often, "the People of God" has been taken to mean "the laity".

In an article published by the *"Osservatore Romano"*, Fr Sullivan, SJ, again underlined this misinterpretation. The expression "People of God" refers, in this context, to the common vocation of all those who have received baptism, including the pope and the bishops; this common vocation had to be discussed before the Council could proceed to an analysis of the diversified vocations of the laity, the religious, and the clergy. We are not making a distinction between "the people" versus "the government." The chapter that deals with the laity is chapter 4, not chapter 2.

It is important to stress this, to put an end to the "democratic" interpretations of chapter 2, which do not correspond to its contents.

This frequent confusion, together with actual ignorance concerning the "mystery of the Church", necessarily had certain consequences at the pastoral level, which was the Council's level.

5. The bishops

Chapter 3 is devoted to the Church hierarchy and more particularly to the episcopate; it is still the subject of much research and ecumenical discussion.

The Council has strongly affirmed the role and the meaning of local churches presided over by bishops, as well as their joint responsibility for the evangelisation of the world. I cannot say that we have as yet sufficiently made clear to what extent local churches today reveal in themselves the mystery of the one Church of Christ whose concrete spatial and historical incarnation they are. St Paul deliberately avoided speaking of the Churches of Ephesus, of Corinth, or of Rome, and always spoke in the singular of the Church in Ephesus, or elsewhere.

II. Vatican II in Perspective

1. Vatican II in an ecumenical perspective

Vatican II was a major turning-point on the path towards visible unity of Christians. I would like to share a few thoughts concerning the origins of the two major breaks which brought about visible separation of the Christian Churches.

Vatican II has helped me rediscover the richness, in our own Church, which we had lost sight of in the course of history, through separation from our Eastern brethren, in particular since the schism of the eleventh century. It would not be difficult to show that the *aggiornamento* has been, in large measure, a re-integration into the Latin Church of values which the Eastern Church has always preserved.

I would like to believe that if we had not experienced the separation from the Eastern Church during the eleventh century, and if the "Eastern" trend of thought and of Christian life had been allowed to develop within the Latin Catholic Church, the Reformation might never have taken place. The Reformation was, to a large extent, a reaction against abuses, and against a legal and scholastic narrowness of the Latin Church.

Because of this complementarity, even if there had been no Vatican II decree on ecumenism, this Council would still have been, in my opinion, eminently ecumenical in its essence. We need only remember the Council's insistence on the idea of Church as People of God, on the collegiality of the bishops and of the local Churches; we need only remember the new emphasis placed on the Epiclesis, on liturgy in living languages, on concelebration, on communion in both species, on permanent diaconate, and so forth.

The full impact of all of this — replaced in its proper context, or re-emphasised — has yet to be felt in the present evolution of the Church, whether ecumenical or internal. The input is full of potential and hope, in particular for the

evolution of the Churches of Africa and of Asia; these must
express themselves in their own proper style, which is
much closer to the Eastern style than to ours. They need
to draw on this common heritage, which can be for them a
source of enrichment.

2. *Vatican II and future perspectives*
We all remember Pope John's prayer: "O Holy Spirit, renew
your wonders in our time, as for a new Pentecost."

The key words in this prayer are a call for Vatican II to
be the vehicle for this "New Pentecost", so that the Church
may be renewed and strengthened in our time.

We have yet to fully understand the implications of "baptism in the Holy Spirit and in fire", which was promised by
Jesus to his own, in accordance with the Father's promise.

Vatican II will remain in history a universal "pentecostal" experience, which for every Christian must be
translated into a personal pentecostal experience.

Georges Bernanos once said, "The only way to hold on
to an old grace is to welcome the new grace." These well-
known words have many implications.

We live in an age of grave turmoil and of new hope. I
believe that in time it will become increasingly clear that
Vatican II was indeed a great moment for the Church. I
gladly subscribe to the words of Maximos IV, the valiant
Patriarch of the Greek Melchite Church, whose statements
at the Council were often a breath of fresh air; he once
said, "The Holy Spirit has opened doors which no one will
ever be able to close again".

The death of Cardinal Benelli
My friend Cardinal Benelli died on October 26, 1982; he was at
the time Archbishop of Florence. His sudden departure was for
me the most significant event of the year; it brought back many
memories of a long and faithful friendship.

Earlier that year, I had stayed with him on the occasion of a
Conference of Italian Theologians, which he had asked me to

address. His pastoral activities were prodigiously intense. Five years earlier, he had left his post as Substitute at the Secretariat of State under Pope Paul. I was amazed to see how totally he had since become involved in his new mission.

We had discussed his possible appointment as Archbishop of Florence when Pope Paul had first mentioned it to him; the Pope had given him complete freedom to accept or reject the appointment. Benelli phoned me in Malines, in the middle of the night, to ask for advice. I suggested that he should stay where he was, in the Vatican, out of regard for Pope Paul, who was sick and needed more than ever his faithful and trustworthy assistance. Benelli rejected the offer. Pope Paul, however, was unable to find anyone else who could adequately fill the position, and a year later, he again offered it to Benelli, in a moving letter which Benelli read to me. We decided together at that point that he had to accept Florence – and he did.

When I stayed with him briefly, in Florence, in February, I was struck, moved and concerned by the intensity of his pastoral involvement. His life was a constant round of meetings with priests and visits to parishes – some of which were in the mountains, in places almost impossible to reach. In vain I preached moderation; and it was surely because of his devouring pastoral zeal that sickness overcame him, on his return from a visit to his priests in Brazil.

The memory of this man is still very much with me, and goes back over a period of more than thirty years, rich in encounters and exchanges.

Benelli went to Paris at the end of his assignment as auditor at the nunciature in Dublin, where he had met Frank Duff, founder of the Legion of Mary, whom he respected greatly. When Veronica O'Brien tried to introduce the Legion in France, she met with many obstacles. The first door that was opened to her, after that of the Bishop of Nevers, was that of the nunciature in Paris, in the person of the young auditor Giovanni Benelli. He intuitively understood Veronica O'Brien's mission in all its dimensions, and became the regular confessor of the house in the Rue Boileau; he persuaded the architect of the nunciature to provide help, free of charge, for the construction of a magnificent assembly-room; and he obtained an important grant from Pope John XXIII.

Our friendship was born in this context, and lasted, faithfully, until his death. We corresponded during his many diplomatic postings. In Brazil, where he spent some time at the nunciature, we had a friend in common — Dom Helder Câmara, whom he saw once a week.

During the Council Benelli was Apostolic Delegate in Dakar, and was therefore unable to take part. He followed events from afar, however, and sent me a memorandum on the internal reform of the Roman Curia — a reform which he ardently desired, to eliminate what he called "careerism". I handed his detailed and precise paper to Pope Paul, who did not ask me who had written it; since it was in Italian, however, he probably guessed.

Having spent some time in Spain, as auditor at the nunciature, Benelli returned to Paris, where he was delegate of the Holy See to UNESCO. We worked together, for some time, to provide aid to the Third World; Veronica O'Brien was a member of his consultative board in Paris.

After that, he was called back to Rome, where he occupied the key position of Substitute at the Secretariat of State. His role was in fact more important than that of the Secretary of State, Cardinal Villot, because of his very close relationship with Pope Paul over many years.

Finally, he was promoted to Archbishop of Florence, and soon afterwards was made Cardinal. Benelli was a model pastor — devoted, attentive, daring. He literally died at work, on November 26, 1982. I was present at his funeral, as was Dom Helder Câmara, and I was able to hear on the spot many tales of his profound commitment.

It was John Paul II, however, who found the right words to describe him: "He was a great servant of the Church, who never made use of the Church to serve his own interests. May he rest in

Memories and Hopes

the peace and joy of the Lord."

Ecumenical contacts in England

Tom Smail, who had presided with me over the Dublin Ecumenical Congress, later became Vice-President of St John's Anglican Seminary in Nottingham. He invited me to preach a retreat, at the Seminary, for students and professors together. This involved three brief homilies, preceded and followed by singing; and later, in the evening, a brief talk followed by a question-time. It was a friendly and relaxed day. At the end, the President of the Seminary publicly expressed his admiration for the Catholic Church, "which has succeeded in guiding the Charismatic Renewal along a steady path, avoiding the vagueness of the official Anglican position." He had personally written and published a very balanced study on the subject.

After my day in Nottingham, I travelled to Brentwood, where I had been invited by Bishop Thomas McMahon to give one lecture to the clergy and another in the city; these were to be followed by a day of Renewal. I received a very cordial welcome from a true and fraternal friend. He is still young, and is also parish priest in Stock, the little village where he lives. Together, we went to have a drink with the Anglican minister in the village; in the evening, he arranged a quiet dinner with the Anglican Bishop and my friend Butler, Auxiliary Bishop in London.

Bishop McMahon very kindly drove me to the University of Exeter, where I had been invited to give the ecumenical speech which traditionally opens the academic year; this address was, in fact, the main purpose of my trip.

1983

Germany

During 1983, I made several brief trips to the Federal Republic. I had been invited to Bonn to participate in the work of the German commission appointed to study the question of exorcisms, and to prepare a revision of the Roman ritual. I had agreed to give a talk dealing specifically with the Renewal, entitled "Renewal and the Powers of Darkness", which was also to be the subject of Malines Document No.4.

The Anglican bishops had, for their part, formed a similar commission, and had also asked me to participate in their work; I was, however, unable to do so, due to lack of time.

My main contact that year was with the University of Würzburg, which had awarded me a doctorate *honoris causa*. The University officials had come to Malines to present it to me; by way of thanks, I accepted to go to the University and give a talk on Vatican II. I met the Bishop, Mgr Scheele, former Professor of Theology at the University, who was in charge of ecumencial matters for the German Bishops' Conference. I felt very much at home, both theologically and spiritually.

1984

Scotland

In 1984, I had the opportunity to help prepare a diocese for "the coming of Pentecost". The Scottish Bishop, Mgr Vincent Logan, had proclaimed "a pentecostal year" for the pastoral renewal of his diocese. The opening event was a Congress in Dunkeld from June 8 to 10. He asked me to give an introductory lecture.

I was warmly welcomed, not only by the Bishop, but also by the priests and by members of various lay councils. Dialogue was a joy, at every level. There was a prophetic note to all that was said, and Vatican II was no longer mere theory — it was gathering life and growing wings.

Rome

In Rome, that same year, six thousand priests gathered for an international retreat; they were brought together at the initiative of the Renewal Movement. I was asked to celebrate the opening Mass, to give the homily, and, later, to deliver a lecture on priesthood.

The paper I had prepared was a doctrinal statement; but as I stood before those six thousand priests, who had come from every part of the world, I felt a personal challenge from St Peter, who had asked the faithful "to be ready at all times to justify the hope that is in you". And so I set aside my outline and my written speech, and spoke about my own lived experience as priest and as bishop in witness to the Lord. This was a powerful moment in my life, and the response I received filled me with joy.

1985

A medical alert

One evening, as I was dining by myself, I fainted with no warning whatsoever; they found me when they came to clear the table. The village priest was called in and gave me absolution; the doctor thought for a moment that I had died; I was taken by ambulance to the intensive care centre, where I woke up at about five o'clock the following morning, none the worse for the experience, wondering what I was doing there. The doctors kept me in the hospital for a week, while they did all sorts of tests; then they sent me to Brussels for more tests. There seemed to be nothing wrong with me at all.

My schedule for the holidays was very full; I went ahead with it, missing none of the planned activities and taking no medication. I travelled to Bamberg, in Germany, to Graz in Austria, to Cagliari in Sardinia, and finally to Rome to give the jubilee speech on the twentieth anniversary of the Council for the Laity. I also took part, with no problems, in a synod to which the Pope had convened all the cardinals.

It was a strange adventure; my friends decided it was a miracle, and concluded that I still had a few things to do here before going to Heaven. In any case, it will be one of the puzzles to solve up there, in the final peace of the Lord.

1986

Stormy ecumenism in Ireland
The Cardinal of Armagh invited me to participate in the Ecumenical Week in Ireland, and to preach first in Belfast, at the Church of Ireland Cathedral, and then at his own church in Armagh. I accepted, in gratitude for all that I owe to Ireland.

As soon as I arrived in Dublin, the Cardinal took me under his wing; he drove me everywhere I had to go, and never let me out of his sight. Due to a misunderstanding, we failed to meet our friend Van Cauwelaert at the airport (he is the son of the former President of our House of Representatives, and a most devoted person). We also missed Sr Mary Duffy, who is the very incarnation of Charismatic Renewal. They caught up with us in Drogheda. During my stay, I was asked to preside over a Renewal meeting, in Dundalk, which involved the entire diocese. Sr Briege Murphy, of the Medical Missionaries of Mary, was on the organising team; she welcomed us to their community house, "Bethany", and made us feel very much at home.

On Monday the 20th, we attended the Greenhills Ecumenical Conference; then we left for Armagh. Along the way, there were military patrols, vindictive inscriptions on the walls, traces of violence; all of these reminded us of the calvary of this torn people.

In Armagh, the Cardinal settled us in. He was very attentive, joyful, quick in his every reaction; he speaks very fast, in quick, short sentences interpersed with witty comments. Together we went to pray at the tombs of Cardinal D'Alton and of Cardinal Conway (who had been my friend during the Council days), both of whom are buried in the garden surrounding the church.

On the following afternoon, we left for Belfast. We had dinner

365

that first evening with the bishop of the diocese, Mgr Daly, also an old friend of mine, who has since been appointed Primate of Ireland. He informed me that my most recent book had just been published in English, under the title *Nature and Grace, in Vital Unity;* with great kindness and humour, he added that these words would have made a very appropriate motto for me.

After the meal, we left in darkness, with the Cardinal and the Bishop, for Belfast Cathedral. It was surrounded by a few hundred protesters; they carried insulting posters against the Pope and the bishops, shouted "No popery!" and waved their torches. About fifty of Paisley's followers had managed to mingle with the faithful in the crowded cathedral. Paisley himself was there, to excite the crowds outside, while, inside, his daughter had positioned herself under the pulpit.

The master of ceremonies whispered that it might be better if I did not attempt to reach the pulpit, and instead addressed the crowd from the ambo. It was wise advice, but it did not prevent the uproar. The Ecumenical Prayer Service for Unity had no sooner begun than it was drowned by shouting from every direction. The powerful notes of the organ resounded in an attempt to override the shouts, and managed to do so a couple of times; as soon as I started to speak, however, the shouting resumed.

Policemen calmly expelled the protesters, who left in small groups and were met by loud cheers from Paisley's troops, still massed behind their barricades.

I waited, in prayer, for a moment of silence which never came; finally I brought the evening to an end with these words, which were heard over all the noise: "God bless you all, and may he bless twice those who created all these troubles."

There were about one thousand faithful, Protestants, Anglicans and Catholics, in the church; together they expressed their disapproval and their ecumenism with a long and moving ovation to the celebrants, who, at the end of the office, walked down the nave – now quiet at last.

A second ecumenical service had been scheduled for the following day, this time at the Catholic Cathedral of Armagh. There were no incidents here. The Archbishop, President of the Church of Ireland, was present at the service; he said goodbye to the Catholics, since his mandate was coming to an end and he was anxious to tell them of his hopes for visible unity among the Christian Churches. In private, he told me how much he had suffered the previous day in Belfast, and how deeply he cared about ecumenism.

An ecumenical lecture in Marseilles

I was invited to Marseilles by the Archbishop, Mgr Coffy, to give a talk during the Week for Christian Unity. The audience was largely Catholic, but there were also a few Protestant pastors whom I had already met before this conference.

Because the atmosphere was particularly friendly, I decided to run a double risk, giving my talk a new and unexpected turn. Speaking first to the Catholics in the audience, I said that I had something to say to them alone, and I asked the Protestants in the audience not to listen! Having taken this oratorial precaution, I stated to the Catholics: "My friends, do not be afraid of the Holy Spirit. Dare to believe in the Pentecost of yesterday and of today!"

Next, I invited the Catholics to close their ears, while I begged the Protestants in the audience, "Let the words of the Angel of the Lord to Joseph be a challenge to you: 'Do not be afraid to take Mary home as your spouse, because she has conceived what is in her by the Holy Spirit'. This message," I added, "is just as valid, in spiritual terms, for us today: the spiritual maternity of Mary, who conceived by the power of the Holy Spirit, is entirely 'christocentric'. Do not be afraid; Mary is not an obstacle on the path of ecumenism, but rather a meeting point. Let us not separate what God has united."

An interview in 1986 about the year 2086

A Belgian theologian, Philippe Weber, asked me a series of ques-

367

tions for *La Foi et le Temps*, a publication put out by the franco-phone Belgian dioceses. The last of his questions went as follows: "If we were to ask our imagination to transport us one hundred years ahead, to the year 2086, what do you think would be the most obvious differences with respect to our present-day lives?"

Here is my answer:

> 2086... that's a long way off! If you were to ask me about the year 2000, perhaps I would hazard a guess. No one who is not a prophet should attempt to prophesy, but what I see gradually happening – as I look at what is actually before me, with human eyes which are badly equipped to read the future – is that Europe is no longer going to be the centre of things. Rome, yes!... But there will no longer be councils run by European bishops, with their universities behind them, and so forth.
>
> Europe itself is no longer divided into Northern and Southern Europe; there is also Eastern Europe. This fact alone will have an impact on the future.
>
> I also see the African Churches becoming stronger and more vigorous, with all the problems of adaptation to their cultures. This will raise a great many problems. Perhaps there will be mutual enrichment; in any case, it will be a delicate matter.
>
> I can see Latin America taking new pastoral directions, faced with the challenge of an enormous task and specific needs.
>
> As for what the world will look like concretely in the year 2000 and beyond, you will have to ask others, later on."*

1987

A goodbye to Vatican II, and good wishes for the future
I was invited to the Commemorative Synod for Vatican II, where, in a few words, I expressed my dreams for the future, before the

---

*La Foi et le Temps – September-October 1986, p.422

Pope and the assembled bishops. I thought of this as a farewell from "the old guard" to the new generation which is taking over where we left off.

Every word I said would require explanation; let me just say that this very brief message was a cry of hope for the "new evangelisation", a reminder of its urgency, and a prayer that it might remain consistent with its starting-point – the Jerusalem Cenacle, at the hour of Pentecost, early in the morning.

My speech began with these words: "I am here to speak on behalf of the four moderators of the Council, three of whom have already gone to Heaven, and who are thus more present here than any one of us. With their permission – presumed if not canonically granted – I shall deliver our message. It is the following:

Scripture tells us that "the young have visions and the old have dreams". This gives me the right – at my advanced age – to share with you the dreams I have for your work and for the upcoming Synod on the Laity.

Years ago, I proposed – and Pope John XXIII supported my proposal – that Vatican II should be centred on the Church *ad intra* and *ad extra*.

My dream for the present Synod is that it may be centred on Vatican II, of course, but beyond that, and more deeply, on the Cenacle – *ad intra* and *ad extra*.

Ad intra
I would like to see the Synod insistently stress the need for Christians of future generations to relive the experience of Pentecost – in other words, to receive that "Baptism in the Spirit" which created the Church and gave it its vital breath.

Before we catechise the Christians of tomorrow, we must tell them who Jesus Christ is. Therein lies the first and prerequisite Kerygma. They must live the experience of the Cenacle – and I do mean the experience – which is an experience of profound conversion; of recognition of the resurrected Christ; of openness and availability to the Holy

369

Spirit, to his gifts and charisms, in the fire of Pentecost.

Christians must rediscover Jesus Christ, meet him, or —
better still — allow themselves to be met by him.

It is up to us to outline the necessary teachings, to pre-
scribe some form of neo-catechumenate. In past years,
parishes were re-Christianised by missions; today it will be
necessary to break up the large crowds, and to invite Christians to enter into the Cenacle in small groups. We can
devise all kinds of retreats — provided that they are animated by the Spirit of Pentecost, carried and sustained by the
fraternal communion of our brethren in the faith, and that
they teach Christians to go out of the Cenacle and carry to
others the fire which has been lit.

Ad extra

This brings me to a review of the scope of our apostolic
tasks. Some are to be situated in the dimension of the
Incarnation, in the continuation of the mystery of Jesus,
who identifies with his human brothers and sisters, and
who will judge us on the basis of love lived out in solidarity with our neighbours.

But we must also offer the message of salvation explicitly, in word and in action. We must provide the *means* to
survive — in this respect, the situation is today a tragic
one, on a world scale — but we must also, at the same time,
give people *reasons* to live. We must respond to material
suffering — that of the body — but also to the challenge of
spiritual suffering, whether it is consciously experienced or
not.

We must never forget that we were created not only (as
the old catechism tells us) "to know, love and serve God"
(end of sentence!), but also to make him known, loved, and
served by others. We still have a long way to go before this
obligation and this sense of urgency become an integral
part of our Christian way of life.

* * *

This, I believe, is "what the Spirit is saying to the Churches"; it is here that we are called to act.

The permanent temptation is to think of the renewal of the Church in terms of reorganisation, of adaptation of external forms, of a reform of existing structures — as is the case with human institutions. A French Bishop, Mgr Matagrin, once wrote the following words to me, and I have never been able to forget them: "We can build canals and pipelines, but we cannot make the water surge."

John XXIII, who did not deny the need for reforms, went straight to the heart of things, to the spring of living water. He invited Christians to be receptive to the gifts of God, so that the Church might experience a new Pentecost. The Church always needs to be refounded where it was founded — in the Upper Room, in the founding experience which was the event of Pentecost. His Holiness Pope John Paul II addressed this very same message to the symposium of the Council of European Episcopal Conferences. May that document be a charter for the future!

Finally, I wish you courage and confidence!

The twentieth anniversary of the Pentecostal Renewal
This year also saw the celebration of the twentieth anniversary of the Pentecostal Renewal which was born in Catholic groups in the United States. People frequently ask me about this. Here are some of the questions that I am asked most often:

Eminence, you once wrote a book on Charismatic Renewal: A New Pentecost?, with a question mark at the end of the title. Today, the Renewal celebrates its twentieth anniversary: does the question mark remain?

When we are dealing with grace, we must always distinguish between grace that is offered and grace that is received, lived, and fully integrated by us.

There is no question mark on God's side. On our side,

however – on the receiving side – there is more room for uncertainties. If you were to ask me whether Vatican II was indeed a new Pentecost, I would say "yes" – in terms of grace that was offered – and "yes and no" in terms of grace received.

In your opinion, what are the positive points, the negative ones, and the ambiguous ones of the Renewal?

I will begin with the positive, if I may. I believe that the Pentecostal Renewal (I prefer this term to "charismatic", which is far too ambiguous and narrow, since the whole Church is charismatic) is a very precious grace, which completes, and extends, at the level of the people of God, the pentecostal grace which Vatican II represented at the level of the bishops.

Aside from this correlation, however, I believe it is a precious actualisation of the workings of the Holy Spirit at the heart of the Church; and this includes charisms. We are far from having fully discovered the Holy Spirit, whether in theology, in spirituality, or in our pastoral applications. We still have far to go to situate the Holy Spirit at the heart of the new evangelisation. The title of Pope John Paul II's encyclical on the Holy Spirit – *Dominum et Vivificantem* – is in itself an invitation to emphasise his life-giving role.

I know that, when you became bishop, you took for your motto the words "In the Holy Spirit"; were you already anxious to stress his role?

Yes, it was an act of faith and of hope in his active, concrete and renewing presence, which can be revolutionary when that is called for. It was a way of reaffirming the priority of grace, and therefore of prayer. No one has a monopoly on the Holy Spirit; we can only be glad of the new emphasis that the Renewal has placed on prayer in its many forms.

372

Which forms, for example?

For instance, in the form of communal prayer, where there is room for spontaneity, and for the freedom of the Holy Spirit, who prays in us, as St Paul tells us, "with sighs too deep for words".

I know that it is possible to take these things too far, and that prayer also requires moments of silence. But I believe that we are too afraid of expressing our prayers outwardly, visibly, with our whole beings – body and soul. It is a matter of balance and common sense; but do not forget that we are in greater danger of being too lethargic than of being too exuberant.

We seldom realise to what extent our liturgies are still rigid, ossified, formalised. The important thing is not whether we raise our arms to pray, but whether we can be detached from our selves; whether we are able to overcome our timidity, the inhibitions which we prefer to describe as "reserve" or "discretion".

What is "normal"? If you sit in a train at the station and watch the train next to yours begin to move, you cannot be sure which train is moving.

Ask a few young people, if you like, or people from cultures outside Europe – ask them a few questions about our customs and ways. You'll be surprised!

Is this a discreet defence of "prayer in tongues"?

We must first of all agree on what we mean by this expression. Pentecostals see it as a gift of foreign languages, a sign of authentic baptism. We cannot accept this interpretation; it is not a gift of unknown languages, but rather the grace of prayer in a formless, unstructured style. I wrote about this in detail in *A New Pentecost?*, but there still remains a great deal of ambiguity on this point, even among our own people.

Charismatics often use the Bible; is theirs not, all too

*often, a fundamentalist reading, or a way of turning to
the Scriptures randomly in search of an answer to some
immediate personal problem?*

A fundamentalist reading of the Bible, one that does not
take into account literary forms, is a danger which must be
avoided. We all need to be guided by the Church in these
matters, in order to avoid the double danger of being too
literal and of mythologising.

As for the practice of opening the Scriptures in search
of God's Word; for me, today, this is part of my spiritual
life, as I open the Missal to the day's readings. It is acceptable to do this, so long as we do not turn it into some sort
of challenge to God, defying him to give us an answer.

*"Prophecies" are a frequent occurrence at Renewal meet-
ings; does this disturb you in any way?*

Yes indeed, if the attitude behind them is "God has said
this to me...," "Listen to me, my children..."; or if they claim
to predict future events.

Vatican II speaks of all Christians as "a prophetic people" — that is to say, as carriers of the word of God. We
must beware of the apocalyptic manner, but there is nothing strange in sharing with others a word which we have
received in prayer and which has struck us — if this is a
spiritual sharing, and nothing more. There is no private
line to the Holy Spirit.

*Prayer groups are often criticised for living in isolation,
closed off from the world, with no social involvement.*

I wrote the third Malines Document, in collaboration with
my friend Dom Helder Câmara, specifically to insist that
prayer must lead to action, on the apostolic level and on
the social level. We must "act out" our prayers. I think
there has been considerable progress in this direction within the Renewal.

374

The theme of the International Renewal Congress, which was held in Rome in May 1987, was "Evangelisation of the Poor", and the main speakers were Mother Teresa of Calcutta and Jean Vanier; I think this is very significant.

Is the Renewal not, to a large extent, marginal to parish life?

This is a two-way problem of responsibility. The members of these groups must be open to the parish community, but the latter must in turn be receptive to integration. Much depends on the people involved, and on the priest in charge. If the priest has personally experienced a "pentecostal" baptism in the Spirit, it is likely that an osmosis will take place. I have seen such cases in Germany, in Austria, and in England.

You speak of baptism in the Spirit; is this some sort of super-baptism?

Of course not! It is an experience of the grace received at baptism and at confirmation, and is therefore rooted in those sacraments.

The first "pentecostal" baptism can be traced back to the Cenacle in Jerusalem; there, in the Upper Room, the Holy Spirit transformed the apostles, and outward evangelisation began.

Every one of us must "meet" the Lord in a life experience; therein lies the key to the "baptism of the Spirit" of which we speak, and without which prayer groups would lack vital depth.

Are you made uncomfortable when, during "healing sessions", it is annouced that so-and-so has been healed, or is in the process of being healed?

I would prefer a certain discretion in these matters, and I would be happier if people waited for the announced healings to be confirmed – or not confirmed – by time. I do believe, however, that the Church should give more space to prayers of healing and to the ministry to the sick. Redemption is a mystery of the healing of human beings at the deepest level; the Eucharist is a promise of healing, for the soul and for the body. All of this should be an ordinary part of our daily pastoral work. Changing the "extreme unction" to the "sacrament of the sick" was a great step forward. I believe that the Renewal can be an instrument for progress in this direction.

I continue to have reservations concerning "resting in the Spirit", where a direct intervention of the Holy Spirit is implied. I am also pleased that Rome has warned against wild exorcisms. There is no doubt that we must ask God to "deliver us from evil", in accordance with the Lord's Prayer; however, we must avoid challenging evil spirits, except in extreme cases – which should be left to the discretion and wisdom of the bishop, or of one who has been duly mandated by the bishop. This was the theme of the fourth Malines Document.

Does the Renewal have a role to play in bringing about the unity of all Christians?

Certainly, provided we avoid all ambiguities. By this I mean that "ecumenical" groups are "an opportunity for unity", provided that each faith respects the identity of the others, even in prayer.

Authentic ecumenism does not require that we set aside our specific identity – leaving it in parentheses, as it were – and meet at "the lowest common denominator". I have written about this in greater detail in the second Malines Document.

If we are to progress towards genuine ecumenism, we must head straight for "union of the Churches", rather than for "union of Christians among themselves, outside and beyond the Churches", into a super-Church of the Holy

Spirit. We must begin by trying to unite the "episcopalian" Churches, those which have preserved the apostolic tradition which, in our case, means apostolic succession through the bishops.

In concrete terms, this means giving priority to union with the Orthodox, Anglican and Lutheran Churches. Dr Fisher, the first Archbishop of Canterbury to come to Rome to see the Pope, shared this belief.

This was also Pope Paul's feeling, when he was Archbishop of Milan, and had regular meetings with the Anglicans, for whom he had a definite sympathy.

I feel that the Renewal could be very helpful in expressing our ecumenical hopes by bringing out all that is implied, for all of us, in the "mystery of the Pentecost" and in its celebration. I wrote about this – in response to a specific request by Vincent Synan, Secretary General of the All Holiness Churches – in the third Malines Document.

What are your hopes, concerning the Renewal, for the year 2000?

That the river should reach the ocean, and that all of this should become common property shared by all.

That the Renewal should no longer be viewed as a "movement" alongside other "movements", but rather as a breath of the Spirit, an act of the Spirit.

That we should rediscover the secret of Pentecost, which is a mystery of conversion (*ad intra*) and of apostolate (*ad extra*).

And that we should not be afraid of the symbols of the wind which shakes the house – without uprooting it! – and of the flames which kindle from a spark.

Once, after a lecture I gave in Würzburg, a lady from the audience handed me a small package, saying, "Open this when you get home; it is to tell you that we have understood your message". The package contained a box of matches!

FIAT initiatives throughout the decade

In the course of this last decade, I have helped promote a variety of evangelical initiatives which emerged from a small international group: the Family International Apostolic Team (FIAT). If the Lord gives me time, I hope someday to discuss these at length and in depth, as they deserve.

Two of my collaborators, Roger and Cecile Matthys, whose home is known as "Nazareth", have given their lives with apostolic devotion to this enterprise; around them hinges the work of this apostolate. The success of their activities throughout the world owes much to the assistance provided by a Dutch foundation – *Getuigenis van Gods Liefde* (Witness to the Love of God), established by Piet and Trude Derksen.

Some of the inititatives they have taken are described in my booklet, *Spiritual Journey*, which exists in French, English and Spanish editions. I refer the interested reader to this booklet for more detailed information.

The FIAT message is essentially an invitation to become more open to the "New Pentecost" as a key to the New Evangelisation to which we are all called. This message emphasises that the secret of all apostolic fruitfulness is in our own openness to the action of the Holy Spirit, which in turn brings into play Mary's maternity of graces and our union with her.

What brings life and unity to all of this is the desire to give practical and concrete expression to our faith in the Holy Spirit. He inspires the New Evangelisation which is demanded of us, and which originates in the mystery of Pentecost, lived in union with Mary, Mother of the Church at its birth.

FIAT is not a movement; it is a pastoral service available to all Christians, and especially to families, parishes and apostolic movements.

During an audience with John Paul II, Veronica O'Brien, who has been at the heart of this group, received much encouragement from the Pope. He expressed his gratitude in a letter he sent to me on the occasion of one of these intiatives; the goal of this particular project was to give new significance – in particular for Christian families – to the feast of the Nativity of Mary, which is celebrated on September 8. Here is his letter:

To His Eminence Cardinal Leo Jozef Suenens,
Former Archbishop of Malines-Brussels

In thanking you cordially for your letter of August 19, I wish to make known to you the joy with which I welcome Your Eminence's recent initiative, in collaboration with the FIAT group, whereby you are helping Christian families and Christians of many countries to prolong the spirit and the benefits of the Marian Year 1987-1988 – in particular through the fervent celebration of the Nativity of the Virgin Mary, "who brought to the world the dawning of hope and of salvation".

May the Very Holy Mother of Christ the Redeemer assist you in your apostolic endeavours!

I bless you with all my heart.

From the Vatican, October 5, 1988

Joannes Paulus II

Of the many FIAT initiatives, I will mention only the most recent one, which is still being developed. A small book is in preparation; it is intended specifically for our Christian brothers and sisters in Eastern Europe, who are stepping out of the catacombs, and who are asking us to share with them the best of our religious literature.

The book we have chosen is *Abandonment to Divine Providence,* by Fr de Caussade, SJ. This book has been for me – as for many others – a liberating experience. The author proposes a secret of holiness, which is none other than total abandonment to the loving will of God, in all circumstances of life. The power of his message lies in its inflexible simplicity, which leaves no room

379

for escape; he tells us over and over again, on every page, that God loves us "relentlessly". He invites us to live out this assent to the love of God – which is identical to the will of God – in the spirit of Mary, and in filial dependence on the one whose FIAT, at the hour of the Annunciation, was a summary of her entire spirituality, and of her entire life.

By accepting to live, as she did, in this spirit, we are placed at the very heart of our faith, of our hope, and of our love.

Our faith discovers God working his wonderful graces, hidden in the camouflage of what we call "the coincidences" of life.

Our hope recognises, with St Paul, that "everything works to the good of the one who is loved by God" – and that "everything" really does mean "everything".

Our love, which finds its source in God's own love, leads us to love our brothers and sisters with a love that is unwavering, inventive and creative.

I was very happy to participate in this effort to make this work known again, and I am pleased to testify – on the basis of experience – that there is in those pages a teaching which is a source of unshakeable joy. I feel that in encouraging this FIAT initiative, I am in a way discharging a debt. I am very grateful to Fr Jean Meeûs, SJ, who has been my closest religious collaborator within FIAT, for all his help with this project.

In concluding this very brief summary of current pastoral activities, I would like to mention that the present volume of my reminiscences will be followed by a second one in which the reader will find a key to certain events, and will be able to understand them in their full and vital spiritual dimension.

1990

The Lord beckons
In January of this year, a minor heart problem forced me to work a little less, but did not put a stop to all of my activities. In Febru-

ary, I went to see a friend of mine, a cardiologist; during our conversation, I asked him if he could tell me how to speed up my recovery. Suddenly, there was a dramatic development: my friend examined me rapidly, and announced, "You must go to the hospital immediately — you are having a heart attack." He telephoned ahead and I was taken to the hospital. I spent eight days in intensive care, followed by eight more in ordinary care, in a room with several other patients.

I discovered that medical services, even when they are technically perfect, can be completely lacking in humanity. Take, for instance, the anonymity of it all; this is a heavy psychological burden, and makes conversation very difficult, since there are no points of reference. I remember an excellent orderly with whom I was talking about the diocese of Malines-Brussels; I remarked that the name "Malines" probably meant little to him, to which he responded, "You're joking! Brussels means very little to me. But Malines — everyone knows the Malines soccer team!"

One of the men in my room was a mason. He had been a mason since the age of thirteen, and he was then sixty-three. He helped me to understand what it means to do one's work with passion and with pride. He spoke of nothing else, and only when his relatives came to visit him was I able to talk, with them, about religion.

Those fifteen days in hospital made me see for myself that Christianity has barely touched the surface of the people's souls, and that Jesus Christ has ceased to be for us a common denominator. The world is in need, more than ever, of a "New Evangelisation".

A Christian who is King
Gradually, during the months of March and April, I returned to life. I decided not to go back to the Brotherhood of "Le Rocher", where I had been welcomed for a quarter of a century, where I had lived unforgettable hours of human and spiritual communion, and where I had written a dozen books.

During my convalescence, Belgium lived through a crucial hour of its history: the King, in the name of his conscience as a human being and as a Christian, refused to put his signature to a law which he considered morally unacceptable.

I remember a sentence in Spaak's memoirs about a French Minister whom he respected, he tells us, but who lacked "a sense of grandeur and the courage of the impossible". King Baudouin revealed to the members of our Parliament, and to his country, the meaning of moral grandeur. By refusing to sign the law on abortion, he pointed out to the whole world the primacy of moral imperatives, the primacy of the absolute, which must be respected over and against every kind of relativism, even that instituted by parliamentarians. In a world where our vital truths are at the mercy of a play of numbers, left to the random accounting of majorities, what rare royal grandeur was required to call us back to respect for essential values!

The King also had need of "the courage of the impossible"; for at stake were his throne and the future of monarchic rule in the country. He measured and accepted the risks. To the very last moment, and against numerous opposing opinions, he stood by his decision. It will be a landmark in history, to help men and women of all nations to understand that the witness of one weighs more than the conformism of multitudes.

His was not the gesture of a "Most Christian King"; this title has been tarnished by history, as we have seen more than one "Most Christian King" lead a private life that was a negation of this title, and a political life that was no better. No, King Baudoin does not belong to this category. He proved himself to be not an honorary "Christian King", but very simply — and very meaningfully — a "Christian who is King".

Thirtieth wedding anniversary
Today, December 15, 1990, Belgium celebrates the thirtieth wedding anniversary of the King and Queen.

The King's sixtieth birthday, celebrated recently, was marked by widespread expressions of popularity. In the papers, much was made of Maurice Béjart's admiration for the King, to whom he dedicated his new ballet. "I love your King", he is reported to have said. "He is very human, and there are not many people in high positions who are... I have never met anyone who has retained such freshness, such humanity, such depth. He is a rare person, and Belgium is very fortunate to have such a King."

Today, we can add that our King's encounter with Queen Fabiola was also a most fortunate event — or, in Christian terms, a special grace for our country.

This anniversary brings to mind a memory. The King once came to Malines for the opening of the town museum. As I walked with him through the main square, we heard people shouting "Long live the Queen!" I was somewhat taken aback, since the Queen was not with us, and I remarked to the King: "How strange; they are shouting 'Long live the Queen' rather than 'Long live the King.'" He replied: "Oh! it happens quite often; once a man came up to me in a crowd and said, 'Your Majesty, do you know why it is that when you go by we all shout 'Long live the Queen' rather than 'Long live the King?' And he explained: 'Well, Your Majesty, we do it because we believe it will make you happier!'"

Later, I told the Queen about this, and she confided: "I have a little story of my own to tell you. Once, as I was visiting a hospital, a sick woman said to me, 'Madam, do you know why we love you so much?' And before I could answer, she went on: 'It is because you make the King so happy.'"

Today we celebrate the royal couple, a model of authentic love, of mutual tenderness and faithfulness. This deserves a vibrant *Te Deum*.

On the threshold of eternity

Every day, I am struck more and more by the relativity of what

383

we call the past, the present and the future. It is all one in God; it is only from our earthly point of view that there is a sequence and a diversification. The sun is always the sun; the earth gravitates around it, passing from light into shadow.

Death, in Stanislas Fumet's profound words, is "the end of our exteriority". Freed from time and space, which hold us prisoners here, we enter into the depths of God and of his Mystery. God instantly becomes "the shortest path between two beings" who meet on another level, who participate in spiritual compenetration in the trinitarian life itself. We enter into a world in which anonymity no longer exists, and where the coexistence and juxtaposition of beings become communion. It is God who becomes all, in all of us. We enter into the world of the Living, of the Super-Living. We must repeat, with Claudel, "Blessed is death, in which every petition of the Lord's Prayer is answered!"

As for the rest, we await the future: it is in the hands of God. Lord, we know that your prodigious love and your infinite tenderness watch over our every step, our every breath. The future belongs to You alone, for the simple reason that You are the Future, the "Absolute Future". Thank you for leading me to the very heart of your Being. Amen.

I would like to end with a prayer for the year 2000:

Looking at the World

Lord, we are afraid of the world of tomorrow.
We have lost faith in ourselves.
We no longer believe in the boundless progress
which was to ensure our happiness,
nor in science as the salvation of all mankind.
We no longer believe that Man is the supreme end of
man,
Nor that death is the last word of life.

And we know, too, that if, tomorrow,

Another nuclear disaster, like Chernobyl,
were to befall us, whether by accident or by design,
there might be an apocalyptic explosion:
no one among us would live
to count and bury the dead.

* * *

Looking at the Church

Lord, if I turn my eyes to the Church,
Who received from your Son the promise of Eternal
    Life,
I see all the poverty and weakness there is
in us, your disciples,
so poor and so un-Christian!
And I hear, on every side,
the pressing call of our Pastors
to a new and second Evangelisation
to make us true Christians,
conscious of the imperatives of our Baptism.

Help us to find again the fervour of the early
    Christians
and the power of the first evangelisation,
which began that morning of Pentecost,
in the Cenacle of Jerusalem,
where your disciples, gathered in prayer with Mary,
awaited the fulfilment of their Faather's promise.
Give us the grace to be renewed
"in the Spirit and in fire".
Teach us to speak to the world in tongues of fire,
and let there be an end to this time of timid, silent
    Christians.
who anxiously debate the problems of today
as Christians did long ago
on the road that led from Jerusalem to Emmaus
unaware that the Master is Risen and Alive.

Memories and Hopes

A Prayer for the Future

Lord, open our hearts to welcome your Holy Spirit.
Teach us to wait for His coming,
as Mary did at the hour of the Annunciation,
and again at Pentecost – the Nativity of the Church –
when she became our Mother as well.
Teach future generations that Jesus Christ, your Son,
is the Saviour of the World for all times.

Help us to proclaim, loudly and boldly,
that He is "the Way, the Truth and the Life" –
the Way – leading us to our final goal;
the Truth – lighting our path through the night;
the Life – giving us profound peace, serenity, and joy
which nothing created can destroy.

May your disciples, at last,
on the eve of this third millennium,
hasten their step to obey the Master's command,
to be "One" in the Unity of the Father, the Son and the
    Holy Spirit.
May they together draw close to the Lord,
so that, radiant in His Light,
their faces may be free of shadows,
and the world may recognise Jesus Christ
alive in his disciples
now and forever.
Amen.

Index

Hallinan P.J., Archbishop 170, 171, 172, 174
Hamilton E. 236
Hare R. 302
Harmel P. 167, 244
Haubtmann P., Mgr 107
Haughey J., SJ 300
Heath E. 181
Hebblethwaite P. 213
Heenan J.C., Cardinal 218, 219, 240, 242, 243
Hello E. 14
Hemeleers E. 14
Herrmann F. 230
Heylen V., Mgr 160
Himmer Ch.M., Bishop 22
Hume G.B., Cardinal 204, 226, 240, 302, 329

J

Jacques J.
Jadot J., Archbishop 55, 110
Jeannne D'Arc, Sister 291
Jenkinson R. 309
Joliet O., Bishop 23
John XXIII, Pope 44, 55, 56, 59, 60, 65, 66, 67, 68, 69, 70, 71, 75, 76, 77, 78, 83, 85, 86, 87, 100, 101, 102, 103, 104, 105, 106, 107, 108, 109, 110, 111, 112, 113, 114, 115, 116, 117, 118, 119, 120, 121, 122, 123, 125, 128, 129, 131, 138, 148, 170, 176, 177, 178, 180, 198, 199, 222, 231, 232, 237, 247, 251, 281, 286, 294, 318, 320, 321, 326, 359, 361, 369, 371 (*see also* Roncalli A.)
John-Paul I, Pope 316, 322, 323, 324, 325, 326, 327, 336, (*see also* Luciani A.)
John-Paul II, Pope 251, 285, 316, 328, 329, 331, 353, 361, 371, 372, 378 (*see also* Wojtyla K.)
Josephine-Charlotte, Grand-Duchess 34
Journet Ch., Cardinal 306, 317, 333
Jousse M. 24
Jubany A.N., Cardinal 329
Justinian, Patriarch 258

K

Kaiser R.B. 145
Kasper W., Bishop 281
Keller 343
Kempf W., Bishop 69
Kerr C. 302
Kitchener, Lord 237
Knox J. 344
Koenig F., Cardinal 243
Krol J., Cardinal 56, 69, 254, 257
Küng H. 229, 246, 277, 341

L

Labourdette M., OP 145
Lambe A. 347
Lambilliotte M. 198

Lamotte E. 24, 28, 40
Landazuri R.J., Cardinal 322, 324
La Taille M. de, SJ 132
Lauge 300
Laurentin R. 213, 218, 279
Lebeau P., SJ 277, 280, 284, 302, 303, 305, 335
Lebbe V. 21, 175
Lebreton J., SJ 24
Leo XIII, Pope 22
Lercaro G., Cardinal 85, 126, 127, 130, 131, 354
Le Roy E. 39
Levie J., SJ 38
Liénart A., Cardinal 68, 69, 83, 84
Logan V., Bishop 363
Lorscheider Al., Cardinal 329
Lousse E. 33, 40
Lubac H. de, Cardinal 76, 175, 211, 237
Lubich C. 301
Luca G. de 100
Luciani A., Cardinal 322, 323, 328, 330

M

Mackenzie R. 240, 340, 341
McCord 336
McCormick R., SJ 300
McDonnell K., OSB 277
McMahon T., Bishop 362
McNutt F. 301

Maistre J. de 14
Malevez L., SJ 38
Maloney G.A. 300
Malula J. A., Cardinal 212, 213, 254
Mamie P., Bishop 305, 306, 333
Marella P., Cardinal 57, 93, 97
Maritain J. 237, 317
Marmion Dom C., OSB 24
Martin R. 240, 260, 268, 292, 296, 299, 313, 315
Marty F., Cardinal 286, 329
Matagrin G., Bishop 371
Matthys R. and C. 378
Maximos IV, Patriarch 359
Meeûs J., SJ 380
Meliton, Metropolitan 245
Mercier D.J., Cardinal 17, 19, 20, 21, 22, 26, 28, 29, 53, 73, 101, 161, 175, 178, 180, 206, 207, 275, 306, 310, 349
Mersch E., SJ 24
Mertens E. 41
Messori V. 336
Meyendorff J. 245, 247
Meyer A. de 40
Meyer A.G., Archbishop 69
Meyers, Mgr, Bishop 187
Mimmi M., Cardinal 56, 57
Moeller C., Mgr 38, 135, 246
Molinghen P.-H. 303, 305
Monléon A.-M. de, OP, Bishop 272, 277
Montague 300